Taking Charge in Japan

Taking Charge in Japan

Thomas J. Nevins

President, **TMT**

Author of *Labor Pains and the Gaijin Boss*

With Strategic
Rules of Employment
and the other "Four R's"—
Recruiting,
Rewarding,
Rehabilitating, &
Reducing (as last resort)
Japanese Staff.

The Japan Times

First edition, December 1990
All rights reserved.
Copyright © 1990 by Thomas J. Nevins
Design and typography by Omega Communications, Inc.

Cover art by Masaru Ishikawa
For information, write: The Japan Times, Ltd.,
4-5-4 Shibaura, Minato-ku, Tokyo 108, Japan.

ISBN4-7890-0553-4

Published in Japan by the Japan Times, Ltd.

This book and many other books on Japan and the Japanese culture
and language are published by and for the Japan Times, Ltd.
located at 4-5-4 Shibaura, Minato-ku, Tokyo 108, Japan

PRINTED IN JAPAN

Dedicated to Rules of Employment as Your Primary and Most Powerful Management Tool —a Totally New and Different Dimension

For the Businessman, our gift is a lot of insight and practical usable advice, and more specifically help with turning your conventional and dry Rules of Employment into a powerful solution, inspiring your staff and enabling you to manage Japanese employees effectively.

We would like readers to focus on the tremendous strategic advantages to be gained with improved Rules of Employment, pay and retirement practices. If combined with built-in "applications software" and guidance they can help prevent strategic mistakes from being made on into the future and long after you left Japan—Strategic Rules of Employment can be your on file around the clock Personnel Consultant/Manager, combined with strengthening your supervisor's skills and leadership.

For those fighting business battles this book will give an awareness of and point-out a number of areas where new or changed practices can be implemented in surprisingly easily changeable policy language in your Rules of Employment.

This will:

1. Save (or even earn!) you hundreds of thousands to even millions of dollars each year (depending on your size).
2. Energize and motivate your managers and staff.
3. Prepare you better for recent and future legal/policy changes effecting your corporate human resource management.

Reading *Taking Charge in Japan* can embolden, then assist you in achieving real and measurable results in areas such as:

1. Take advantage of legitimized systems of performance pay and flexible bonus as practiced at the biggest and best Japanese firms but probably not at yours.
2. Largely eliminate the poor performer problem and the deadwood safely, cheaply, and with legal (and moral) mandate.

3. Effectively discourage unwanted turnover and drastically reduce the actual costs in retirement benefit paid out to those who jump ship. (This alone could save a firm of even 75 staff a million U.S. dollars or more per year, and is particularly essential in a tight labor market with today's roving headhunters.)
4. Give (thoughtful and fair) top management the powerful tools to freely transfer, reorganize and restructure work and positions with commensurate pay adjustments (if required).
5. Slash costs, improve productivity and create a legally acceptable (and employee lauded) no overtime corporate culture.
6. Become able to manage freely and with control over even a feisty union or in the face of uncooperative employees.

Measurable bottom line gains in these and many other areas may seem only remotely interrelated but they can all in essential ways be governed by a pioneering Rules of Employment solution. For the *gaijin* boss one of the concrete and practical aims of this book is to establish an awareness of the importance of this turnkey solution combined with conventional Rules of Employment. (Not as they are now, but after they become a dynamic living and breathing management tool.) The difference that good strategic Rules of Employment, compensation, retirement and implementation policies can have has been misunderstood and greatly underestimated.

Each and every expatriate boss must understand what he's got—what's good, what's bad, what needs to be changed. This boring document after metamorphosis and with enhancements can and should be your most powerful management tool.

(This is another one that unfortunately cannot be left to your subordinates!)

Client Testimonials

Once in a while in the career of an international executive managing multinational operations in a number of different countries with different cultures, laws, and practices, you can go into a new situation in a new country and face a strong organized challenge from certain groups of employees. Maybe it tends to happen after a termination or some other crisis, or when top expatriate management changes.

I would say that depending on how we managed this particular situation, it could have been either very bad and debilitating to the firm, or with the proper advice and management, the problem can be overcome to make the company even stronger and improve solidarity.

It should be a great comfort to any corporate owner or professional management, particularly to the multinational community here in Japan, to know that in his particular area of expertise, a consultant as experienced and competent as Mr. Nevins exists. Not at all wishy-washy, he knows what has to be done and takes a clear and firm position. He has done it before, and the confidence and clarity of strategy as well as means of implementation are precisely the input which the new multinational manager needs when coming into a new country with new practices and different corporate environments.

Mr. Nevins has a way of reducing all the nebulous information and contradictory advice you receive into a common sense and clear position, allowing the expatriate manager to confidently make the most of his intuitions and innate leadership to put out the fires, seize and maintain control, and to get on with the job of managing and building the business.

I recommend you give Mr. Nevins a call if you are facing a challenge from a handful of radical troublemakers, unsavory staff attitudes, unreasonable demands in terms of benefits, work conditions, and work rules; or the other kinds of unpleasantness one would normally associate with the wrong kind of collective action, sometimes characteristic of certain unionized environments.

Roland M. Bischoff
President
Kuehne & Nagel
March 1989

During the last two years Mr. Nevins has worked with me and two of my predecessors in conceptualizing and beginning to permeate and implement throughout the organization new ideas, perspectives, and systems to motivate, improve communications, and further enhance productivity and morale.

Employees and the union are more aware of the constraints the bottom line imposes on all of us, and that only peak performance of each and every staff will guarantee corporate health and survival.

Mr. Tom Nevins has an ability to assess critically yet constructively the assumptions and plans we make. He has experienced what works and doesn't work, and brings you this "street sense", along with of course, knowledge of the law and legal constraints. It is helpful to have Tom on call to bounce ideas off him.

It is easy to forget, and/or realize, that TMT is also a major force in Executive Search with a large and effective team of some 15 professional Recruiters. Obviously the consulting perspective brings value added to TMT recruiting activities. This makes Mr. Nevins a pretty special headhunter as well!

R. Bruce Norris, Jr.
President (former)
A.C. Nielsen Company of Japan Ltd.
July 1987

You and your firm have made many contributions to the ARC group over the past six years, and I thought it timely to acknowledge "officially" the contribution you have made.

The late Dizzy Dean said, "it ain't braggin' if you've done it." I believe that you and your staff could justifiably do some "braggin'." Based on the results you have produced for ARC in personnel consulting and executive recruitment, I can recommend you without reservation to any businessman interested in maximizing his people/performance effectiveness in Japan.

Based upon your past successes, your clear vision for the future and your investment in people, I believe that TMT is going to experience tremendous growth. I am proud to know you and to be a customer.

Robert White
President/Founder
ARC International Ltd.
October 1986

I can heartily and most strongly recommend Mr. Nevins as a personnel/management consultant to give you the general guidance as well as detailed analysis, strategy, recommendations and concrete assistance with execution of some of the most difficult steps that need to be taken when it comes to rationalizing and revitalizing an organization.

Although our bank has had many successes in Japan, due to our long history, the aging of our workforce, and changes in financial markets with the need to accommodate to new and different skill mixes for investment banking products, it became necessary not only to review past practices, such as compensation by age and service, but also to change some internal rules sometimes resulting in adverse impact on our staff.

Mr. Nevins played an instrumental role in allowing us to fulfill these difficult organizational needs successfully. He has rich past experience, strong principles, and the ability to pass both this vision as well as specific plans to the Japanese implementing officers with his fluent and convincing Japanese communication skills.

With his guidance and inputs we educated and persuaded employees as to the need for change, and ended up making significant adjustments in pay and personnel practices culminating in his creation for us of new Rules of Employment, Salary, and Retirement Regulations. We also succeeded in significantly reducing staff such that we are now in a much stronger competitive position.

/Bernard Delage
General Manager for Japan (former)
Banque Indosuez
July 1987

Shortly after arriving in Japan in August 1985, I had occasion to meet Mr. Nevins and the TMT group. Over the past two years, TMT has been of significant help on a variety of personnel related/organizational issues. It has been instrumental in our effort to recruit key staff including some of our most senior and capable executives.

TMT's contract terms are fair and largely performance oriented. There is the right balance between success contingency and financial commitment and support from the client. Their approach is flexible and meets a wide range of client recruiting needs covering all operational areas of the company.

It's a pleasure to recommend Mr. Nevins' services based on his positive performance and integrity. He and the TMT group can offer a client, especially a newcomer, the perspective and insight he needs to get things done and manage effectively in Japan.

Mitchell P. Cybulski
President
Bristol-Myers K.K.
June 1987

Since 1984 we have gone back to TMT to fill some of our difficult professional trader positions. They consistently produce viable candidates in a difficult and tight market.

More recently (Spring, 1987), I worked with Mr. Nevins in reviewing some of our personnel and compensation practices. He has a full knowledge of not only textbook law and practice, but also thoroughly knows the specific details of how tens of companies manage and pay their staff. He can always give specific examples of successful strategies and solutions he has used in the past.

A couple of hours with Mr. Nevins can answer many questions (point out what questions to ask) and provide you the solutions, complete with document implementation.

David R. Johnson
Controller (former)
Cargill North Asia Ltd.
June 1987

Ecco is a major temporary help dispatch firm originating in France and now with a worldwide network. We got off to a rocky start in Japan with the wrong locally hired national making some bad hires, business decisions, and practices. Luckily, within a few short months we got on top of this, and with Mr. Nevins' help, were able to sort out and solve these problems.

As with most expatriates, I did not know all the ins and outs of Japanese business and what I could and could not do. Mr. Tom Nevins backed me up all the way, including winning our case at the Labor Standards Office, mediation proceedings, and even assisting me in cleaning the people out of an office and closing it down. Now the company is running smoothly with a good team, and we are making money. But without our decisive surgery, in a very short period of time the cancer could have spread and permanently damaged our Japan operation. We have learned a lot, and I must say "merci" to Mr. Thomas J. Nevins.

Eric Abramson
Representative Director (former)
Ecco Japan Co., Ltd.
June 1989

I had heard many stories from other banks about how difficult and costly it was to rationalize their Tokyo operations by cutting-back poor performers and head-count. Contacting Mr. Nevins, he showed me that there were better, and less costly ways of doing it, without losing key staff, or jeopardizing morale.

With his assistance, I was able to cut costs, increase profits and come in with a positive program that further enhanced already high productivity. At the same time, we made adjustments in personnel regulations where needed, being sure to have good personnel systems that will work well for the bank in the competitive Tokyo financial services environment.

David L. Munson
Vice President and
General Manager (former)
Wells Fargo Bank, N.A. Tokyo Branch
June 1987

TMT and Mr. Tom Nevins have been working closely with Federal Express since 1985. I have known Mr. Nevins for years, and just since I joined the company in July 1987, I have seen his signature on many invoices.

Whether it be initially setting up our Rules of Employment, salary and retirement practices back in 1985, or the many issues that we have consulted him on since, including the more recent merger of Federal Express with Flying Tigers here in Japan and around the world, he has always impressed me as a foreigner who really knows Japan. I have known very few foreigners who could really hold their own both in Japanese and against Japanese on questions of pay and benefits, employee relations, and the other areas in which we use his service. He is one of the few foreigners you can deal with who actually makes you forget that he is a foreigner.

I can see that Tom is a powerful ally who brings truth and understanding to otherwise unknowing expatriate managers who can easily lose their way in Japan or be taken down the primrose path by well meaning—or sometimes not so well meaning—Japanese advisers or colleagues.

You can't get away with this when Mr. Nevins is around. He is tough, but he is fair. I have learned a lot, and he is a good, honest man you can trust whether you are a *gaijin* or a Japanese.

Yasunari Tamura
Personnel Director (former)
Federal Express Japan K.K.
June 1989

When Kohler came into Japan to do more business on a direct basis we depended on TMT to build-up our staff and to consult with us on personnel and compensation matters. TMT was able to scout and place successfully for us seven people from the top executive positions down, in the one year period between the summers of 1985 and 1986. The great majority of these staff came out of the leading Japanese competitors.

Mr. Nevins also was an excellent resource when it came toward not only giving needed advice, but he also was able to define, design and set-up all of the documents and regulations required by the authorities in terms of Rules of Employment, Retirement Regulations and Salary/Allowance Rules.

TMT brought us success and results. Its approach to headhunting—the scale, depth and quality of its effort—was a refreshing change after initial false starts with others.

David P. Whittingham
President (former)
Kohler Company
June 1987

In the winter of 86/87 TMT filled our most senior position in marketing and sales in a timely fashion.

I have also found Mr. Nevins to be most useful, effective and convincing in interacting between the head office and senior Japanese management in plotting strategy toward difficult personnel problems—avoiding mistakes and successfully and cheaply obtaining the needed results.

Mr. Nevins' approach toward the handling of poor performers is simple yet profound— and most effective at keeping those remaining on their toes. We are also getting some useful inputs from him towards improving the language of our personnel documents, and systems.

Ryo Yonemoto
President (former)
Wyeth (Japan) Corporation
June 1987

In the one year period between November 1985 and October 1986, TMT worked with us in our recruiting effort for several mid-career senior research positions.

They were successful in filling seven positions, including several of our most critical senior technical management jobs. TMT showed an ability to meet our uncompromising standards and introduced us to key, line performers from several top Japanese corporations and government organizations.

Howell A. Hammond
Vice President (former)
Research and Development
Kodak Japan K.K.
June 1987

During the 1985 period, I worked closely with TMT as both an executive search firm and human resources consultant in Japan. TMT assisted in recruiting a number of staff for our Tokyo office, and over a three year period, was instrumental in the recruiting and placement of three senior Japanese at the director level. TMT consistently scouted and assisted in recruiting managers who met our requirements.

Mr. Nevins' extensive knowledge in the human resources area, including labor relations, personnel consulting and benefits, provided valuable perspective to strategic organization issues facing the company in compensation, retirement, benefit and other employment policies. As a consultant, Mr. Nevins consistently demonstrated a vigorous commitment to ensure that foreign companies operating in Japan are able to remain competitive in the human resource aspect of their operations.

His experience is well balanced between the practical, theoretical and legal aspects of labor relations in Japan.

Robert B. Kennard
Director Business Development, Asia
Chairman (former)
Monsanto Japan Ltd.
July 1989

It is extremely convenient and helpful to have Mr. Nevins available in Tokyo as a sounding board on my ideas and to obtain advice and perspective on the various challenges posed in the area of effective union management and the many other specific personnel problems which come up in the course of our work each day. For the last 18 months or so, particularly during the "*shunto* base-up" period in the spring, I have periodically gone to him for answers and to seek coaching (the confidence factor one needs) to carry out strategic policies to make sure there is a fair balance between employee/union interests and the realities of effectively and profitably running an airline.

Without boring you with details of our own situation and the progress we have made, let me offer you a couple of interesting quotes from a policy paper Mr. Nevins presented to us after having analyzed our Rules of Employment, compensation, retirement scheme, and collective bargaining agreements, etc.

"Strikes are indeed counterproductive. By definition, a strike means that there is a loss in productivity and economic damage to a business such that it becomes less possible to offer employees a higher pay increase. Any past pattern where strike action resulted in management being forced to meet union demands must end, because rewards for such behavior will obviously merely result in continued unreasonable demands on the part of the labor union and will encourage a union and its membership to continue to go out on strike or engage in a wide variety of other forms of collective action."

I believe this is a refreshing if not even innovative concept. To make a lower offer after a strike should thus not necessarily subject one to an unfair labor practice and can instead be justified with a computer's calculation.

Another pioneering concept that is remarkable in the simplicity of its truth and clarity is his following position as presented to me:

"An employee, whether a union or non-union member, who insists upon wearing an armband, or in other ways distracts and makes customers feel uncomfortable directly resulting in real economic loss, or who refuses to work overtime when the company is in need, or will not pitch in and switch holidays to accommodate the company with holiday work, certainly has no right to expect to be rewarded the same bonus or annual pay increases as a more cooperative and accommodating employee. If the uncooperative employee happens to be a union member, this is not a question of union discrimination but it is a question of employee discrimination and the right of management to discriminate between good employees and not so good employees."

Hans-Eberhard Schultz
Controller/Japan and Korea
Lufthansa German Airlines
July 1989

I strongly recommend Mr. Nevins as a highly experienced, creative, and convincing advisor. He really cares about the client, identifies with his and employee needs and is committed to smoothly solving problems and this can include hands-on and direct interfacing with employees in his very functional and convincing Japanese.

My company established the Ore-Ida frozen foods business here in Japan in August of 1983, and we have been quite successful in penetrating the market. Ore-Ida brand fried potatoes are the market leader by a large margin having achieved 38% share in Tokyo and 32% in Osaka since the company's founding. However, due to a desire to achieve "low cost operator" status our parent company, H.J. Heinz Pitt. PA., asked us to look at ways to become more efficient. As a result, we elected to consolidate Ore-Ida Japan and Heinz Japan. Certainly our objective was to do so smoothly, but even with that intention the task was not easy.

Since there was overlap in some job areas, a limited workforce reduction was necessary. Furthermore, we faced some transition dislocations and challenges in that benefits and pay levels between the two companies varied considerably, and these matters had to be resolved along with winning employee acceptance.

Mr. Nevins was most helpful in isolating the issues, clarifying legal points, local practice, and in meeting with the employee group, assisting us to reach an amicable and constructive solution to this major organizational adjustment.

Larry D. Blagg
Japan Branch President (former)
Ore-Ida Foods Japan Inc.
June 1987

The Sandoz Group has a strong position in Japan with some 2,000 Japanese employees. Sandoz Yakuhin, K.K. has some 1,000 employees, and formally established in 1960, it is certainly one of the leading foreign capitalized pharmaceutical companies in Japan.

We had no problems and did not even particularly anticipate the discovery of any problems when we asked Mr. Nevins to nonetheless review our situation, and give us a report. Fundamentally, we came out of his check-up with a clean bill of health, but just as a company should never rest on its laurels and should insure that quality improvements and product differentiation are constantly taking place, we were sufficiently impressed and convinced by Mr. Nevins' discoveries and recommendations that we took it upon ourselves to revise certain policies and sections of our Rules of Employment language.

Mr. Thomas Nevins worked closely with our Japanese officers in charge of personnel and compensation, and was flexible in reflecting their ideas and compromise language into TMT's original recommendations. Along with our Japanese personnel officers, Mr. Nevins completed his input in the exercise by making two presentations in both Japanese and English before our Board of Directors.

At the end of the exercise it was clear to us that there are always better ways to do almost anything. Many companies must be assuming that they are implementing the best of standard Japanese policies, sometimes combined with variations influenced by the foreign capitalized parent. Mr. Nevins has a way of taking one step back and divorcing himself from both typical Japanese and Western practice. After objective analysis, he has learned to integrate concepts and develop alternate innovative approaches that make even better sense and are more strategically sound, and meet the realities and needs peculiar to a foreign capitalized firm in Japan that is growing fast and has had to do some mid-career hiring over the years with a resultant blend and mix of different corporate cultures.

Fridolin H. Leuzinger
Vice-President
Sandoz Yakuhin, K.K.
July 1989

Teisan, a subsidiary of L'Air Liquide, has been a leading producer of industrial and special gases and related equipment in Japan since 1907. The business is strong and profitable, but with 1,400 employees, and changes in the industry one can never be complacent; and along with some of our competitors, we are carrying out a rationalization program with staff cuts.

I first engaged Mr. Nevins in November 1985 soon after I arrived in Japan. He played an instrumental role in confirming that my goals could be accomplished even in Japan, and went on to interface effectively between myself and the Japanese executives, impressing them with his ability to also relate to their needs on shared terms and in their language.

We were better able to comprehend each other and with his initial guidance have been able to carry-out an effective staff rationalization program with employee understanding and the union's cooperation.

Mr. Nevins also efficiently designed and set-up the Rules of Employment, (personnel practices, compensation and retirement benefits) for a new L'Air Liquide subsidiary.

Although our mid-career recruitment needs are extremely limited, TMT also can be highly recommended for the timely delivery of extremely well qualified managers who were carefully screened and scouted for us. We successfully hired our man.

Herbert R. Wollgiehn
Chairman and C.E.O.
Teisan K.K. (L'Air Liquide)
June 1987

Our Alternate Underground Inside Title

Taking Charge in Japan

—with or without an M.B.A. and without the B.S.*—

(*The Author does have the Bachelor of Science degree.)

Contents and Chapter Introduction
in a Nutshell

I. Recruiting—Everyone's Bottleneck to Success ———— 39

A blueprint to success and a wealth of practical information for the businessman. Even for the job applicant, a little reading between the lines will provide invaluable insight to anyone seeking a position, hoping to interview better, structure their pay package or succeed on the job.

This exactly follows the outline of a speech of the same title I made at the International House on November 16, 1989, sponsored by the *Japan Times* and A.T. Kearney.

A rather similar presentation was made at the Capital Tokyu a month later on December 14, 1989, before the French Chamber of Commerce. They asked me to write it up, and the French version of this appeared in the Spring and Summer 1990 issue of their excellent quarterly magazine, *Japon Eco*.

3. Avoiding Costly Mistakes in Offer Letters, Contracts, and Compensation/Benefit Packages

4. Timely Solutions to Problem Employees and Cutting Back Losses When Necessary

5. Conclusion

II. On Why They Win and How to Become a Winner

1. Why You Can't Beat the Japanese at Their Own Game—It's Because There Are Different Rules

A fresh perspective and behind the scenes in depth look at the differences between Japan's and other countries' legal and regulatory systems. America is strangling itself with litigation and compliance with teeth. In certain areas Japan is more tolerant of the flexible application of the rule or guideline.

This article appeared in the *Spring/Summer 1990 Cornell Enterprise* published twice a year by the Johnson Graduate School of Management, Cornell University. The 1989 Business Week Survey of American M.B.A. programs placed the Cornell Johnson School within the top five.

2. Little and Big Tricks of Any Trade for Japan or Anywhere — 97

On the lighter side, new ideas and tips to help you to reach your potential and succeed in business in Japan or anywhere.

3. Managers and Monday Morning in Tokyo and New York — 102

Walks you through a typical day in the life of a manager in Tokyo and New York, so you can empirically experience the pressures, forces, environmental factors, motivators, and demotivators that each one has to live with and respond to in very different ways—Always focusing on how and why the Japanese organization works the way it does.

III. Twenty Questions and Answers on Recruiting, Selecting, Attracting, Rewarding, Managing, Motivating, Controlling Costs of, Disciplining, and Rehabilitating/"Firing" the Japanese —————————————— 115

Even if you're not running a business yourself, you can get a lot from these 20 questions. If you are trying to "take charge" and make a difference in Japan you have combined here, what the Bible is to the worshiper and the treasure map is to the pirate.

Most of these articles appeared in serial form in the *Japan Times* in the mid 1980s. They are very different in writing style and content from *Japan Time*s serialized articles of the early 1980's appearing in *Labor Pains and the Gaijin Boss—Hiring, Managing, and Firing the Japanese*. (Japan Times, 1984)

IV. For a Change of Pace, Other Views on Japan and How It Works ———— *189*

1. What's Wrong with America? What's Right about Japan? — All Over Dinner and Drinks ———— *190*

In a hotel room and restaurant you can join a fast paced and dizzying dialogue between a business visitor seeking orientation and the labor/personnel consultant who is being pressed and stretched to not only present why Japan works so well within the company unit but also how business and government etc. work so well together.

2. Economic Growth Is Fine.... But More Important the Japanese Must Wake Up and Join the Human Race ———— *207*

For the many foreigners struggling with the Japanese language or for those who have already paid their dues but are frustrated and feel they are not being let in, here is an empathetic piece—you may not be the only one! Things have been getting better, however, during the ten years since this article was delivered in Japanese speech form before a Japanese audience.

Since I wanted this message to go to a Japanese audience at the time, it was published in the Japanese language by *Shukan Diamond* in 1981.

3. The *Gaijin* Boss and Japanese Women—New Opportunities - 215

Working or non-working women will be particularly interested in this article appearing in the March 30, 1986, *Japan Times* "Guest Forum" in connection with the passage of the Equal Employment Opportunity Law taking effect from two days later, April 1, 1986. When there's too much protection, there can be no equality. If anything, some legal protection— overtime, holiday-work, authorized type of work were lifted or loosened while companies were asked to stop discriminating. Progress is being made.

At TMT we used April 1, 1986, as a trigger date to set up a separate organization to place secretaries and female clerical staff. ABA (Access Business Associates) is "managed for women by women."

V. Case Studies and More from Behind the Bamboo Board Room —————————————————————————————— 221

1. Absolutely Required Reading for the Serious Businessman— the ¥ and $ Lifeblood and Guts of Your Company ———————— 222

You discover you are by no means the perfect salesman when you find (unfortunately former) clients enthusiastically selling you on the value of your product! Two or three clients over a two month period told me about the millions of dollars in cost savings and opportunities, sales and profits gained because of my management policies and, more concretely, our strategic written policies in the form of Rules of Employment, pay, and retirement policies.

They said I can and should charge more, and the clients would appreciate it more because I would have to sell it better and demonstrate its value. The client would, in turn, understand it better and use it more effectively.

We have made dramatic changes in the traditional and conventional approach to Rules of Employment (and salary and retirement regulations) with the addition of our unique and pioneering "Application Software."

This probably represents the single biggest breakthrough to assist and strengthen foreign capitalized firms in Japan since market liberalization measures in the early 60s! Required reading for the expatriate executive and his head office.

2. Headhunting the Samurai ———————————————————— 230

Tom Peters of *In Search of Excellence* fame is an older fraternity brother of mine from Fiji (Phi Gamma Delta) and Cornell (along with Ken Blanchard—*One Minute Manager*) although I never met either of them. Tom's newsletter on *Achieving Excellence* had me write a piece on the headhunting scene in Japan.

3. The Japanese (Asian?) Executive Search Trap ——————— 233

If this article saves even a handful of executives from hiring the wrong man for the wrong reasons, I will have been rewarded many times over for the time and energy I spent to write it.

In fact, it was from feelings of frustration at the mistakes even our own clients make that drove me to give this gift to you. Well worth a serious read the night before you interview a slate of candidates.

4. *Gaijin* Boss Beware! of the $400 Commuter Allowance —— *237*

We are talking here, not only about ¥ and $'s but also about equity and fairness among employees. Before the law changed, I made sure this message was aired in the *Japan Times*, and this article appeared there on March 6, 1989.

  It is surprisingly easy to fix this problem and make a strategic adjustment the way I had to do at my own firm.

5. A Neck Cutting Leads to Revolt—West Clashes with East — *240*

Everything here down to the last detail is a true story—an actual case study. I wrote it many years ago, and it remained unpublished until now as the client asked me to hold off for "at least five to ten years." Names, places, and nationalities were changed to protect the innocent!

  As a sequel to the story, you may be interested to know that within six months of the incident the Japanese president, who was fired and rehired, went to a worldwide sales conference, where he was one of those asked to make a presentation and proceeded to tell all the Frenchmen and other Westerners assembled why they were (sexually) impotent.

  I heard he was fired for the final time within a year or so after that.

6. If the Headhunter Could Cry on the Client's Shoulder— or What the Client Should Do for a Successful Recruiting Campaign so the Headhunter Can Make No Excuses —————— *258*

All the orientation information and concepts are fine, but when it comes to succeeding at recruiting something as simple as selling well, along with treating candidates and your headhunters well, is probably more important than anything else.

  We have placed over 60 executives and staff into one client and even when they went into essentially a one year hiring freeze, they insisted on paying us our non-deductible retainer. Client/vendor relationships can't always be like that, but I think we did have a big role in making them number one in their field within a couple of years. All of us at TMT will be forever thankful, and we buy their products every chance we get! Here we would like to supply you with the actual excerpt from our TMT bimonthly "How Are We Doing?" Client Survey. These reminders are presented to clients for reference along with our survey requesting they evaluate our service during the period.

  I think it might also assist non-TMT clients with their recruiting program, and help improve your relationship and the results you can enjoy with the executive search firm you are now using.

VI. A Helpful Summary—So as Not to Forget the Key Concepts and Strategic Tools —————————— 263

1. A New Trend in the Japanese (Labor) Market—A Nationwide NHK TV Interview ——————————— 264

This is from a half hour interview show appearing in April 1986 on nationwide NHK television. The government subsidized national TV network—perhaps similar to the British BBC.

At the time, Mr. Tatsuya Komatsu was president of Simul International, reputed to be Japan's leading interpreting and translating service with excellent training facilities in these areas. Mr. Komatsu was born in 1934 in Nagoya and is also a well-known author and commentator.

2. Strategic Tools for Managing Japanese Personnel—Local Practices, Policies, and the Law. Using Them in Six Key Areas ——————————— 274

This is largely based on the video text accompanying a three hour video of the same name. Produced by and available from the *Japan Times* (1987, ¥19,600 plus ¥400 postage).

We had been talking about producing a video, and I happened to have two speeches/ seminars at the American Club within three days. The title comes from the Saturday morning seminar, which was sponsored by the American Chamber of Commerce in Japan (ACCJ) and the University of Maryland.

Material here is capsuled and focused, making it easier for the businessman to readily apply the powerful Strategic Tools.

Introduction on How to Read and Use the Book

What's behind the Book's ("Alternate Inside"*) Title and What I'm Trying to Give You

(* See the preceding title which we were tempted to initially use.)

This is the fourth book I've written, and there has been a long six years between this one and the first printing of *Labor Pains and the Gaijin Boss—Hiring, Managing, and Firing the Japanese* (Japan Times, 1984).

One of the reasons I've held off is that *Labor Pains and the Gaijin Boss* still serves a very useful purpose, is selling well and is definitely worth keeping alive. Another reason for holding back in coming up with another book in spite of having a lot of excellent content already lined up for publication was the inability to come up with a title I, and, hopefully, readers, could get excited about.

The underground title was essentially presented to me by a European client who came to TMT in the Spring of 1990 just after the cherry blossoms finished fluttering to the ground, in our area along the Palace, near the British Embassy. We are over near the Ichibancho crossroads, and one of his Japanese colleagues said as long as he was coming over here that he could get a glimpse of the cherry blossoms. As he entered the office, hot and sweaty he declared that these two locations were not that close and that he had fallen for the 'Bachelor of Science' again. Coming from a European at the first meeting I was a bit surprised, and in our discussion he went on to tell me how "When I asked to get a copy of the Rules of Employment, Salary Regulations and Retirement Regulations in preparation for this meeting, I was again given the 'Bachelor of Science'."

As I listened to him, suddenly I could envision and see graphic and detailed images of scores of expatriate executives. The true but tired *gaijin* bosses streaming through my office over the years with similar comments: "I have worked in the States, throughout Europe, did a stint even in South America and just came from Singapore but never cease to be amazed why in this country (Japan) we cannot just focus on the issues, on what is good for the company, on how to build sales—Why we can't argue about and reach a decision over real business issues?—Why is it always this 'Bachelor of Science'? Or it could be the other American businessman who blurted out in anger "Why aren't we able to get things done here through people, make a change, get the right distributor, rationally discuss the possibility of moving out a manager and replacing him with someone who is big enough to do the job and face these issues like businessmen instead of putting up with all this 'Bachelor of Science'?"

And then there was another European who had worked for American companies in the States and in Europe as well as for European companies in Europe and in several other countries around the world. Over wine and cheese at his house recently, he quipped "It really is interesting to watch Tom, isn't it? Those American businessmen are so tough when they go to Europe, yet they fall apart and crumble like cookies at the feet of the Japanese. Here they cannot seem to be able to tell the difference between sound strategic business issues and decisions, getting results, and instead become drugged by or even emasculated by this constant flow of Japanese 'Bachelor of Science'."

Recently an Australian businessman told me that he was tired and ready to go back, and he met a British businessman at a party the day before who commiserated and said the same thing. "At every turn I am thwarted. With every initiative I am stonewalled. I cannot live with this 'Bachelor of Science'."

I know that every expatriate businessman does not feel this way. I also realize that given the way TMT markets and because of the solutions and services we provide, we may be scooping up even an uncharacteristic percentage of discontents—people that are facing resistance as they try and make their companies better and succeed at the mandate, which is often their reason for being sent to Japan in the first place. I think we also must realize that a lot of this deep seeded conservatism, or lack of cooperation, or even fair play when it comes to managing your business better, does not just necessarily come from impulses of turf protection or self preservation but from a genuine belief on the part of Japanese people that a foreign businessman cannot, and will not, understand how Japan works and thus is in no position to make any sort of a useful and meaningful contribution.

Of course, such a parochial view is annoying, smug, condescending and luckily not at-all accurate. The fact is you do have a mandate and a business to run, and your energy, creativity and inputs probably are just the thing that is needed to energize your firm, build the business—and at some point, depending on how this is done, it will be welcome and you can be a leader and hero to everyone on your payroll. This we have seen many times.

Let me emphasize that the 'Bachelor of Science' in the "alternate inside" title is not just coming from Japanese sources—your internal staff and managers, joint-venture partners, lawyers, and consultants, government regulations, your distributors or popularized Japanese stereotypes and ways of thinking. It also comes from *gaijin* sources—including fellow expatriate businessmen, popularly held mis-understandings in the west of Japanese practices, including, more specifically in my field, the unrealistic and improbable position that there can be no "negative change" or employees "must give their consent" to any changes, when not to fix what is wrong will preclude your firm from ever being able to compete and hold your own in Japan against powerful Japanese firms.

In this book then I am trying to give you information, insight, techniques, strategic tools to get the job done, and even reassurance that you are not the only one facing this same challenge in a far away land with a different culture and language. If anything has helped our business at TMT, it was my realization that you must enrich others before you can enjoy riches of even the modest dimensions known to us. As I help managers in their every day working lives, I have faith that as they read this book they will appreciate what we have written and done, and they will want to come and work with us and watch us do the same thing for them.

I hope to show you that there is a way to accomplish anything on your agenda. If you are discontent, there is a reason. If you even sense that things could be better, they can. If sales are growing 30% per year; but if you hear of a competitor who has been in the market for only two or three years and is already pulling in 30 or 40 million U.S., you begin to ask the big question "Japan is a tough market and all that, but what if we had a few more (or other) managers" or "What if our company really understood and was taking advantage of the tremendous strengths of Japanese companies in areas such as (even unlimited) performance ranges on summer and winter bonus or good flexible Rules of Employment and Policies, which would give our supervisors and managers the tools to manage flexibly and decisively as enjoyed at Japanese firms?"

And if you are focusing in on your business, trying to do lots of it and do it well, there is no place where business is done as well as it is in Japan. The Japanese need make no apologies or excuses for their corporate cultures, management style, decision making process, compensation, and reward systems. It all works just fine here; but if it's not working right at your firm, that may be a separate but very solvable problem.

If you are an expatriate executive (or Japanese manager, of course) who has even a sneaking suspicion or hunch that this can't be the real world and the Japanese wouldn't have been able to build their empires if it had to be like it seems to be at your firm, perhaps you should start to think about *"taking charge in Japan"* slowly, carefully, deliberately, and perhaps in only selected areas. Everything is not and cannot be wrong with your business and the way you are doing it. There may be debilitating weakness in only 20% or even 10% of your operation. Most foreign managers have rather universal experience in areas such as finance, manufactur-ing and even distribution and marketing. It is the area that TMT specializes where you are weakest, and that is why your hand went to this book and you pulled it off the shelf. I hope we can help you "take charge" where it counts and only as appropriate.

How to read and use the book

For starters, I hope you will skim the Table of Contents. We've done something a little different here, which makes our Table of Contents longer than what you're used to. You'll find there is a brief explanation and commentary on each article, to assist you in focusing on subject matter which may be most germane to the tasks you face on the job. For friends, students and scholars of Japan that want to absorb more from a nuts and bolts, labor and personnel consultant solving real problems, this commentary will also assist in selecting reading material of interest to you.

As with *Labor Pains and the Gaijin Boss*, this book need not be read at a furious pace in one sitting. Based on various seminars and sometimes previously published works, and due to the way it is compiled, there is some overlap and reinforcement of content. This dovetails well with the needs of the *gaijin* boss for example. As he begins his exciting adventure within his Japanese organization, as the months go by each chapter will be read with a new and different relevance. For the same reason, I guess, nowadays very few M.B.A. schools will take their students directly after university graduation. They want them to be out in the business world with working experience. And each business (or any resident) reader will grow and glean new and different things from the book as time passes.

For anyone interested in case studies and real life accomplishments in various foreign capitalized firms, I would encourage you not to skip a reading of the testimonials at the front of the book as they show you in black and white how we have changed compensation, retirement plans, and other benefits, even when this meant adverse impact or negative change and even without the so-called required "consent." Our motto is always, "forget the stereotypes and inaccurate myths. Do what must be done."

How does *Taking Charge in Japan* differ from *Labor Pains and the Gaijin Boss—Hiring, Managing and Firing the Japanese* (Japan Times, 1984)?

The content is totally different in that no two articles are the same or even actually very close at all.

Some of the articles or submissions in *Labor Pains and the Gaijin Boss* were the result of speeches and writings made as early as the late 70s and early 80s. I will stand by them, but an increasing wealth of experience in actually solving the problem and getting the client there has added a certain maturity and change of perspective to *Taking Charge in Japan*. For example, all professionals in the field of personnel or human resource management talk about "Paper Trails" when it comes to terminating a poor performer or problem employee. In anticipation of inevitable litigation perhaps such a paper trail is helpful; but the whole process of issuing written warnings, trying to get signatures, filing documents, is a bit weak. So whenever dealing with an employee with credibility and power, if possible, it is nice to avoid the legal tit for tat.

In the meantime, essentially, I have learned never to terminate, yet we end up with the same result without litigation, at no expense and in (generally) even a shorter period of time. Also in reality many clients never have the paper trail but our coaching combined with the "power talk" and our style of "rehabilitation" will get you exactly where you need to be, and even faster.

Taking Charge in Japan also gets into some new areas of self development and improvement to help you manage yourself and others better. It is more involved with positive motivation and business-building, but there is still the needed dose of the "how to" and technicalities of the TMT style "cut and chop." When you really have your back against the wall, when you're right and the other party's wrong, and you are also acting under the best of faith to protect the interest of your employer and the vast majority of your good well-meaning employees, a little well placed "cut and chop" is not to be avoided and has a way of realigning things and moving up and away in the right direction.

People, however, should always be given a chance to become a winner, or go out as a winner, and our flexible rehabilitation policies are better than the "hire and fire" approach. That one definitely does not work for you here. There are other options as used by the Japanese that must be available to the foreign capitalized firms to keep the playing field even and enable you to compete effectively at reasonable fixed cost levels and free of any debilitating litigation.

Indeed we have developed more subtle (and even more strategically powerful) alternatives to "cut and chop"; but the more we work with foreign capitalized businesses in Japan, the more convinced we become that people want good, tough and firm—discipline leadership and that the Japanese employee works best under the kind of tough and taut (yet warm and even personally obsessive) management as it is practiced in good Japanese firms. More people will leave your firm because there isn't enough recognition, room for growth, self-actualization and the demands of a disciplined yet free and energized environment—and they will inevitably be the wrong people that leave you. Those that leave seek those challenges and want to work in a company that makes them measure up and even draws out their own positive self expectancy of themselves. And in this process, I don't think I have to tell you what you end up being stuck with. This is why you need strategically sound, reward systems, Rules of Employment, retirement benefits, a high level of supervision, and leadership in your firm day in and day out.

What's happened since *Labor Pains*?

You can say that a lot has happened. You can also say that not much has changed. The statutes themselves are not adjusted as often as, for example, in the United States, particularly when it comes to the Labor Standards Law and Trade Union Law, which are two key statutes affecting the areas we discuss in this book. Also since court decisions do not create binding legal precedents, the 'rules are not changing as quickly and inflexibly in Japan as they might in other countries such as the United States.

From April 1, 1986, the Equal Opportunity Employment Law was passed, and women are slowly but surely making progress in the world of work. Organized labor in Japan was divided up between Sohyo, the more left wing largely government affiliated national center (upper body trade union), and Domei, which is largely private sector along with a couple of lesser national centers. As of November 22, 1989, most of these national centers and major trade union groups were united in an organization called Rengo. There were great hopes that in their first shunto—Spring Wage Offensive, the Rengo united front would help to bring in a bigger increase, but there was no great change here, so the union movement will continue to be moderate and cognizant of from what side their bread is buttered.

Moving into the decade of the 1990s, one of the most severe labor shortages in 20 years, the laws of supply and demand, a stronger yen, and the discovery of Japan through networking, etc., and word of mouth has caused a great influx of legal and illegal immigrants primarily from other Asian countries and the subcontinent (Pakistan more than India). There has been great contemplation and hand wringing on all of this, and from June 1, 1990, employers employing illegal immigrants can be subject to a fine of two million yen and up to three years in prison. Japan will only incrementally and very slowly become a less homogeneous nation.

People talk about the changing attitudes of younger employees, and it is true they are more interested in taking their vacations, and would more easily consider changing jobs with a growing interest in their private lives. Still though, comparatively speaking, there is tremendous dedication on the part of many to their firms. According to an annual Management Coordination Agency survey, out of 59.04 million employed workers, 2.47 million changed jobs between March 1988 and February 1989, or 4.2% of all employees. Among this number, 1.82 million or 74%

of those job changes were for reasons of personal fulfillment (i.e., they quit their firm voluntarily). As many as 26% or 650,000 employees (1.1% of total) were forced to change employers due to restructuring or through terminations/"rehabilitation" of poor and problem performers. As many as 8.58 million or 14.5% of all employees wanted to change their jobs. A much lower percentage of 3.6% or 2.13 million had actually tried to do so during that year. Therein enters the executive search consultant or headhunter.

Headhunting is still hard, labor intensive work in Japan; but at least when an employee is discontent and would consider changing his job, when the executive search consultant places his call and dangles an enticing offer in front of such a less-than-fulfilled fellow, we have a chance of doing some business and building your business.

My soul food continues to be the labor and personnel consulting that I have pioneered and developed in this market place. But another change since *Labor Pains* in 1984 is that the last few years TMT has consistently had over 15 executive search consultants on our payroll, and the last year or so the number has hovered just above and below 20 good men.

As long as you're reading a textbook of the "Three R's"(plus!), what is a valuable lesson you should pick up?

If you are a businessman, you should read all of this book; but you're probably also results and task oriented. You'll learn lots within these pages, but be sure and read the first chapter in Part V entitled "Absolutely Required Reading for the Serious Businessman—the ¥ and $ Lifeblood and Guts of Your Company." Underneath this charming title I will admit there is a bit of a hard sell, and please be sure to read the Summary Statement at the end, as it will help you understand how these approaches can work. Clients and friends have always told me that reading my articles and books are an eye opener; but since they are results and task oriented businessmen, they want all 15 years of my knowledge and experience in solving the tough ones in the form of a usable product. Well, this product is partially described here, and we are trying to demonstrate the value that it can bring. This will help TMT, but I hope I will be forgiven because many of you do very much need it. It has a shelf-life of some 30 years or more, and your firm will enjoy its benefits long after we spend this money.

We've been lucky at TMT and haven't had to go out and sell. Clients have told me we should, and that as part of servicing the community in which one lives and runs his business, we would really have an obligation to get out into the community with our message and to help more people concretely in a practical way that sticks and allows a defined and permanent change in their corporate culture and the way they supervise and reward their employees. What we describe here is indeed big and powerful and will make a significant difference in the success and prosperity of your firm, your employees, and will help you achieve the results you're targeting as a manager stationed in Tokyo.

This chapter of "Absolutely Required Reading" is something you can write home about, something that will make your life easier and is a powerful strategic gift that you can give and leave forever behind for your organization. So in this way *Taking Charge in Japan* leaves you with not just lessons but with a tangible architectural blueprint, a reinforced steel structure, and all the building blocks you need to succeed with people in Japan. People are 60 to 70% of your costs, and you can do nothing without them.

The two biggest lessons I've picked up in years

My Lesson One for Me and You—Create and you'll never have to compete and make sure people know the value of what it is that you sell.

That's really the key, isn't it? Whenever you come up with something new and better, you're in business. No product has an intrinsic indisputable value. The value is in the eyes of the beholder, and it's a great shock to someone who thinks he is good at consulting (sales) when the beholder or the client recognizes and appreciates the value of your service more than you did.

As we enter the decade of the 1990s and just as I hit 40 years of age, it took one of my clients leaving Japan, to tell me that I should get more money for what I do because the client will value the service more, the salesman will have to sell it better, the client will have to understand it and then will use it and take advantage of it, if both parties become clear about its true value. He went on to give me examples of the millions of dollars our written policies, coaching, and practices allowed him to earn and save during his six-year tenure in Japan.

That gentleman and some close clients I have subsequently talked to have encouraged me to create software, which prevents strategic mistakes from being made, even into the future, and provides the client with "an on-file around the clock Personnel Consultant/Manager at a fraction of the cost." It does much more than that and gives your employees and supervisors built-in guidance and instructions on what is expected of them, allowing them to do their jobs better, work better together. It can also define a program of corporate revitalization providing the needed direction and permanence.

Once we got going it did not take long to develop these new and very different solutions which are in no way comparable nor are in the same league with the conventional dry and boring version of Rules of Employment. Yet the thing that is so amazing, and the lesson for me (and for you too perhaps) if you think about your own situation is that although I had been making good conventional, strategically sound Rules of Employment that were head and shoulders over anything else available, and had been doing this in a serious way for over ten years, it took me that long and to reach the ripe age of 40 before I finally saw (or was shown) the light and a very different and innovative approach to my business.

Can you do the same thing for your Japan operation? (We'll make sure the head office appreciates and understands your efforts, accomplishments, and the value you are bringing.)

My lesson two for me and you—on how we think everything is o.k.,... and we're doing fine, or there's no way to do things better, but we're totally wrong on all three of these points

This is really an extension of Lesson One, and it is the stuff that all discovery and progress is made of. Inventors and all people who are catalysts for change are discontent with things the way they are. Maybe they also have an ego and want to make their mark on the world (sometimes they're also paid to do so!).

In my own case, since about 1982, we had been operating an executive search unit as a division of TMT. Although we are Tokyo based and have deliberately stayed away from affiliations with worldwide search firms, in Tokyo we have been a good sized headhunting firm placing senior and middle managers with at least 15 staff and at least ten executive search consultants since 1985. We are now a firm of about 30 staff and 20 full time executive search consultant employees on salary with supplementing incentives. With all the innovative changes that a good consultant must make in his client firms, I had been chugging along, running this executive search operation, believing that it was pretty difficult to build a good strong organization out of a group of hungry headhunters. Well, I was wrong. The trigger and catalyst for change didn't primarily come from within myself and good men and women within our organization came up with many unique innovations as part of systematizing headhunting and building an organization where consultants truly share and work well together. We also developed detailed and complex systems for taking out our own poor performers nicely balanced with a rich and varied reward system for the producers.

Indeed it is a microcosm of what I have tried to do in clients' shops. No need to come in with firing. Instead develop concrete performance targets measuring both level of activity as well as the bottom line yen earnings results per consultant.

This allows us to come in with subtle jabs giving people strong messages, sometimes a kick in the pants, and if at all possible, turning them into winners. And we have seen within our own organization that people can be turned around and made productive, and it would have seemed miraculous until we demonstrated and proved that it could be done. It took good leadership and good "followership." It meant never walking on eggshells, calling a spade a spade, and working with an open glass box when it came to performance, standards, and means of appraisal.

There are no surprises and no room for feelings of unfairness or favoritism. If somebody is "fired," everyone believes that was the only way to go. If someone leaves, people are disappointed, but they usually understand why. We got tougher, but we also got more fair. We created team work. We serve the client better. We make and enjoy richer rewards.

As I look back at all the innovations and changes, even within the confines of our own little business, I see that many of these innovations and adjustments have become an important and an indispensable part of our client service and internal performance-based management. Yet we didn't know that they existed and never missed them before we made those changes in how we run our business. And now I know there are still many things that we will discover, implement, and do better in the future.

I guess there is no big news here. We must never forget that we can always manage and run our businesses much better than we are. There are many areas where you can "take charge" and make a difference in your firm, and in this book I hope to give you the awareness, insight, confidence, passion, strategies, and techniques to do so.

I

Recruiting—Everyone's Bottleneck to Success

1

Manpower-inventory-planning and Sourcing Alternatives

Position creation, organizational and titling decisions

You want to determine if the search is really necessary and take advantage of each recruitment to examine your organizational structures. It can serve as a trigger or excuse to restructure and streamline. If you work with a thoughtful executive search consultant accustomed to working in areas other than just headhunting, this recruitment process helps to define with the client the job and executive specifications as well as give an accurate assessment of your current corporate culture or the nature of your current staff's background and their management quality. Don't get someone who is either over or underskilled. Recruit a second-rate executive at a lower salary, and you'll have no performance. A candidate from a large structured organization may not be able to perform in an unstructured one.

You have probably already decided whether to bring an expatriate from your home office or to replace an expatriate with a Japanese. One other option is to look at the growing number of bilingual foreigners who could be hired locally in Japan not requiring the full expatriate benefits, but rather a "transnational" package and status. Of course, there is no Japanese company in the world that would manage an overseas operation purely with non-Japanese local hires. They realize a valuable investment cannot be completely left up to others. My recommendation is that any foreign-capitalized firm also be sure and have expatriate representation in Japan—not necessarily at the chairman or president level, but at least it is important to have someone from the home office who is on a different career path from the Japanese executives. Otherwise, it is unlikely that better executives than those already hired will ever be identified, introduced, and placed into your organization. Indeed, it takes a very good man (if not a saint) to go out on his own initiative and hire a man better than himself, especially when the incumbent has complete control on the subsidiary organization and virtually all inputs and information flow to the home office. Even a rather young expatriate or locally hired foreigner in the financial, technical, or marketing area can be a good check and alternate information source on what is happening and the inputs available to the head office.

The age specifications on your job profile are of absolutely critical importance. Although foreign businessmen are aware that age and seniority are important factors in Japan, still with only rare exception, clients continue to expect high-level business or profit-centered department managers (*bucho*) and often even country managers to be aged between 35 and 45. Most often we are given an even more confining age range of 30 to 40. The other day a client came to us complaining that his headhunters have not been able to serve him and that the level of staff he is able to attract is extremely low. He is looking for a technical service manager (*bucho*) and another business development manager at that level. The problem he is facing primarily boils down to the fact that their initial hire and the man they expect to continue to have the key role in the organization is only 37 years old! He is doing a great job, but in Japan he would lack the confidence to manage older men. There are very few seasoned executives who would want to work underneath such a young man. I also might add that a 37-year-old is too young to be at the head of an organization. If he has a high-level title commensurate with his role, the fact that he has that title at his young age and with his background makes the company look small, unsophisticated, and unimportant in Japanese society. This is extremely crucial. Please stop and think about this. Even if your maximum age specification is 45, that really is a shame and makes things difficult for us headhunters. First of all, it unnecessarily precludes essentially everyone over 45. Yet this is the age group that has the most experience, the most contacts; and age in itself does not necessarily mean that vitality is lost. Secondly, if the 45-year-old is a *bucho*—or worse yet a country manager, very few individuals above 35 are going to be excited about joining that firm simply because, with a 60-year retirement age, the 45-year-old has 15 years left in either role.

Yes, I would recommend that for senior manager positions, clients refocus on the 45- to 55-year-old age group. Experience shows me that 50 to 53 are all the more preferable because you are able to bring in good managers throughout the 40-year age range. Still another problem with focusing on the 35- to 45-year age range for your senior managers is that the foreign capitalized and Japanese labor market is after those people. Yet at those younger ages, many of the managers are not yet sure where they will end up in their firm, and the good ones are still actively engaged on the line in very interesting jobs. Essentially, the younger the man, the larger the salary differential has to be in order to attract him. With executives in their early 50s, however, reasonable salary increases of 10 to 20% will often suffice.

Please also be aware of the common problem in foreign-capitalized firms which fail to create organizational structures to accommodate senior Japanese managers. It amazes me, but even in some very large foreign firms with several hundred employees and, in the case of one our clients, Japan sales alone of over $1 billion, there was not yet a knowledge or exposure to the importance of creating a Japanese *torishimariyaku-kai* (local board of directors at the Japanese K.K. subsidiary). Boards of directors at many companies throughout the world tend to be made up of outside directors—people from other industries, bankers, a variety of prominent individuals. In Japan, however, there are virtually no outside directors, and the boards are quite large. *Torishimariyaku* boards generally have between 15 and 30 or even 40 members. Thus, securing a position on the board of directors is a reasonable goal for the top performers in these firms, yet still the title is scarce enough to bring great distinction, recognition, and status within Japanese society. Certainly if a high-level candidate were already on the board of directors, he would not join your firm unless you were able to give him the same, or preferably, a higher board title. (This is especially true if you are a smaller firm. It would only be natural to jump two or three ranks in board title.) Just within the *torishimariyaku* board there are six levels: *hiratori* (lowest board level), *jomu* (managing director), *senmu* (senior managing director), *fukushacho* (vice-president), *shacho* (president), and *kaicho* (chairman). It is basically a pyramid structure, and in some firms the *fukushacho* title is not used. You would basically have one chairman, one president, perhaps two or three *senmu*, four to six *jomu*, and about double that number of *torishimariyaku bucho* or *torishimariyaku honbucho*.

I would like to encourage foreign firms in Japan to shoot for the stars. With a good executive search firm that has enough manpower to keep on top of the very labor intensive job which we have, we can bring you senior people at this level. Their connections and their very presence will serve as a magnet in bringing in and relieving the apprehension of future managers and staff that need be recruited. Making the most of these senior executives in their 50s is the only way to bring in equally excellent successors in their 40s and have them willing to join your firm. I cannot overemphasize the importance of age and titling (including *torishimari-yaku* possibilities) if you are to build a successful organization in Japan. I realize *gaijin* are not particularly concerned about these titles because it is not part of our culture and it is not a shared expectation. Recently we were completing the negotiation on a foreign expatriate who crossed over to another firm within his industry on a local basis here in Japan. I asked, "What about the board?" He answered, "What about the board? I don't do boards and windows!" But for senior Japanese it is no laughing matter.

Job posting and internal applicants

It's a good thing to do and when in doubt, give your own staff and managers the benefit of the doubt. Employees are almost always better than their jobs and benefit and get remotivated from a good stretch. Posting can either be done on a formal posting board, or the word can go around through department meetings or by way of circulating memos (*kairan*). Obviously, people don't have to post their own names, but they will start to talk to the appropriate decision makers. Yes, there is the risk that you have to turn them down, but presumably you have good reasons (otherwise you're accepting their bid).

Rather than have someone suddenly surprise you by quitting the firm, why not at least hear about their desire to take on the new job. Then you've been given forewarning and can stay in touch with that manager and give him some informal recognition, psychological massaging, and maybe even a pay increase.

My rule of thumb for an organization to stay young and fit is not to hire anyone until everyone is overworked. That way everyone will welcome the newcomer no matter who he is! When the overall impression in the organization is that the hire isn't necessary, people wonder what's happening and whether or not they are on the hit list to be tapped out of the organization. In any case, anticipate those feelings and reassure your good people. There are, of course, exceptions to this rule, and sometimes you have to do advance hiring in order to have people fully oriented at the head office and to get trained up and to be ready to take over from, for example, an expatriate manager.

Advertising

TMT has never run an advertisement in any newspaper or magazine in order to secure candidates that are introduced to our clients. I have always believed that if this category of candidate is being introduced, the client might just as well do it for himself. Whenever a client has any kind of feeling or propensity toward wanting to try out an ad, we certainly encourage him to do so. That will make him a better client for us and one that understands the labor market is indeed tight, and the only way to get good people is through using good headhunters. While the most widely subscribed and copious classified ads appear in the *Japan Times* on Monday, for major Japanese newspapers (primarily *Asahi* and *Nihon Keizai*), it is the Sunday edition where such ads are usually run; and businesspeople might have time on a Sunday afternoon to mull over their futures. There are also specialized recruitment magazines available such as those published by Recruit and Nihon Keizai Shimbun.

Depending on the position, these ads may be worth trying. You may be lucky and be able to pick up one or two good people who happen to be in some psychological or transitional state so that they're looking. Of course, the common line from executive search professionals is that busy, productive people engaged in their work and appreciated by their employers are certainly not looking at help-wanted ads. There's got to be truth in that. In my opinion the greatest danger faced by the rare firms which try to staff solely through advertising is that such firms have not discovered or may not be aware that the quality of their staff could be, should be (and must be) higher than it is. I have come in contact with any number of companies where top expatriate management has simply reconciled itself to hiring and putting up with subpar performance and people who are not big enough to do the job and to take advantage of the potential which really could be awaiting that firm and its product line in this marketplace.

If you are going to run an ad, take it seriously. Put yourself in the potential applicant's shoes to determine whether or not that ad would be attractive. Don't write up a long, dry laundry list of job requirements. Instead it is best to appeal to the kind of individual you want to attract. Only mention key qualities—not ones such as adaptability or cooperation. Naturally most candidates will decide that, "I'm adaptable" and "I am also cooperative. I guess I'll apply." But we know it really takes more than that. When writing the ad copy don't attempt to clone for the incumbent, and be sure not to set up too many prequalifying screens such as unnecessary educational degrees, experience, age constraints, etc. Realize, for example, that in Japan there are many fewer individuals with Ph.D.s, M.B.A.s, and M.S.'s. For example, in the United States in pharmaceuticals or chemical research, it is difficult to get very far in these technical positions without a Ph.D. Yet in Japan many of the key heads of R&D and clinical research certainly do not have Ph.D.s. When I first arrived in Japan years ago, one of the first bits of advice I got from a Japanese Ph.D. was that, "You really shouldn't be all that impressed with my degree. Please don't call me doctor. As a matter of fact, the main reason why people like myself get these degrees is that we were not able to get into the ministry or company of our choice, so we saved face and set up our own cushy fudge factor by staying on at the university and taking a shot at getting into a top employer again on this different basis."

I guess the main reason getting these advanced degrees is not so popular in Japan is that receiving the degree in fact is not rewarded by corporate business. After three or four years of additional graduate work, at best, the degree bearer will only come in at a salary level equivalent to the bachelor's degree holder at that firm with the same three or four years of experience. Often the degree experience is even somewhat discounted. Good internal technical training, lab work, and team approaches to development and design work must make up for this lack of individual excellence in the form of the Western model Ph.D. hire.

If you are going to try an ad, sell yourself as an employer rather than the job. Also be sure and talk about the worldwide operation in terms of head count and sales level. If the possibility exists for training abroad or to work abroad in the near future, be sure and take advantage of that.

Headhunters

Probably many of the readers have had mixed experiences using Tokyo headhunters. It is a tough and challenging business for us. Unlike our labor and personnel consulting service at TMT, which gets involved in compensation—design and change, Rules of Employment—set-ups and adjustments, problem employee solutions/terminations, staff reductions/cost-saving programs, and union/staff relations, it really is hard to maintain a 100% record in the executive search area. There are so many variables, and headhunters can't do the job by themselves. Indeed, it requires an excellent and close working relationship of cooperation with the highest priority placed on the search work by the client. Although the client intellectually knows that he desperately needs these people, when it gets right down to it, often reporting pressures to the home office and business and operational matters cluttering one's desk and awaiting one in the field manage to take priority over being able to give feedback on the resume sent from your headhunters, and the absolute necessity to have adequate time to be able to meet candidates and sell your firm to them.

Executive search fees in Japan are also expensive, generally 35% of annual income with up front commitment fees and perhaps ongoing retainers. Therefore, headhunting is costly, yet there are even greater costs engaged when trying to do business with a less-qualified workforce. Since candidates that are scouted are not looking for a job and really didn't need such a call from a headhunter at all, they are indeed passive candidates to say the least. Therefore, the headhunter who made the cold call must first be persuasive enough so that the individual will agree to a meeting. Then it is a question of our side basically selling your firm (along with yourself) to the candidate. This gets expensive because a passive candidate needs some good reasons to move if he is already in an interesting enough job at a prestigious Japanese firm. A significant pay increase for younger candidates, often as high as even 50% or more, is not uncommon. This extra money is one thing that can be rationalized to one's spouse and family. The good news about scouting these passive candidates is that they are generally unlikely to take a job if they do not have the confidence to carry out that job successfully. This means that you should certainly not walk on eggshells around them, and if you have any doubts about a candidate's ability to do a certain aspect of your job requirements, you should vividly describe these needs and attempt to screen out the candidate or scare him off. If after all that, he is still willing to join you even though he is happily employed, chances are his expectations and abilities are in line with your needs.

How to pick your executive search firm is a headache, and there are quite a few. Nowadays, I imagine, there may be some search firms which go to you with resumes in hand on sales calls. Such firms are probably not requiring any up-front fees or retainers. Since in any line of business, reputation generally seeps through and referrals come, I think you should seriously question why it is necessary for these firms to be selling to you. Such selling missions that lack mutual commitment on both your parts can also result in scouting missions! Actually, at a recent speech made to the French Chamber of Commerce, I was asked if "being involved with headhunters might not lead to such activities where the client's staff would be poached later on." I had to think about that and basically give an answer similar to the one I am giving now. If the executive search consultant is unknown to you, not particularly well known in the community (not a part of your social circle), and lacking a reputation to protect (which by definition is the case with any search firm which must engage in sales), I think you run a risk in too easily opening up your shop to a number of executive search firms.

Kindly stop and think about the significance of the "commitment fee." A leading search firm gets a number of calls from prospective clients. Those clients who have talked to people they trust who have used the firm's services and been pleased generally become clients. We prefer to work with people on introduction and people who know people we know. A reasonable commitment fee means exactly this: it means the search firm is not listening to all of them and is not spreading itself too thin. A fair and reasonable commitment fee and retainer are specifically designed to screen out less serious clients and to make sure we can manage controlled growth where we always have enough executive search consultants to stay on top of the number of assignments we carry on our books.

Some executive search firms require as much as 2/3 of the projected 35% fee of a hypothetical income level within the first two months of the arrangement. TMT does not like to take that much money up front because, frankly, it takes the fun out of the search, and the thrill and impact of placement is somewhat diluted. We can only stay in business and have our business grow if we keep making placements. I think you should also look for the kind of creative and flexible terms that we have, for they assure that no client fees paid should be left outstanding. We will deduct interview fees (or the initial up-front commitment fee) off 35% of annual income of the first or the next candidate hired, regardless of position and at any time in the future.

I think the most important factor in choosing your executive search firm would be to ask to visit their facilities and meet them on their home turf. Ask for a tour of the operation to get a feeling for the kind of consultants working there, whether or not there is enough PC power to type up the resumes of freshly scouted candidates, if there is a good computer data bank maintaining records on candidates scouted in the past. Also get a flavor on their home ground for how they work and why they think they are good.

Generally, if there is not much action form your executive search firm within the first month or two, you should not expect to enjoy a successful and active search. Let's face it; if an executive search firm is seriously in the business and has worked on similar assignments, there are going to be a number of candidates already on stream. Years ago at our initial detailed client presentations, I would never allow our consultants to present resumes at the first sitting. It seemed to me that if a client were going to pay 35% of annual income, he should get the feeling that the search is being carried out from now and that a large number of man hours are involved. We still will run into a client who feels that way. Nowadays, however, most of our clients realize that just because we are able immediately to present resumes does not mean that these candidates are in any way inferior or are actively looking for a job. It simply is a question of some six months or perhaps even years earlier having scouted these people, and generally those candidates turned down the assignment so they are still with the executive search firm. Be sure not to turn up your nose at a candidate who has surfaced too quickly. If you meet a candidate and he seems suitable, and if ethical and professional executive search recruiters indicate to you that that is about the best you will do, given the attractiveness of the job or your firm's position in Japan, etc., scarf that man right up. Luckily, many of our clients know one when they see one. It is not uncommon for us to describe a candidate at the initial client meeting, have him meet, whisked off to the head office and have him hired immediately. I guess that takes some salesmanship, some credibility, and a sophisticated client who is decisive and knows what he is looking for.

As the leader of a group of headhunters, I would also ask from the bottom of my heart that you take care of your executive search consultants and be sure to treat them well and keep them motivated. The other day, after having an assignment for less than two weeks and after having already succeeded in having three interviews with the client, without giving us any forewarning by telephone, a fax threatening termination of our contract was sent to me. I kept that fax to myself and know that if I showed it to any of our consultants, they would not want to work for that client. Whether it comes to successfully working with people in your families, on your corporate team, or even with key vendors that you depend on, the triple AAAs of acceptance, approval, and appreciation are extremely important. Honey attracts more flies than vinegar.

If I may, my final request to good clients in this section would be to be sure to stay on top of your own assignments and place pressure on your executive search consultants. Clients may say that it is the headhunter's job to stay in touch with the client, but if this article is designed to help foreign corporations successfully recruit in Japan, I must say here that that is certainly not enough. When the headhunter sits at his desk at 9:00 in the morning, he inevitably has two, three, or more assignments that he is working on. He mentally lists his own priorities for the day. If you call him at 9:15 a.m., give him helpful feedback with the reasons you're choosing not to meet the candidate of resume, give him a little praise for coming close and apply pressure on him to come through for you; believe me, he will begin name-collecting and following up with cold calls on your assignment that very morning. Of course, we try and do our part of the job. TMT sends retained clients a report each month with all the resumes attached to the report that were sent during that month. But this is not enough. We must be at least in weekly contact. Many of our serious clients plan a review session with us once a month. A headhunter will hesitate to make those kinds of demands on your time unless there's also an indication from the client side that he is clear on his priorities and he deems it important to spend that kind of time on the recruiting assignments, and with his executive search consultants.

College recruiting

The common sense is that it's very difficult to secure new school graduates starting with you from April 1 unless you have been in Japan ten years with 200 employees. For example, there are 6,000 companies trying to recruit 4,000 Keio University graduates. While some get over 100 recruits, only 900 companies are successful in hiring even a single Keio grad. In the case of Tokyo Institute of Technology (TIT the MIT of Japan), a recent report revealed that 139 companies made 3,450 job offers to 226 TIT engineers. If you begin to recruit from the universities, dealing with professors and the *gakuseika* (administrative organization responsible for placing the students), you must consistently go back to them each year, or credibility will be lost. In a formal sense, companies cannot go to the university campuses to set up desks and recruit. You are not supposed to allow the graduates to visit your firm until August 20. In reality, by as early as September 15, usually most major firms have sewn up their new graduate hires. According to this gentlemen's agreement concerning recruiting from university campuses, the company paper tests are not supposed to be administered until November 1. But this is a mere formality, and mutual commitments have generally already been made between students and firms.

Foreign capitalized firms should take a serious look at the female graduate sector. Although job offers are several times out of balance for male graduates, actually there are female four-year university graduates who cannot secure employment. The labor market becomes tighter with more job demand for two-year university graduates and female high school graduates. But there is an oversupply of four-year graduate women, presumably because Japanese firms feel that entering the company at 22 or 23 is too close to the anticipated age of marriage, company training will not sufficiently bear fruit, and the negative impact of premature turnover will be too great.

I would recommend that multinationals in Japan not be overly concerned with getting people from the very top universities. I believe that intelligence as determined by an ability to pass the difficult paper entrance exams required to secure enrollment—at least in the top national universities (no side-door donations are possible)—certainly will always take a backseat to effort, drive, and a good personality. The other day I was in the office of a major European multinational, and they claimed that their German president was insistent on trying to recruit some people from University of Tokyo (Todai). I was at a meeting in front of five or six Japanese personnel managers and staff. We all had a chuckle knowing that it is not all that important (two of them were from Todai). Since that firm has some significant sales and/or research and development facilities throughout the country, we agreed that it made more sense to try and bring in students from the outlying national universities rather than trying to compete with everyone else for University of Tokyo graduates.

Think twice, however, about feeling the necessity to recruit early on from the universities. If the size and stature of your organization preclude getting good graduates (or you don't have the personnel staff and manpower to recruit properly from campuses), don't bother to do it. Rather than bring in a dreg among the bunch and be stuck with him for life in this land of "lifetime employment," you might be better off using professional executive search firms to bring in mid-career hires. Also remember that if you hire a new school graduate, it becomes even more difficult to weed him out during the probationary period because the way judges and courts of law look at employee security and corporate responsibilities to new school graduates is different from the status of probation and its relationship with the hired gun mid-career entrant. This is because traditionally Japanese university graduates only had one chance in a lifetime to secure employment with a major employer from April 1. The notion that this student gave up his chance to join a prestigious firm to work for you—his only chance of a lifetime—places more of a moral pressure on you not to dispose of your problem.

Finally, if you are a firm that within just a few years plans on having much more impressive facilities in terms of bricks and mortar, employee head count, etc., rather than go off to the universities at this point and tell your story (which is not yet an impressive one), I believe you should wait until you have something to really brag about. Unfortunately, first impressions are indelible ones. Even if you rapidly grow in the next few years, the professors you deal with and those staffing *gakuseika* will envision your operation as it was initially and may not steer the best students toward you. Another key point—don't spread your limited line and personnel staff resources too thin. Since you will only need two or three or at most a handful of new school graduates, initially work with only one or two universities and deal intensively and closely with only one or two professors. This is particularly true in order to secure good engineering students. Many firms wine and dine these professors to try and establish good relationships. A creative foreign-capitalized firm in Japan could go one step further in producing a special interest on the professor's part, making him more cooperative. Trips to your head office in Paris or New York, along with consulting arrangements and/or contributions of computers, equipment, etc. to assist his research work will certainly pay off. If it doesn't, try another professor because I know of cases where it is effective.

Temporary help

Here I have in mind the *jinzai-haken*, dispatchers of temps who remain on the payroll of the dispatching firm and work in your company for time periods generally of a minimum four hours going on into contracts of several months. While the hourly rate for these staff is rather high, considering that it is not necessary for you to pay the social insurance costs (amounting to some 11% of wage) and in that if the staff is not performing adequately, you should be able to get a replacement within fairly short order, for work in marginal positions this route is not a bad one. Manpower Japan is the pioneer of this business. It was introduced to Japan by the president of Manpower, Mr. A. F. J. Finnerty who is also the first president and continues to be president of the Temporary Help Service Association. There are a number of strong competitors, and the business has grown by leaps and bounds. Legislation was passed several years ago under pressure from labor unions that were concerned that the growth in this industry would make inroads on full-time employment of staff and presumably whittle away at union membership. Of course, another advantage of using temps is that unionization itself becomes impossible because the staff is not even your employee and can merely be sent back to the dispatcher with no conceivable grounds for an unfair labor practice charge (although believe it or not, several years ago a client consulted me on this issue and did have a problem with a dispatched staff until we sent her packing!).

There are some companies who try out a temp, like her, and then either directly, or after a period of time, try to bring her directly on the payroll. That, of course, is the anathema and great headache of the temp service firms. If no contractual arrangement is available for this contingency, I would nonetheless recommend that a fee of at least 10%, and perhaps 20 or 30% be paid to the dispatching firm. Please accept this as a helpful suggestion from a headhunter to our brethren in the temporary help sector!

By the way, the commission payable to the dispatching firm is generally 30 to 35% with the remainder going to the staff you are using

Employee loans and outplacement gifts

We are talking here about *shukko* commonly translated as secondment. This practice has been rather common among foreign banks that have either asked for or been asked to absorb managers and staff from corresponding Japanese banks. It is also common in joint venture firms or wherever there is a rather close relationship with a Japanese party. The idea is that the *seki*, or the official place of employment of the staff you are borrowing, remains with the other employer. This should mean that the retirement benefit is probably ruled by the other firm's Rules of Employment although working hours and conditions at your shop would be governed by your own Rules of Employment. Sometimes you pay the salary directly to the seconded personnel, or the other company pays and bills you for the charges. I would certainly recommend this latter approach in that it tends to assure that as time goes by you do not get stuck with employees who are not very good (it usually takes several years to realize that they are not very good!). You discover this when you start to use good executive search firms and hire good people on your own from the outside. Sometimes, however, by then it is too late.

What happens is the lending company often welcomes these relationships in order to pass off second- or third-rate staff on your firm. The lending firm begins to let the employee know that he is not welcome back, or the employee knows that and begins to tell you that he is now your employee. This is then backed up by word from the original lending firm. In the meantime, the expatriate manager changed; there may or may not be surviving paperwork, and unless you are a rather in-charge *gaijin* manager on such an issue (which is rare), you often end up being stuck.

You can develop special and specific contract and, more importantly, Rules of Employment language which help to protect you under these circumstances. Another problem with these *shukko* relationships is that often after a number of years the pay levels become much higher in the joint venture or in the foreign firm. This makes it more difficult for the employees ever to be able to go back to the original sending firm. In one case several years ago, the employee costs at the joint venture became so high that it contributed, along with other reasons, for making the firm's profits begin to dwindle. The Japanese partner told the American in charge at the joint venture that it was his job to bring the pay levels of the Japanese managers and staff down to the proper Japanese parent-company levels. Easier said than done. When I got the phone call and after asking a few questions, we determined that if there were going to be a union organization drive and bloodshed, at least it should take place in the parent company. We clarified that those employees were still on secondment basis. After all, the Japanese parent was also in a better position, both culturally (and in terms of the Japanese employees' view of where legitimatized authority rests) to do this nasty job. We insisted that the parent company managers carry out this exercise with their staff at their office location. That also took the poor *gaijin* boss off the hook.

Year after year experience confirms for me that very few joint ventures are successful. If your main reason to go into the joint venture is to staff up instantly and to get around the challenges of having to manage Japanese employees with unfamiliar Rules of Employment and compensation packages, I would recommend that this be rethought. Joint ventures are rarely mutually satisfying. Inevitably, one partner tries to buy up more or get out altogether. You can do it on your own—both the personnel management side and the staffing up aspect. Obviously, it will take longer, but it will be your baby and you will nurture it and make it grow without unnecessary frustration and friction.

It was only a couple of years ago that I made the rather profound discovery that it doesn't really matter how much of the Japanese joint venture the foreign partner owns. He still can't control it. Lately when my clients tell me that they are thinking of moving there 50 or 51% up to 65 or 85%, I often discourage them from doing so. Since the foreign partner still does not have control of the Japanese people, their minds, and their hearts, it doesn't do you that much good to own a majority share. Certainly, you will proportionately get a larger percent of the profits. But if the Japanese don't want to go your way, they can dig in their heels, make life miserable, and you end up selling out for a song. (Of course, there are exceptions to this scenario.)

There can even be a negative destructive influence when the foreign partner buys up a larger percentage. As he goes from 49 or 50% up above that, if he begins to say thing and do things as though he has control (when in fact he does not), that merely creates problems with the Japanese side. They may cooperate less, and they will probably care less about the joint venture and put less into it simply because they own less of it. Come to think of it, perhaps my recommendation would be to go for and stay at 50 or even 49%. Since you can't really control it in an operational sense anyway, let the Japanese take pleasure in their JV and make the most of it.

2

Getting the Right Person for the Right Job— Matching Up Profiles and Interviewing

Evaluation of applications and initial screening

In the United States and other countries companies may be used to receiving a number of unsolicited resumes. I would not be surprised if even foreign-capitalized major firms in Japan also received unsolicited resumes from other non-Japanese nationals. Unless you run an advertisement, the likelihood of receiving resumes fron Japanese candidates is probably rather limited. Even when you run a very well-written newspaper or recruiting magazine ad, the number of qualified candidates is indeed few. In Japan in particular, you must be careful when it comes to evaluating applications. For one thing, the traditional Japanese-style application and English translations thereof merely indicate the months and years that an individual worked in a given position, with the name of that department and the individual's title. There is then some personal information at the end of a typical Japanese form resume obtainable at the stationery store, including information on family members and hobbies, etc. I can say with confidence that most Japanese— this is even more true of Japanese in major Japanese firms where the closed or internal labor market prevails—have never written or even thought about writing their resumes. If they did, inevitably you would get no detail and no mention of accomplishments. Thus because a resume received says nothing and is not at all impressive by Western standards, be sure not to reject the candidate. Look at his university, the name of his company, his job progression, and track record.

When evaluating resumes, look to see if the months and years are given. The Japanese tend to write up their resumes with the first job appearing at the beginning, moving on through the last job. I personally prefer this method, for it allows you to more easily track the career and make sure there are no blank spots. While many professionals in the West prefer a resume that discusses accomplishments such as designed blah blah blah, or cut back costs by..., or increased sales by X%, I think that information is okay, but I believe it makes more sense to have it in a detailed write-up together with the months and years that the individual was in the given position. To make a resume helpful for you, it is good to have the English title and the romanized Japanese title appearing in parentheses. You should look for whom the individual reports to, how many subordinates there were. If possible, it is good to know how quickly the man was promoted in comparison with his peers. Sometimes even on our resumes this information is not as clear as it should be. Don't hesitate to ask. If in fact the man was in the first group to become *kacho* at his age level, the headhunter should have asked that, known that, and sold it to you. Likewise, rather than say that an individual is in equity sales, it is good to mention the volumes and how he rates with his peers. If a young man or woman has been the computer salesperson of the month rather consistently, it would be a shame not to know that. I would hope that the executive search consultant would convey such useful information to you. They may not, so it pays to ask. Otherwise, that resume sits on your desk along with all the others, and no action is taken.

Manpower staffing succeeds when a client's rule of thumb is, when in doubt, meet. I can give you inside information that executive search consultants rapidly become demotivated when they believe they have adequate candidates—the best they can put up considering the attractiveness of the position, salary level, and social standing of the client in Japan, etc. Yet feedback is not received, or the client is over particular, or simply may not have enough time to meet candidates. If that is the case, the problem has to be fixed. So initial screening should move over to the personnel department to a younger staff member with more time and less travel, or another person should be hired to work closely with the executive search firm, stay on top of assignments, and make sure the decision makers meet the candidates.

Please do not screen out candidates because their language skills are not up to par or because they haven't tried to sell themselves to you. There are exceptions, but it really is true that very often in Japan the best people with good backgrounds who have done a good job throughout their careers simply will sit tight and will not feel they have to prove this to you, especially when they don't need your job and are just as happy staying where they are. If the interview normally plays an important role in making a personnel decision in the West, possibly even accounting for 70%, with track record and references weighing in at about 30%; in Japan perhaps the interview itself should be discounted down to a 35% weight.

I have just seen too much pain and unnecessary suffering when hiring mistakes were made because an adroit and skillful job hopper was able to talk himself into a job whereas good, solid performers were passed up because they are poor presenters in English. Remember if the chemistry doesn't seem right, maybe it doesn't have to be completely right. However, their chemistry is very likely right for their culture to get along with your employees and managers and to make the right impression on your Japanese customers. In fact, it would not be an overstatement to say that if one's resume is too detailed and well written, and if one also presents himself extremely well, antennae of caution should go up. The resume may have been written by a professional outplacement agency. These are regularly distributed to executive search firms, especially tending to go to those firms that take advantage of this outplacement service. It is generally not to your advantage to do so unless we are talking about a complete closure or reorganization such that it is possible that a good man is tapped out.

In a word, discount the chemistry of the interview, the quality of the resume (whether written by the individual or the executive search firm) and instead check up and check into the positioning of the firm within the Japanese social/business hierarchy and determine the exact Japanese title of the candidate, making sure that he is on the line and not off in a staff function. Generally, it is a good idea if you need a powerful line manager to watch out for words like *taigu* ("treatment" like a *bucho* but not a real *bucho* with subordinates), or *tsuki* (simply attached to, for example, a *bucho*), *hosa* ("assisting"), or the various status titles given to staff specialists such as *sanji* (a man may be a *sanji* but not a *kacho* (line section chief), *fukusanyo* (without the responsibility and authority of *jicho*), *sanyo* (who could be, for example, an off-to-the-side window-type version of the *honbucho* who would normally have two or more *bucho* under him). Remember, English-language titles may be all that are familiar to you, but the English title on his card is essentially irrelevant. For most candidates, so is the English title you select to give him. "Director" means nothing and is not the same as a member of the board of *torishimariyaku*.

If you are a large, established firm with several hundred employees, there is even less room for you to experiment flexibly. It is basically safe for you to scout only from employers larger than yourself. Above all else, look at the track record, the Japanese title, learn what it means, and know what the man is actually doing. For goodness sake: discount those resumes and interviews.

Describing the position and selling the company

Don't give it all away. Make sure you do not describe the position early on in the interview. A clever candidate will then be able to tailor his answers and self-presentation based around the candidate you are looking for. Do, however, begin your interview not by asking the candidate questions, which go down very hard on these passive candidates that are happily employed and are simply coming because a headhunter did a reasonably good job of selling your situation. Instead, be extremely warm, polite, full of smiles, make him feel at ease, and begin to tell your company's story—what you are doing worldwide, what you stand for, what you are in Japan, and what you plan to be.

After 10 to 20 minutes of that, you can begin to ask questions, but it might even be smart to allow the candidate to ask you a few first. Passive candidates are always more willing to give information after they have had a chance to listen and ask a few questions of their own. If they do not have questions, do not be alarmed. This may be *enryo* (self-restraint) and a general feeling that they should not be seizing control to that extent. That does not mean that they will not aggressively sell your products and build your business. Describe your position honestly pointing out some of the challenges as well. That will give you credibility in the candidate's eyes. Sell your company with great enthusiasm. The energy and confidence in your company and its business plan displayed by you will be infectious. In any case, it will be very difficult to convince a candidate if you yourself do not believe that you will succeed in Japan.

Think about the things that make your company special, whether it is in the area of benefits, corporate culture, niche, product categories, allowing international subsidiaries to have a rather free hand at managing themselves, new products in the pipeline, your own growth and sales, the quality of people you have already been able to scout and from which companies (if this information is, in fact, impressive). This will all help to put your candidate at ease. Especially for more senior candidates, it is helpful to initially meet over lunch or dinner. Probably a passive scouted candidate is feeling so self-conscious about even considering leaving his firm and has such ambivalent feelings about even talking to you that the faster you meet his ego needs, the easier it will be for him to begin to step across, listen to you, like you, trust you, and consider sharing the rest of his life with you and your firm.

Interviewing techniques—asking the right questions on adaptability, decision making, delegation, initiative, integrity, leadership, and technical ability

Again, track record is most critical. In the West, it is certainly said in professional circles that the interviewer must avoid speaking and that the candidate should talk at least 70% of the time. That is probably true in Japan too, but it is a greater challenge to get the individual to open up and express himself to that extent. As much as possible, questions should draw out information on how the applicant has performed in job-related situations. One helpful mechanism to assist you in doing this is the STAR concept (S = situation, T = task, A = action, R = results). What this means is that if the individual mentions a result, you are trying to determine the situation or the task in question for which the applicant was responsible when achieving that result. You will also want to find out the actions the applicant took. Similarly, if an individual mentions a situation, task, or action taken, you can then ask about the result if that part was left out of the explanation.

ASK is another helpful interviewing technique to remember (A = accomplishments, S = skills, K = knowledge.) What skills or knowledge were or would be used to accomplish a certain task? Or what did the individual accomplish using those skills and knowledge he claims to have?

Another technique which would especially be more viable with candidates who are actively looking for a job, such as those who sent you an unsolicited resume or answered your advertisement, would be to leave the candidate with a copy of the job description (preferably, job model), give him five to ten minutes to read it over, and then get back together and ask what similarities he sees with the current position being offered and his current job or past work experience, or what is different about the two? Aspects of a good job model can be incorporated into a job description; but rather than describing the duties of a job, make sure that you also get into typical job model aspects which include discussing the results that will be required, the priorities of the job, the obstacles which can be expected to be encountered, and particular or unique aspects of the work environment or management style (of the company or the style that will be expected of the candidate given the tremperament, etc., of his boss or the main players surrounding him).

Ask open-ended questions, using keywords such as how, when, who, what, in what way, which. Avoid asking leading questions which essentially supply the answers you are after. The Cone System can be helpful as you allow the individual to be expansive and then can gradually tie him down to detailed specifics by asking questions. For example, you can start out by asking, "Tell me a little bit about how you...," and then focus in on the details and specifics. Make sure you observe body language, eye movement, nervousness, voice changes, eye dart, etc. Don't hesitate to use your sense of humor. More than relaxing the candidate, we are also trying to see if he comes back with a little humor of his own. I once looked over the client's job model while I was interviewing a candidate. I made a joke, saying to myself so that he could hear me, "Ah, it says here that the candidate must have common sense," and asked him if he had any (with a chuckle, of course). He sat back in his chair, looked up at the ceiling, and quipped, "I must have some because I haven't used any yet." He got the job and went on to be a winner. Years ago, one of our consultants asked a young candidate what his grades were like in school. The young man looked very serious, almost belying the twinkle in his eye. He came back with, "Yes. I see. I was in the half of the class that made the top half possible." Again, he is already a *kacho* and doing well. Especially when it comes to plying the treacherous waters of a new foreign corporate environment, a sense of humor and a ready smile go a long way. It also helps the mid-career hire break into the established ties of the more conservative multinationals that are not used to taking senior people in from the outside.

Some other good questions to ask a candidate might include, "What is the most critical aspect of your current job?" Or, "If I called your current boss and asked for an opinion on you, what would he say?" (Be careful with passive candidates.) Or, "Describe the type of work environment you feel most comfortable in?" Or, "In your estimation, what is a good boss?" "What are your three most outstanding skills and abilities?" These are some pretty tough questions, and I must say that asking them and expecting good answers to them contradict my firm position that interviews in Japan with Japanese generally should be discounted. Keeping that in mind, you might try and ask them to candidates who have particularly good English. It does become easier to ask them to those who have answered your help-wanted ads.

Even if a candidate's English is not very strong, as long as you are patient, listen carefully, and never interrupt, you might try suggesting, "Take your time and spend 10 to 15 minutes describing your work and accomplishments over the years, with more emphasis on later jobs." Among native speakers such a question does test an individual's ability to express himself and communicate logically. These kind of open-ended approaches are what we are after as opposed to asking questions which can be answered by yes or no. If there are long moments of silence, don't worry about that. The Japanese tolerance for silence is probably three or four times longer than that of a Westerner anyway. Try saying nothing and see what happens. At some point, candidates might ask you some good questions. Look for that, but don't write a man off because they don't come. "Who held this job before?" "How about the career path you have outlined for this position?" "How would you describe yourself as a boss?" "How would you like to see the department (or company) positioned in the next three to five years?" "How does one advance in this company?" "Describe the ideal candidate for this position." (This one should only be answered by the client after the client has time to assess the candidate independently to see if the candidate matches up with the job needs.) A good question from a candidate might also be, "Why is this a good place to work?" "Are there any particular policies or rules that confine the way a manager can get his job done?" You are probably getting the same feeling I'm getting. While some impressive candidates might ask these questions in the West, it certainly is unlikely that you'll get them from a Japanese candidate.

When evaluating the candidate, ask yourself a few questions before you make the hiring decision. Do I see him fitting in our environment? Does he have the right image? Can he gain the respect of the people we have on board? Can he lead? Will he follow when necessary? Is he smart enough to do the job? Will he be influential with key people? Can he handle heavy responsibility? Is he trustworthy? Does he have the knowledge he needs? Can he make the right decisions in tough situations? Does he have the right energy level? Is he resistant to stress?

Certainly keys to executive success include a degree of inner self-motivation and ambition, emotional maturity, judgment, common ideals, loyalty, and identification to your corporate goals, someone who has a good plausible reason why he wants the job (money shouldn't be the only reason), someone who can channel hostilities and has a sense of humor, a manager with perseverance and a determination and need to finish a task begun.

Although all of us have done a lot of interviewing, some times we get sloppy and fail to ask good or the right questions. A few candidate traits or qualities with a question or two assessing that quality should form a helpful list of questions that you can refer back to. Let's go in alphabetical order with a few key traits.

Adaptability—Which supervisors have you found the easiest to work with, the most difficult? Why? *Control*—What do you do to keep track of your subordinates' progress on delegated assignments or execution of tasks? What do you do when you find that a subordinate is not meeting your standards? *Decision-making*—What was the toughest decision you had to make in the last year? Why was it so difficult? *Delegation*—Describe a job or project that required a major effort by many members of your staff. Who did you have participate? Why did you choose them? What assignments did they have? *Identification with the job*—What did you like best about your previous job? What did you like the least? *Initiative*—Tell me about an idea you generated. What did you do? How did things work out? *Sales initiative*—What is the best method you have found to obtain new prospects? How do your selling techniques differ from those of others you know? *Leadership*—What did you do to help your subordinates set performance objectives last year? *Management interest*—What part of your work have you found the most frustrating or unsatisfying? *Technical ability*—Give me an example of a particularly difficult assignment or project. What was your role? How did you accomplish this? What do you think is the most important development in your field today? What impact do you think it will have? *Work standards/performance*—Are you satisfied with your department's performance? Why or why not?

It might be helpful to try and remember to end interviews by asking, "Is there anything else you would like to say about yourself or anything you think you should let me know?"

A final word about some interviewing methods. Probably the most typical approach is the so-called sequential interview, which would have the candidate meet a lower-level person. If approved, the candidate moves on up the ladder to the higher-ranking decision maker. In contrast, the serialized interview does not allow any single lower-level or higher-level person to reject a candidate. Rather, a number of interviewers meet a candidate separately and then compare their notes or summary sheets and make a decision after discussing each other's perceptions and perhaps even essentially voting. A panel interview should probably not be used for a first interview, as the company, its business, and the position should probably be somewhat described in advance. In the panel format, a number of interviewers would meet the candidate together sharing a uniform experience and supplementing each other's questions. It is important that no one person dominate the panel. Consensus is reached among panel members after the interview. Somewhat smaller and less intimidating than the panel interview would be the consecutive interview where two people would meet with a candidate taking turns interviewing while the other person sits in and listens.

Keep this article. A lot of the tips and pointers here will be useful for you in any country where you secure a future assignment. Frankly, a lot of these techniques are a bit too sophisticated and professional for the interviewing purposes of Japanese candidates. Again, the all important bottom message is to discount the interview and don't be overconcerned with presentation skills, his lack of ability to sell himself, and a failure to hit bingo on chemistry. Often when the chemicals mix well between a Japanese and a foreigner, there can be a heated reaction between that same individual and the Japanese executives/staff already on board.

Checking references and employee testing

Some references are obviously more useful than others. The pattern of the friend from the university, an associate from a club, a famous man the individual happens to know, someone from the church or PTA are obviously not relevant and impressive references. In former employers where the candidate no longer works, it should be possible to check references in any detail without damaging the candidate (unless it is done to such an extent that the word could leak back to the candidate's current employer).

If your executive search firm does business on a scale of significant dimension, it is very possible that it has already recruited some one from the candidate's firm. Often the candidate was initially identified or introduced to the consultant through his industry connections as a key player at his company. When checking out a candidate's background, we also make efforts to bring in another employee from the same company in a lower-level position but from the same division. You can then rather casually and unobtrusively mention the names of a few of his seniors including the candidate you are trying to check up on. Usually people even at lower levels in the organization have considerable information on top players. This is even true of female clericals who could be met.

It is also possible to investigate professionally a candidate using a *koshinjo* (private detective agency). Actually this is quite common practice in Japan. In large first-class employers, especially in banks, etc., even new school graduates beginning on April 1 are routinely investigated, including checking with people in the neighborhood where the individual grew up. Although a client could rightfully expect that such an investigative cost come out of the executive search fee, I would strongly recommend that the client take control of such an investigation and have it done himself. If the investigative agency wants to get repeat business from the executive search firm, they may not be completely objective and may hide, or at least express euphemisms for some of the qualities or reports they have discovered on the candidate.

Frankly, in the case of most hires, such *koshinjo* investigations are not carried out. They are only really necessary when an unsolicited resume is sent to you, and the candidate is an unknown factor who may have a spotty background. If you have any reason to doubt your executive search firm or the candidate, or under any circumstances, you could just routinely have your secretary call the company where the individual is supposed to be working to see if in fact he is working there. There should be no risk there in blowing the candidate's identity as someone who is being presented by headhunters. Just make sure your secretary is coached to handle such a sensitive call properly.

On the subject of employee testing, if a candidate is applying to your job after looking at a newspaper ad, or if he has sent in an unsolicited resume, you could consider some form of intelligence test. Certainly, for most of the candidates that we scout, it would be totally inappropriate and would be rejected by the candidate.

One of our clients had a good strong candidate interested in joining him until he mentioned that he wanted the candidate to take "some kind of an IQ test." The candidate laughed and said, "Excuse me, sir, but I don't want to know my IQ at this point. I've done a good job; I know my field; and if you can't figure that out for yourself, maybe we should take the test together." I really cannot blame the candidate for his comment. This cautious, conservative attitude by that particular client, as manifest in many other ways on many other occasions, has essentially demotivated our consultants so that they have lost their will to continue to present candidates.

Even the client did not want to breech this subject himself. He cannot expect the executive search firm to test or screen out candidates in this way. Since all of our candidates are scouted and essentially remain rather passive to change, we would lose at least 97% of them even if we nicely asked them to take such a test.

Massaging egos and keeping candidates warm

If you deal with an executive search firm that does pinpointed targeting into the firms you have identified as likely and preferred sources for your candidates, you may very well meet essentially the best candidate available at your first interview. Clever and scheming headhunters or executive search consultants might try and put some second-rate, lower caliber filler candidates up first and then have the superior candidate sweep it away. In reality, however, with the rush of the moment and with speed and decisiveness being the ever most important factor in successfully meeting a client's needs and assuring that the executive search firm gets the placement, it is likely that you will meet an extremely well qualified candidate early on. Hopefully, you will know it when you see it and make your decision without having to compare the person with a handful of individuals.

Sometimes clients will ask, "Do you expect me to hire the first person I meet?" Honestly speaking, we headhunters will answer, "Yes, please do." That candidate may be the first person the client is meeting; but in an indirect sense, with us working as his agent, he has already sifted through and screened out a number, if not tens, of candidates. However, if you feel you simply cannot yet make your decision, then you have the problem that you will lose that strong candidate if you let too much time go by. First of all, the candidate is no dummy. He knows that by definition if you're waiting, it is because you are not sufficiently impressed with him and you want to meet other candidates. Just as in a love affair, no one wants to be hurt, and so the candidate immediately takes two or three steps back just like the clam who is picked out of the water to face the hot sun.

Periodic meetings to massage the ego are critical. It also would make sense to stretch second and third lunches and dinners out with a couple of weeks in between each one to buy time if the client is insisting on meeting other candidates. If your headhunters believe they have already put up the right candidate, however, you have another problem. Since they know it is only cosmetic and basically an exercise in futility, it is pretty hard for them to motivate themselves and to justify the time it will take to put up inferior candidates that they know will not be hired anyway. Let's just hope that the consultant in charge of your account is frank enough with you and can communicate well enough with you to stand his ground and steer you toward hiring a good candidate presented early on.

The clients that are the most successful in securing the largest number of top-quality hires are the ones that really appreciate the difficulty of coming up with even one or two good men. Good candidates do not grow on trees. Once they meet a good man they recognize it and put a tremendous amount of energy into wining, dining, and courting that candidate. First of all, often a client has to be extremely accommodating especially when it comes to interviewing very busy executives or young engineers. After work interviews, even an after-dinner drink at a hotel, after dinner at home, meetings on Saturdays and Sundays, sending the candidate to the home office, often along with his wife if at a senior enough level, are all ways to help clinch the deal and get the candidate. I remember in one case with a very reluctant candidate, before the candidate agreed to join, the client went ahead and secured an American Express company Gold Card in the candidate's name and mailed it to him. That was the straw that broke the candidate's back, and he joined.

On the other hand, last month a strong and interested candidate was scheduled to meet the chairman of a worldwide corporation as he visited in Tokyo. This was to be the top Japanese in charge of the operation and a man who could significantly improve this company's fate in Japan and then eventually in the Asian region. This company is also not at all attractive considering the caliber of individual they are insisting on attracting. Yet instead of scheduling a nice dinner at the chairman's hotel, they met in the lobby and had a drink at the bar from 6:00 p.m. until 6:45 p.m. with the chairman ending the meeting to have dinner with a not-so-key customer from 7:00 p.m. at the same hotel. Our candidate had expected to have dinner. There was not enough time to listen to one another and express themselves. It also showed very bad judgment on our client's part because as the local expatriate manager admitted, certainly to have met this candidate and taken better care of him was far more important than having the chairman spend time with that customer. The candidate, right before his eyes in that bar, is the caliber of man who can create tens of such customers. We are still struggling to keep up the interest of that candidate and now are in a holding pattern until the vice-president of International visits Japan, hopefully sometime within the next month. Unfortunately, chances are that by then the candidate will be lost, for in these tight labor market conditions and with a number of headhunters springing up, it is very conceivable that an information or introduction to one of those headhunters will bring a more attractive job offer to that candidate. Sometimes the local expatriate manager in Japan has to fight hard for a hire, take full responsibility, and shoulder the risk of a failure. The non-resident chairman or president visiting Japan is much less well equipped to be able to interview and judge a Japanese candidate with rather weak English and presentation skills.

The job of taking good care of the candidate also must not end after he signs the offer letter. Sometimes it can be two months or more before he can join, so make sure you stay in touch. After he joins, it is even more important to see how he's doing.

3

Avoiding Costly Mistakes
in Offer Letters, Contracts,
and
Compensation/Benefit
Packages

Beware of candidate who wants guarantees on paper

It is true that there are some Japanese candidates who have a perception that foreign companies hire and fire and that there is a greater level of risk when moving into the multinational firm. Sometimes an otherwise good, strong, solid candidate will say initially something about a five-year-contract or wanting a "guarantee" until retirement age of 60. That can and must merely be tossed aside by the executive search consultant. In reality, other than the possibility of the common two-year director's term (for *torishimariyaku*), the longest legal employment contract in Japan is one year anyway. Mention in a contract or offer letter of such a three- or five-year-contract or commitment would have some influence if the case went to court in that in terms of fair play, mutual understanding, and mutual expectations, such a stipulation of "guarantee" would be a factor considered. Inevitably, if there were a performance problem for such a high-level person, any termination settlement would likely move toward *chotei* (conciliation). Without a judge ever writing a decision, a reasonable *wakaikin* would be decided. (The amount would not be great if the multinational firm firmly held the line against making a big settlement.)

In this sense, I believe it is unethical of the executive search firm which should know better than to allow a client to write such an offer letter. If I simply brush aside this initial statement by some candidate saying, "Come on, you know there is no such thing as such a guarantee in life. If you join that firm, you have to be a good businessman and do a good job, contributing to the bottom line. Otherwise there is no reason why they should keep you." That will scare away weak candidates, but the good strong ones will simply nod their heads and move on to the next point. On the other hand, cases have come to me in my experience as a labor and personnel consultant handling termination issues in which a candidate insisted on such guarantees, and the executive search firm allowed them to be written up in the client's offer letter.

One case in particular comes to mind where what ended up to be a totally incompetent candidate with a miserable reputation in the marketplace, only finally and reluctantly agreed to accept a job with the multinational client because the "guarantees" looked so good and firm that he and his wife apparently decided that there was little risk in taking the job. The problem is he was only willing to take the job because there was no risk. He would not have taken the job knowing his own abilities without the guarantees. In this case, the guarantees were significant: a five-year "guaranteed" contract with initial salary of ¥23 million and salary over the next four years being no less than ¥24, 25, 26, and 27 million! On top of this, if the client firm closed and left the Japanese marketplace, ¥60 million would be paid to this very man whose responsibility was to be the top Japanese in the organization. Yet, this very man was in the position to preclude any such closure if he merely could go on, run the business, hire good people, and succeed at it.

We have subsequently found out that even the man's wife knew he was no good, but both of them were quite naive and believed that the five-year-contract meant something in a court of law. Actually it does mean something but not enough. Certainly the man will not be successful in winning a *karishobun* (temporary restraining order) to bring him back to his pay level as stipulated in the contract. (For the last eight months or so, the ¥24 million salary by way of contract has been reduced to ¥8 million, yet the individual remains clinging to the company even at this level. Since we did not go for direct termination, even his lawyer is not particularly interested in the case, nor is the lawyer encouraging him to do anything but to begin to consider leaving the firm. When that pay level is further brought down to a ¥4 or ¥5 million level, hopefully, finally, this result will be achieved.)

Furthermore, when a candidate is insisting on an unreasonably high salary, a good search consultant should give him our pitch about, "You realize, Tanaka-san, there is no such thing as a salary that is too high." He then answers, "Okay. Anyway, I'd like a higher salary if we can do it." Then we go on to say that there is a lot of mediocre performance and average contribution at salary levels of ¥10 to ¥15 million in multinational firms in Japan. When, however, salary levels hit ¥18, 20, 25, 30 million, one has to be extremely good, otherwise the company will fix the performance problem much sooner. In other words, about the same amount of management quality, performance, and contribution at a ¥13 million salary level will be tolerated for as long as two years; whereas if that same individual is earning ¥26 million annual income, within one year but probably much sooner, the client will zero in on the problem and take action against the employee, either trying to terminate or using our tried and true recipe of adjusting the job and position and/or cutting back the pay level.

What do the law and practice say about probation, job security, ability to terminate?

Experience cleaning up personnel problems and handling poor performance terminations convinces me that although it is not foolproof, without exception, all employees at the highest and lowest levels should be subject to a six-month probationary period. Six months is still not long enough, but it is about twice as good as three months. There is nothing in the law stipulating the length of the probationary period. Probably in major Japanese firms, the most typical length is three months, but in multinationals that tend to be smaller and can tolerate less fat and dead weight, I would, in any case, recommend six months. If the six months are stipulated in the Rules of Employment, it is not even necessary to mention it is the offer letter although routine mention of a six-month probationary period should certainly not scare away any good candidate. If your candidate is concerned about a six-month probationary period, I would suggest that we have discovered something worth knowing and we should let such a probationary period screen out such weak individuals who lack the confidence to get through probation.

Of course, there is no such thing as lifetime employment or job security in Japan. So-called lifetime employment, in the sense that people leave the university or high school on April 1 and join a firm for life, is something that only applies to some 20% of the workforce. Actually, Japan is a nation of medium and small enterprises to a much greater extent than is, for example, the United States. In smaller firms, there is more job change because essentially there is more of an open labor market between small firms in that they have no choice but to hire mid-career people and to hire from one another because like foreign-capitalized firms in Japan, it is difficult for them to secure new school graduates, against the major Japanese employers. Thus, smaller Japanese firms will also hire a man to do a job at any point during the year. Without a doubt, every day in Japan, people are fired, including Friday afternoon cannings given without even a days' notice. For example, in 1988, 2.47 million people changed jobs during the year, up 5% from the previous year. Of these, 1.82 million or 74% quit their jobs voluntarily, and 650 thousand or 26% changed jobs against their will (essentially meaning there was restructuring, but also a number of selective terminations for performance and other problems). Thus, lifetime employment is or is not a misnomer.

What does the law say about termination? Japanese employers are not considered "at will" employees where the relationship can end at the will of either party without notice. Article 627 of the civil code requires that the employee give two weeks' notice. Article 20 of the Labor Standards Law requires that the employer give 30 days' notice or 30 days' pay or a combination of the two. An employer may not require an employee to wave his termination rights when hired. This is deemed to be a violation of Article 5 of the Labor Standards Law, as well as the prohibition of involuntary servitude in Article 18 of the Constitution. Thus you cannot hope to bind your employee in by way of contract. Certainly there is a moral obligation on an employee to live up to and carry out the full term of a term contract he may be on. As for the employer, one of the disadvantages of the term contract is that unless there is very good cause and strong reason to breach the contract, short of an act of God, the company may be liable for all the moneys during the term of that contract. Of course, the advantage of the term contract is that at the end of the one year, six months, one month (or whatever else—anything is possible), the employment obligation ends and the term contract need not be renewed.

Actually, once an employee gets on the Board of Directors and becomes a *torishimariyaku*, he is essentially no longer considered to be an employee covered by the Labor Standards Law, and his job security is reduced. Although the two-year director's term is more prevalent, if you are not sure of a new hire, a one-year term on the board might make more sense, because again, unless there is very strong cause, once you appoint someone to be a director, there is an obligation for you to pay out all the moneys during that director's term. Of course, in reality, such cases end up being settled out of court, as they are often thrown to *chotei* (conciliation) even if they were initially launched as a temporary restraining order (TRO—*karishobun*) to make pay whole, or if the action was initiated in district court on an issue of either making pay whole or reinstating the director in his job (if the company were unwise enough to terminate instead of adjusting back the pay level).

Although the law states that staff can be terminated with 30 days' notice or 30 days' pay (Article 20, Labor Standards Law—LSO), in reality, if an employee is litigious and secures a lawyer taking action against you in either a TRO proceeding or in district court, your right of dismissal, as stipulated in Article 20 of the LSO, is rarely admitted. The judge can rule that it is wrongful dismissal or abuse of the right of dismissal. Dismissal is referred to as *shikei* or the death penalty. It can and should be avoided in lieu of safer and surer methods of achieving the same result. In reality, even if an action is initiated in TRO or district court proceedings, it usually is pushed down toward conciliation and a settlement is worked out. A company usually has to pay more for the luxury to terminate. The path of less resistance, and one that is more welcomed by the courts, is one of adjusting job function and/or adjusting pay level with or without a substantial change in position or function. (For their own reasons, attorneys will, however, often tell you this is illegal and can't be done.)

Pointers and pitfalls in pay packages offered

Often, out of lack of knowledge, smaller foreign-capitalized firms setting up in Japan make some big and unnecessary mistakes in the way they pay people. On average, Japanese industry pays 5.8 months of bonus (combining the winter portion usually paid in mid-December and the summer bonus usually payable in or around mid-June). Japanese firms do this for a number of reasons including; (1) bonus amount is not calculated into the lump-sum retirement benefit; (2) you can have flexible performance pay in that the bonus amount can vary by employee and also on a corporate-wide basis depending upon how strong corporate performance was that year; (3) in exceptional cases where an employee is not contributing, has a bad attitude, and is not particularly popular enjoying the support of fellow workers, it becomes possible to pay absolutely no bonus at all, which is a good way to get rid of a problem employee; (4) social security contributions (normally amounting to about 11% of payroll) are about 1/3 on bonus amount as compared to normal monthly cash wages.

An employer should not make the mistake of stipulating the number of months of bonus that will be paid in the employee's offer letter or employment contract. Nor should the contract state an annual income figure. Rather the approach should be that the monthly cash compensation and/or combination of allowances amount to X yen. "Since we pay in principle X number of months of bonus at this firm, your total annual income should be approximately X yen. However, it may be more or less since there is a performance range on the company bonus." Likewise, you must make sure that you do not stipulate the number of months of bonus that are payable in the Rules of Employment. If you so stipulate in the work rules and/or the contract, Article 11 of the Labor Standards Law would bind you such that it would become impossible to set up a performance range on the bonus. (Incidentally, if you are a firm which up until now has not had a performance range on your summer and winter bonuses, you can certainly begin this practice. One effective way to do it is to ensure all employees that the company's intent is not to save money and that on a company-wide average and as calculated within each department and/or even section, the average bonus payable up until now will be disbursed. Essentially, what we are saying is, if above-average performers are going to be identified, appraised, and rewarded, each manager has to be on top of his job and know his subordinates well enough to also be able to identify and assign lower evaluations to certain employees.)

If an employee quits on you, hopefully the practice at your firm is such that it would not be necessary to pay retirement benefit for the first three years of service. While this is the most widespread practice in major firms, in smaller Japanese firms, often no voluntary retirement benefit will be paid within the first five years of service. Since there is an open labor market between foreign-capitalized firms and it is rather easy for an employee to get an equally good job in another foreign firm, I am sure many of you have already experienced more turnover than you desire and more than is experienced by the large, first-ranking Japanese employers. The ironic thing is that in most Japanese firms, there is a significant discount between involuntary and voluntary retirement. The rule of thumb is that, for example, within the first ten years of service, if someone quits the firm, only 50% or less of the retirement benefit would be payable. The payable ratio would only slowly go up often only every five or so years in perhaps 5% increments. Even though, there is more turnover in foreign firms, perhaps because the Japanese employees themselves (who may have anticipated the possibility of quitting) were able to have an influence on creating the Rules of Employment, often the discount is much smaller and in not a few cases there is no discount or penalty at all for quitting the firm. I firmly believe that money spent in this way, subsidizing a good employee's departure to perhaps go and work at a competitor, is bad money spent. We have been successful in working with clients and making sure there is a much bigger discount for voluntary retirement. Such a retirement benefit payment penalty may not be enough to anchor in your employees, but a good tight policy can save several million yen every time an employee leaves you with as few as five or six years of service.

I would rather have you put those wasted and precious resources into cash compensation which will make it easier for your headhunters to attract good people to your firm. After all, the fact is that most employees never get details on your Rules of Employment or retirement benefit before they agree to join your firm. Thus, I believe sound, strategic compensation policies dictate that benefits, which by definition apply equally to all employees whether top performers or problem people, should be constrained while the multinational must be able to draw in mid-career hires with attractive cash compensation. If a firm has money to handle both sides of the equation generously, all the better. But I have my serious doubts about that. We have consulted on the closure of a number of firms that gave up on the marketplace because they never got the right people in place. The ones they got were managed and motivated improperly by the wrong reward system.

Clients often come to us asking whether or not they should get involved with the seemingly complicated Japanese-style allowances such as housing, family, meal, or positional allowances, etc. Of course, as with the bonus, one reason Japanese firms have these allowances is precisely to reduce the weight of pensionable income, cutting back the liability when it comes times to pay out the retirement benefit. Such allowances will do the same thing for you. Frankly, most multinationals in Japan do not want to get involved with those allowances and prefer a more simplified compensation package. You can keep all things equal on the weight of pensionable income versus retirement liability if you merely stipulate in the Rules of Employment that a certain percentage of regularly monthly cash compensation is nonpensionable and will not be calculated into the retirement benefit. This is not your typical Japanese practice, but is something that we have developed as a creative and simple solution to this particular problem.

One allowance that really cannot be avoided, given its institutionalized nature within Japanese pay practices, is the *tsukin-teate* (commutation allowance). If we really stop and think about it, this is a most unusual practice and is really not fair, especially in that nowadays an employee who lives very far away will be able to perhaps buy a home and enjoy spiraling personal assets. His commutation pass will cost the company a fortune. The employee who is working late for the firm and realizes that he cannot be tired and also be effective in his job may have to continue to live closer in the city and pay rent. Even though such an employee is in good health for you and be flexibly worked longer hours, etc., he is the one who is also costing you less! This problem was not so acute when most companies held that the commutation allowance would be limited to the maximum tax-deductible amount which had only slowly drifted up in ¥500 or ¥1,000 units to as high as ¥26,000 per month as of April 1, 1989. From that date, however, then the three percent consumption tax was also implemented, in one shot the tax authorities said that this tax-decutible amount is raised to ¥50,000 per month.

Obviously, at major Japanese firms, unions and management had to go into a scuttle and still haven't sorted this one out, for most Rules of Employment and contracts stipulated that the company would pay up to the maximum tax-deductible amount. I can tell you that at our firm I knew about these changes in advance and immediately informed our staff that we would keep the ceiling at the ¥26,000 level. I suggest that clients confront this problem, which is a rather serious equity problem that can create tensions and unrest among employees. I recommend also that you limit to the ¥26,000 rate (at least for now) and perhaps establish a policy such that the ¥26,000 can move up by something like two percent each year on into the future. I hate to spend so much time on this issue, but it is indeed now possible to live ¥50,000 away, and that is as much as 25% or more of the annual income level of certain lower-ranking employees and can represent an even higher percentage of their monthly pay.

When you hire someone, you also need to make no guarantees or statements about an automatic pay increase. I think there is a problem with any candidate who is unrealistic and naive enough to insist on that. I would also recommend that you check your Rules of Employment to see if they are indicating that there is an automatic pay increase taking place at your firm. It should be sufficient to say that there is a salary review once a year, without tying yourself down to such an assumed increase. If an employee is merely coasting along, I believe it is inappropriate to give a pay increase, for that gives the signal the coasting is acceptable. After all, how can we try to terminate an employee if they have had an annual increase? Wouldn't it make more sense to hold back pay to a level in line with the individual's productivity and contribution rather than to have to come in with traumatic surgery of termination (which also would be a more viable option if it were easier to do in Japan without recrimination)?

Although full commissions with no base salary are a tough sell in Japan, creative commission and incentive sales plans should be considered. I have a Japanese friend who is a Keio graduate and quit Kanebo, Ltd. some 30 years ago to move to NCR Corp. while it was still a very small firm because NCR Corp. provided commission sales. As a young man, he was making more money than most top executives in Japanese firms, And, of course, he ended up on the Board of Directors at NCR Corp.. There are people who are attracted to commission work. Although a passive, headhunted candidate will require a good, solid base salary, I believe that a good test of a candidate is to see if he is attracted to an executive incentive plan with trigger bonuses that allow him to reach a considerably higher earnings level.

Even for senior executives, there are really not that many usable and attractive perks available in Japan. Probably the one with the largest impact and one that brings about the greatest personal tax savings is provision of economic rent, which essentially means that the employer pays the deposits, leases with the landlord, and pays the rent each month. Only some five percent of this rent amount should be taxable income to a non-director manager or staffer (if you have a good, aggressive tax account). Even for members of the Board of Directors, if they are not representative directors (*daihyo-ken*) or owners, you should try and get away with only 15 to 30% of that rent amount being taxable to the employee. Since the bonus paid to *torishimariyaku* must come from after-tax profits, most firms do not bother to pay a bonus, and annual income is divided and paid out in only 12 installments. Other common perks for *torishimariyaku* in major firms include commutation by green car, car and driver, and/or use of taxis from home to nearest station and office to nearest return station, home telephone charges covered, golf club memberships, and perhaps some extra retirement benefits combined with a form of golden handcuff.

For example, in order to attract a candidate—whether director or non-director level—who really desires a higher pay level than you are able to pay due to internal balance constraints, you could consider promising the man an extra retirement benefit of even as much as ¥20 or ¥30 million when he hits the retirement age, depending on how many years of service he has left. After discounting for inflation, this really is not all that much money. Of course, this concept can be refined by stipulating that, should you terminate the candidate at some point, he would get 1/2 this payment prorated by the time actually serving you. But if he quits the firm, he would only get 1/4 of the same.

Some firms bringing in a man from the outside do indeed have serious problems accommodating the individual on the salary table, job grades and qualification systems already existing in the firm. Introducing a concept of second-salary, nonregular pay, headhunter's allowance, extra-performance pay, or any other appropriate labeling could be one way to get around this. You can justify the extra compensation by letting the individual or the personnel department know that the higher payments are only subject to continued performance at adequate contribution levels. Other ways to bring in a candidate with some creative package adjustments include offering a few years of automatic extra service toward the retirement benefit, working with either one-shot or delayed sign-up bonuses, or, if you can get away with it, doing something with off-shore payments.

You should not go along with or accommodate candidates who desire employment guarantees in their contracts. Obviously, you also should not have to write in an offer letter that at a certain point, a candidate will be promoted into a certain position. At an interview, even when asked on such promotional prospects, you can talk about expectations or explain specific cases of another employee who was thus promoted without having to make a commitment to the candidate.

Prewarn the candidate and coach him on how to deflect the likely counter offer which will be made at his firm. You can point out that, "You will be seen as a disloyal manipulator. They will be training and preparing someone to take your job in case you leave again."

In working out a good package and in negotiating it, it is important for the executive search firm, the client and the candidate to avoid a pattern of positional bargaining and rather go for a principled negotiation based on merits, objective standards, and shared interests. We should not forget to ask why an individual wants something that he is stubbornly holding out for. If we understand this, there are options that will develop. The negotiations become much more than a one-dimensional split of a fixed pie. The pie itself can grow or change shape.

Remember the story of the two sisters fighting over the single remaining orange. They ended up cutting the orange in half. It was not until several days later that they found out why they each wanted the orange. They had been too concerned with what only they wanted and had preconceived notions. One wanted to eat the fruit, while the other simply wanted the skin to shave up and mix with some cookie batter she was working on.

4

Timely Solutions to Problem Employees and Cutting Back Losses When Necessary

---

After selection responsibilities—mentors, briefings, introductions, orientations, training

If an excellent, proven Japanese executive has worked his whole life in a single corporate environment, think about all the shocks and surprises he will have when he moves over to work at your firm during the first few months. Especially after he has been aggressively wined and dined, if that close, inner-circle contact immediately stops as problems and frustrations build up, you may be in for a fairly serious morale and performance problem. Orientation helps make a good first impression, improves morale and motivation, gives accurate information, eliminates mistakes, and heightens loyalty. A good solid orientation plan should cover (1) what info should be presented; (2) when to present; and (3) who should present. Even simple things such as a seating chart of all the people on the new hire's floor with the name written in on each desk will be extremely helpful to get people's names and faces down.

One reason we have been able to place 61 people into a single firm is because they do such a splendid job with audio-visuals and with the enthusiasm with which that company represents its "five principles" to candidates. There are then periodic follow-up meetings. Check often within the first few days for problems and make sure the person realizes that he can come and speak to you at any point. Unfortunately, just having your door open is not enough. Have a veteran staffer periodically go through your orientation program as a check on quality and impact. It is also extremely important to have your best supervisors and associates working side by side with a new recruit. The initial bonding or influence with this supervisor is extremely important. After one year or even six months, it becomes less important as to who the new hire works with, for he can usually stand on his own two feet and has discovered his own pace of performance, etc. (also thanks to the initial bonding relationship with the excellent supervisor or associate).

In the early months of the relationship with the new employee, it is also helpful to set up mechanisms of *jiko-hyoka* (self-appraisal), supplementing the boss's appraisal. Actually, self-appraisal has existed a number of years in both Japan and the United States, but in the United States its use as a powerful and motivating tool is coming more into focus. It will work better than unilateral supervisory appraisals in any country. Statistics show, for example, that 90% of employees will evaluate themselves lower than does their employer. Next to termination discussions, personnel appraisals are something the most detested and loathed by managers.

Do you see what we have going for us with the self-appraisal approach? Since 90% of the employees will evaluate themselves lower than does their supervisor, the supervisor can see the appraisal session as a good opportunity to get some information, dig his claws in, and learn what's going on in the organization—but more importantly, as a chance to build up his subordinate rather than tear him down. After all, even the most harmless remark designed to help a subordinate can tear away at the sensitive ego and hurt his/her feelings or cause an unnecessary rift in the relationship between subordinate and supervisor. Thus, rather than being an unpleasant task that must be faced, a supervisor mostly needs to listen and primarily dispense ample doses of the triple AAAs—acceptance, approval, and appreciation of his subordinates. Furthermore, after an employee has had a chance to get his say in and explain his side of the story, he becomes willing to listen more receptively and objectively to what the boss has to say.

Certainly part of after-selection responsibilities includes making sure the new hire succeeds. Coaching and guidance must be given. Try and focus on performance and behavior not personality or character. Saying that someone has a bad attitude is not helpful, for it is impossible to manage an attitude. We can only concretely work with and manage behaviors. Guessing about someone's motivations for doing the things he does is also rather unproductive. Know what the new man is doing and remember that the worker performs what the boss inspects. If someone is not performing well, try to take him under your wing and turn what can become a loser into a winner.

Position adjustments and reassignments

New employees and managers get into trouble when their LOE (level of expectancy) is not in line with their LOR (level of reality). If the LOE is over the LOR, the employee may become demoralized and lose his enthusiasm. Employees should be content to do uninteresting and routine tasks once in a while. But sometimes it is important to throw in stretching experiences such that a new burst of energy and enthusiasm is possible. People usually are superior to their jobs.

Remember the story about the bright-eyed and bushy-tailed young M.B.A. graduate who joined a company hoping he had the world by the tail. He had a high LOE indeed. He was assigned to the personnel department and asked to design a new reporting form. He got that done within an hour or two that afternoon and showed it to his supervisor who didn't really react and suggested that he take it upstairs for the perusal of more senior management players. For reasons expressed and unexpressed, the form was rejected, and over a six-month-period, it ended up that one of his major duties was to get this form in shape, with it constantly being resubmitted, altered, and sent for management approval. Our young M.B.A.er was getting fed up and was ready to quit the firm anyway, so he decided to submit the original form that he made six months ago. This time it passed the upstairs management committee, and he thanked them as he handed in his resignation.

Encourage subordinates and at senior management levels, get them to get you to buy into their own 90-day plans and goals. Lee Iacocca identifies that as one of the most important aspects of his management style.

Stay in touch with your people. They should know the rules, your expectations, and how you think they're doing. Find out first how they think they're doing. It's not enough for this to only take place once or twice a year at formal appraisal sessions. How would you like to have to bowl all year and find out your score only once? Wouldn't it be unsatisfying to have to date a member of the opposite sex for months without finding out what your partner thought of you and whether or not he/she liked you? In our jobs and even in our love relationships, at a certain point we expect some appreciation and some rewards! Rewarded behavior is reinforced. Non-rewarded behavior will extinguish of its own.

I know of candidates who were excellent performers at their former companies, but for whatever reasons, ended up being judged as inadequate performers when they changed jobs. Likewise, I know from the termination side of our consulting practice that managers forced out of one firm can go on and become more than satisfactory performers in another. It's a bit scary and a bit confusing. One thing is clear. Performance is not always just related to what the individual can and cannot do. The managers surrounding him, the goal of the organization, their management style, the initiative that is allowed to be taken, the way subordinates are hired, the way that the firm can or cannot spend money and build the business all have a great influence, along with a hundred other things, on whether or not a man is so-called successful.

At least we should do as much as we can to try and keep the playing field even and fair. Certainly after we have hired a good man, let us not cavalierly attempt to fire him. I don't believe in termination, but I do believe in rehabilitation, including change of position or job function, if possible, accompanied with a commensurate pay adjustment. That may end up being tantamount to termination, but in not a few cases, individuals discover that they are better-suited for less pressure at a lower level—they can get a hold of their performance problem and end up coming out a winner. That's something we owe our employees and managers.

Please carefully note, however, that this kind of rehabilitation (which can also end up effectively solving your performance and problem employee situations) is only possible when you have specific language in your Rules of Employment that allows for such demotions, repositioning, or job junction adjustments with commensurate pay level changes. If you check your Rules of Employment, you will probably discover that the pay cut you can make is limited to 1/2 of a day's pay or 1/10 of the pay during the pay period. Our interpretation must be that this is for a given specific infraction or error made, and what we are discussing here is something entirely different, going beyond the scope of the Labor Standards Law pay cut limitation but still a preferable and more humane policy than termination. A court of law will look to see if you have specific provisions for these procedures and also if you have detailed grounds that justify your taking such actions or procedures against your employees.

You do not have to drink all the wine to know it has turned to vinegar—severance policies

In reality, where the rubber hits the road, the fact is no managers can get through to 100% of their employees. When people frown at us, we usually change our behavior. When they smile, the behavior is reinforced. About 10% of the employees in any company are poor performers or problem employees. About 1/2 of those employees are perceptually deficient. They either don't understand the guidance, coaching and signals they were given or they block them out and attach their own meaning to them. Most counseling assumes that feedback will work because the subject wants to change or is capable of changing if they have adequate information. But if a problem employee has a communication and perceptual problem, maybe communication won't work. Maybe only consequences will work, such as pay cuts and/or termination.

If we make a special connection to a person, our limited powers of communication and persuasion can increase. Indeed, patients need to trust the therapist and believe that the therapist is truly interested in the patient and working in the patient's interest.

In any case, sometimes in spite of our best intentions and efforts, lack of time and need to use priorities in other directions dictate that a parting of ways is to mutual advantage. Termination can allow an employee to have dignity, self-respect, and succeed in another environment. In Japan, unfortunately, if there is litigation, termination is not the way to go. We have already adequately described how to handle these problems.

There is no severance law in Japan other than the provision of 30 days' notice or 30 days' pay, along with the obligation to pay the normal retirement provided for in your Rules of Employment. Usually, something extra is offered as a sweetener, but I believe this should not be more than two or three months' pay and certainly less than six months. Otherwise, you are giving the wrong message to the remaining employees that performance problems will simply be bought away. Average performers can get sloppy and become poor performers.

Studies show that 3% of the problem employees in an organization account for 25% of payroll costs. Most managers know how to address these problems, but it is true that some cannot face taking decisive action against an employee. Henry Ford, for example, was good at building Model Ts but not very good at canning his people. In one case, he moved an undesirable manager downstairs directly below Henry's office, had carpenters cut a hole in the floor, and Mr. Ford used the hole as his wastepaper basket. His ranking executive finally got the message, talked to personnel, and got himself out of there.

Exit interviews aimed at reducing turnover and discovering problems

Try and do this because often it is the only way to get feedback about your organization (and perhaps even your own management style and business plan) that is otherwise not available while someone is still hoping to be on the payroll. The interview should take place with both a high-ranking line manager and with some other individual who shared perhaps a better relationship with the departing staffer. Since sometimes the bearer of bad news also loses his head, it actually might be a good idea to allow the departing manager to record his feelings into a tape recorder. That way any interested party (within designated boundaries, of course) would be free to listen to what he has to say, and there would be no filtering out or misinterpretation as the message goes through the notetaking and verbal reporting process.

When it gets right down to it, before we really go after an employee and effect a termination or its more manageable equivalent, as described above, we must realize that in the end we have to answer to our own internal judge and the court of self-respect. It is true that if you can change losers into winners, you will become a confidentand great leader, and this talent will be worth money to you and your firm.

5

Conclusion

In this paper I have tried to show that it is not enough just to recruit good staff, but we also have to keep them motivated and make sure we succeed with them. In achieving this, I think the following eight points are germane, so I would like to leave them with you.

1. *Select good employees*—You'll never be completely sure. Since it's so hard to get qualified people in Japan, I hope you will follow the rule of "When in (reasonable) doubt, hire." That will also motivate your headhunters, get your recruiting effort to snowball, and get your company off to a fast start, which is so critical here where competition is always nipping at the heels.

2. *Give good and complete orientation*—Remember people are 100% disoriented when they first come in. They have to be put on track and not allowed to make mistakes. They have to know the standards of performance. They'll play ball and go after the objectives of the game if they know the standards and rules.

3. *Utilize strong supervisors*—Initially they are the linkpin to the organization. In a Harvard Business Review article, a study showed that employees perform at the level of their superiors. Weak supervision creates poor performers. Bonding becomes less important after six months or a year in the job. If there is no excellent leadership, there can be no excellent followership. Many supervisors hesitate to get into the personal lives of their staff. This is wrong. If the supervisor knows his people, he can make quicker and more accurate judgments that will not be resented by those subordinates.

4. *Use the employee*—"Using people" usually has negative connotations. Make them stretch and remember that the LOE (level of expectancy) cannot be too much higher than the LOR (level of reality).

5. *Conduct ongoing training and education*—The required knowledge base is constantly shifting and expanding. Skills must be updated. Education should be a lifelong learning practice.

6. *Provide continuous performance feedback*—People need to know where they stand. A basketball game is only interesting to play or watch because there is a hoop. Without the target and the hoop there would be no game.

7. *Set up avenues for the solution of personal problems*—Employees want to know they'll be supported by you when they're in a jam. You have to get your people through the rough spots. If a (good) employee uses up all of the paid sick leave provided for in the Rules of Employment, think flexibly and allow him to take personal time off without pay. Go out of your way for the good performers. You don't need to treat the poor performers the same way. In fact, by definition, if you do, you are giving no special rewards to those who are really contributing to your success and that of your business.

8. *Make sure there are firm consequences when the wrong behavior won't change*—Here we are talking about disciplinary measures, poor performance pay cuts, and even very significant salary adjustments accompanying changes in position and job junction. To do anything else, again, is not fair to the good men and women who are killing themselves for the organization. Experience has shown me there are more people who want to bail out of a loose, undisciplined ship than those who desire to leave a tightly run vessel of trim sail and ambitious destination.

II

On Why They Win
and
How to Become a Winner

1

Why You Can't Beat the Japanese at Their Own Game— It's Because There Are Different Rules

A hands-on insider's look at some of the strengths and advantages in personnel/human resource systems, law, practices, and management.

Introductory splash—just a flash of Japanese common sense

One day about a year ago at home in the family room, my Japanese wife of some 13 years broke the silence reading the *Asahi* newspaper about how Honda lost a court case over job and age discrimination at its Marysville, Ohio plant. Fines would have to be paid and a settlement made. In her fluent Japanese she spurted out the equivalent of, "How can America be strong when they don't even allow businessmen to run a business efficiently? The company will be down on its knees if it has to use all those old people in any job they want!" My 11 and 8 year-old boys chimed in with, "*So da! So da!*" They were not asking for a coke. It's the abbreviated form of *so desu*, or that's right. They added, "That's why America has gotten weak. Go back and straighten them out, Dad!"

Well, I don't think I'll be able to do that in this article, but I did want to give you an insight into the typical Japanese way of looking at this issue. For them it is the common-sense way, and indeed the only practical way to see it. Just perhaps as most Americans would see protecting the aged and eliminating all discrimination of equal and fundamental importance.

In this piece I also will not cover many of the now commonly recognized constraints or major structural system-based differences between Japan and the United States, such as Japan's superior educational system, its industrial policy, the long-term strategic view that is primarily possible because profits don't always have to be made with dividends distributed to stockholders who are conscious and protective of their rights. Instead, I will try to focus on a micro view and even limit that to my own narrow field of expertise. I won't spend any time on diverse psychological reasons for the strength of Japanese corporations such as the lack of a need for the husband to spend time with the family, or the cultural orientation toward a disinclination largely to separate work from play, often being blind to the Western notion that time after five is "my time."

Who I am and where I am coming from

I was in the lowly state-supported school in the pit below your fine Johnson school. For me there was no M.B.A., and it ended with an ILR degree in 1972. I was a cheerleader my sophomore year and watched a classmate, Ed Marinaro (later to be runner-up for the Heisman trophy), run with the pigskin. I worked 30 to 40 hours a week at the Straight Desk and was a Fiji (Phi Gamma Delta) with good *sempai* (seniors) whom I've never met: Ken Blanchard (One-minute Manager) and Tom Peters (In Search of Excellence). Our senior year while I was studying Japanese with Professor Eleanor Jorden at Cornell, it was my class's Phi Gam president Pete McCarthy who was the first and only one ever to say, as we worked together at the Straight Desk, "You know, you may never come back from Japan." At the time I just wondered about that, but it looks as if he was right.

When I was 20, I took a trip around the world taking time off from school made possible by Professor Alice Cook of the ILR school setting me up on an indepedent study project in Japan. I was here ten weeks, but thanks to her influential introductions, was able to meet the George Meany-type equivalents as well as the heads of the opposition parties. I came back in the fall of 1972, worked mostly in labor unions, did a lot of translating in the early years, began writing, and became chairman of the Employment Practices Committee of the American Chamber of Commerce in Tokyo.

Because of my specialty in industrial and labor relations, position as chairman of that committee and strong Japanese language skills, the American Chamber of Commerce selected me to represent them on the first investment mission of senior Japanese businessmen to the United States sponsored by the governments and business associations of both countries. A book about American labor relations for the Japanese came out of this and was published by JETRO in 1980. (The notorious MITI-Ministry of International Trade and Industry is called JETRO abroad and comes under MITI control.) This book sold like hotcakes. Some companies bought as many as 30 copies each, even though each cost $70.

But Japan kept getting stronger, and there was more and more of a need to assist foreign-capitalized firms break into the Japanese market. I changed my focus toward working for American and other foreign interests establishing joint ventures and direct investments in Japan. Although I subscribe to a few U.S.-based professional journals, there is little time to read them, and I do not claim to have kept up with legal changes and developments in stateside human resource management. I am sure readers will realize I have been molded by my environment here after being in this country for over 17 years. This though is perhaps the value of my perspective.

One of my books published in 1984 by the leading English daily newspaper, the *Japan Times*, has the subtle title of *Labor Pains and the Gaijin [foreign] Boss—Managing, Hiring, and Firing the Japanese*. Indeed, TMT is doing a lot of the hard ones for the multinational business community in Japan and the "six strategic tools" or services we offer consist of manpower sourcing/recruiting—executive search, compensation and benefits—design and change, Rules of Employment—set-ups and adjustment, problem-employee solution/terminations, staff reduction and cost-saving programs, and union and staff relations/attitudes. I think I can say we have become the leader in our brand of niche-consulting. With a staff of some 25 employees consisting of 15 full-time consultants engaged in executive search, we also have hunted our share of heads for multinational foreign-capitalized firms in Japan.

I myself was cold-called by Dr. Catheryn Obern, Director, Office of International Public Affairs, who put me onto Ann L. Calkins, Assistant Dean for External Relations of the Johnson School. We ended up working together to make the Johnson School Tokyo '89 Seminar a great success in October, 1989. I got to know your Johnson School Dean Merten, and Professors Dyckman, Hass, and Thomas.

As I recall, the question-and-answer period after the seminar presentations was as long as an hour and a half. Since the Japanese do not like to bathe in the limelight, they are not great question askers. With a half-hour remaining and no questions, I had an excuse to seize the spotlight. My "question" lasted some 15 minutes, and Dean Merten asked me to write it down on paper. One of the good professors had already suggested I write for the *Enterprise*, so here we are.

If you are still with me, please continue and read on about what this inferior ILR school undergraduate has to say. Good news to most and bad news to others: he has largely lost that school's pro-labor perspective, mainly because it has not become the preferred way to pay the bills.

The 17 golden precepts (golden because they have helped Japanese companies make a lot of money)

I am going to present these briefly. Admittedly some points might deserve additional explanation. Please keep in mind that generally these characteristics only apply to the largest Japanese employers comprising no more than 20% of employed labor. It is this sector that is characterized by the so-called three pillars of Japanese labor relations and personnel management—lifetime employment, seniority wages, and the enterprise (company) unions. Note, however, that this 20% of the workforce is providing for roughly 50% of national productivity. The difference in productivity between small firms and large firms has been increasing in the last few years.

1. Teamwork. Not working hard but working together is the key. Team spirit starts from April 1 when training begins. (The school year ends the end of March, and without exception, if you want to get a job with a major Japanese employer, you have to join on schedule with everyone else and show up in your navy blue suit on April 1.)

2. Everyone's in the union together—blue- and white-collar--lack of class dichotomy leads to trust and a feeling that we're all in the same boat. Allegiance is to the company rather than to the union. There is no union-protected seniority or cross-company union hiring hall. If you lose your job at the company, you lose your union membership.

3. Lack of union-imposed seniority work rules with workers pay and security irrelevant to job function. This makes for easy plant and job restructuring to adapt to technological innovation or automation.

4. Japanese internal or closed labor markets are consciously and carefully developed, offering a great advantage to industry. Employees don't work out of blind loyalty but because if they leave or lose their job with a major employer, they cannot secure an equally good job in another major firm, they lose their social standing, superior pay and benefits. So all in all life becomes two or three shades more miserable.

5. With Japanese lack of mid-career recruiting there is no threat of or disincentive effect of bringing in management talent from the outside. (Picture again the young man who joined his firm on April 1. If he looks around the orientation room, he can see who he has to compete with. It's a finite group. No future now-invisible man will come on the scene. He knows exactly who he has to fight and beat out.)

6. In the Japanese-style *ringi* system (where proposals can be initiated at any level and bubble up and around for approval) a lack of structured and fixed goals coming top down from management tends to breed more initiative, with young men feeling like managers.

7. Superiors are securely hooked into their jobs by lifetime employment and

seniority. Bosses don't feel threatened by sharp subordinates and don't hesitate to train and participate in the career development of subordinates. (This is because even if the subordinate is sharper and better, he will be rewarded with the tough jobs and informal recognition but will not skip rank and displace his boss.)

8. Although company members of the (internal, employee) board of directors (*torishimariyaku*) often have their own private rooms, they are more highly evaluated and win the respect of peers and subordinates if they spend most of their time out in the big room. They are exposed to grass-roots information and there is constant rapport, improved communication, and all this minimizes disruptive status differentials.

9. The internal labor market means the bargaining unit is limited to parties knowledgeable and sensitive to the corporate profit picture and needs of workers within a given firm. (Even if a company union is loosely affiliated with an upper-body trade union, no one from the upper body sits in on the collective bargaining negotiation.)

10. An emphasis on in-house training helps to create the needed internal labor market. Skills are designed to fit best the special needs of that employer; employees feel they are stretched and are developing, and this reduces the need for job mobility. (A tragic bottleneck to progress in the United States is that no one will hire the unskilled. Job corps programs don't offer very usable skills. A legion of hard-core unskilled fall into the ranks of the permanently unemployed.)

11. American management should discipline itself to keep men at work. Japanese-style lifetime employment demands excellence, innovation, and diversification into new product areas and fields. Lay-off is an admission of failure. (Think about it. If companies A, B, and C are all too easily shaving off staff, the economy itself can shrink and lose its vitality.)

12. Use of frequent job rotation makes managers more well-rounded, seasoned, and makes the overall workforce more adaptable to technological change. Most important, it avoids on-the-job burnout. (This can result in better products and quality. For example, TV set or other design engineers in general must work a year or so on the assembly line and also in the selling and servicing at retail outlets. Employees appreciate each other's needs, problems, and constraints as well as customer taste and preferences.)

13. Japanese management's secret weapon to keep employees scurrying. Everyone feels until age 35 or so that they are headed for a top management position. In their most productive years and while workers are young, management goes out of its way to make as few distinctions as possible in formal evaluation and pay so as to keep the vast majority of employees at an adequate level of motivation and productivity. (This may be the single disadvantage of M.B.A. programs which indeed catapult degree bearers. This in itself may demotivate the vast majority left behind—but you made the right choice in getting one!)

14. The Japanese practice of paying large bonuses in summer and winter (5.8 months average) is largely responsible for the high rate of personal savings and sustaining consumer demand for expensive durable goods. There is also more performance pay element here than in Western compensation systems.

15. Japan was lucky. Industrialization came late. Craft unions had no time to be fostered. The workforce had to come from a rural setting that had no industrial experience.

16. Diffusion of individual accountability and responsibility. The result is that employees and managers are not afraid to take risks and are willing not to have to take all the credit. In fact, new product ideas or plans rapidly become a part of the invisible whole. (For example, in the States where the tendency might be to select one of three proposed designs, Japanese design teams would be working together and trying to come up with the single best design.)

17. Intrafirm mobility in the form of job rotation makes up for the lack of interfirm mobility characteristic of the closed labor markets between large firms.

Differences in governing structures and how laws are made

I believe in the United States laws are primarily drafted in congressional committees by the politicians themselves or with the politicians in control of their professional staff. While politicians are, of course, elected in Japan, it is within the various ministries that career bureaucrats are primarily drafting the legislation and administering government policies and guidelines.

During the summer between my junior and senior year, I got a Cornell-appointed summer internship at the State Department and secured a summer internship for myself at the Department of Labor the next summer. I could see with my own eyes that working in the U.S. government service would certainly be more fulfilling if there were not as many political appointments made. My impression is there may be 10 to 20 political appointments in each U.S. department whereas in Japan only the *seimu-jikan* (political vice-minister) is appointed at each ministry (other than the minister who, of course, is a politician). In Japan it is really the *jimu-jikan* (career vice-minister) who absolutely runs the show and has all the clout. In this sense, politicians, including the prime minister, have virtually no power in Japan. But, of course, I am not suggesting that President Bush ignore Prime Minister Kaifu!

I also believe there are comparatively fewer new laws or changes made in Japanese statutes. For example, in my field those laws governing labor and personnel management within the firm essentially boil down to the Labor Standards Law and Trade Union Law. During some 40 postwar years there were no major changes or adjustments made to these laws. This means that the personnel function is very different between the two countries, and certainly much less money is spent in Japan on catching up with legal changes and in complying to these changes. Emphasis is on people management not technical expertise.

Courts without a jury and very few lawyers

Each year in Japan only 500 lawyers nationwide are turned out. The big stumbling block is the National Bar Exam. There is no such thing as professional graduate law school. Rather, any individual who passes the bar exam then qualifies to go into the two-year National Law Institute.

I think it is generally known that there is very little litigation in Japan. So far no one has given the real reason for the lack of litigation (and I only figured it out myself a couple of hours ago when I worked up an outline for this article). The reason is the payouts on litigation are too small, and there is not enough to gain by going to court. There are no juries in Japan. Depending on the case, generally one to three judges discuss and decide. They make reasonable settlements, and there is no concept of punishing industry or the rich capitalists the way an angry jury does in the States.

It would be difficult to imagine that a Japanese judge would allow a plaintiff to gain more than the amount that any personal injury or ailment would deprive the individual of earnings based on the individual's earnings record. The Japanese must be absolutely shocked and amused at the $20 million, $30 million, and $40 million or more settlements U.S. juries have been known to provide for injustices or injuries committed to a single individual.

Incidentally, the judges themselves are all known commodities who have passed through the government institutes. A judge cannot be a locally elected or even locally appointed lawyer.

I don't want to make a judgment about which system is better, but I wonder if the dangers and unfairness to corporate America and its institutions in the form of such high settlements can be considered a less serious risk or problem than the risk that carefully selected and groomed judges screened out by rigorous national testing would seriously conspire to thwart democracy or block human rights.

One other interesting aspect of the Japanese court and legal system is the lack of binding court case precedent. Even if the Supreme Court rules on an issue, it doesn't mean that everyone must fall into line and adhere to that ruling. For example, in the early 80s the Supreme Court ruled in the Nissan Motors sexual discrimination case concerning retirement age that it was illegal for the retirement age to be 55 for males and 50 for females. While Nissan adhered to that ruling and brought the female retirement age up to age 55, there are still many companies in Japan with unequal retirement ages even though that also runs in the face of the

April 1, 1986 Equal Opportunity Employment Law. I guess the emphasis is on flexibility and giving institutions and corporations a chance to work these things out if they can, without an unnecessary and paralyzing burden.

Indeed there is an underlying consensus that what is good for business will be good for the people—a lot of guidance but few rules that have to be followed

In 1980, the Ministry of Labor began to give guidance that by 1985 companies should increase their retirement age from the traditional age 55 up to age 60. Yet it was only recently this year in 1989 that for the first time, over 50% of Japanese companies had a retirement age of age 60 or more. Virtually no retirement age goes over age 60 although since 1985, the Ministry of Labor once again has given guidance that by 1990 the retirement age should start to move up above 60 and on toward 65.

As mentioned above, since April 1, 1986, the Equal Opportunity Employment Law was passed primarily focusing on sex discrimination issues and ruling that there should be no sexual discrimination in hiring, training, promoting, compensating, etc. between men and women. Japan is a country where too much protection of women was effectively precluding equality. For example, women, even if they were executives, were technically not allowed to work on holidays, and overtime had to be limited to two hours a day, six hours a week, or 150 hours a year. With the April 1, 1986, legislation, some of the compulsory protection was loosened up and women in supervisory positions now can work unlimited overtime along with men. In spite of this legislation, however, the fact is there continues to be often even blatant discrimination. Since the law provides for no penalties unless there is specific litigation at each establishment, old discriminatory practices can continue at a number of firms.

It may also be the women's fault because they often do not complain and hesitate to litigate. Note, however, that in postwar Japan even tens of years before the April 1, 1986, legislation, whenever there was a court case where women pressed for their rights and accused employers of sexual discrimination, the courts without fail always backed up the complaining women and ruled that the discrimination be eliminated. However, it was only in late 1989 that the first case of sexual harassment hit the courts. From the fall of 1989, for the first time, a sexual harassment hotline was set up under the auspices of an association of lawyers.

Other examples of where there is guidance but a lack of firm laws with teeth would cover such areas as encouraging employers to provide equal benefits or government social insurances to part-time and contract employees. Yet many firms continue to provide for these categories in different ways. There is also no national minimum wage. Rather, there is a combination of flexible regional minimum wages and minimum wages affecting only certain business sectors in a flexible and limited sense.

In a seeming contradiction with the concept of lifetime employment and a perceived inability to terminate staff, there is in fact no severance law in Japan, no requirement to provide a retirement benefit. As for termination, the statutes per se in the form of Article 20 of the Labor Standards Law merely provide that 30-days' notice or 30-days' pay or a combination of the two need be provided. In reality, however, due to this absence of firm rules, should a termination go to court, an employer will not fare well. His Article 20 right to terminate will rarely be admitted.

The legal minimum overtime rate in Japan is 25%, and virtually no firms pay more than this. (With Japanese employees' propensity to work, imagine how much more overtime might be registered if the rate was as attractive as the 50% premium commonly provided in the United States? Similarly, the legally required minimum vacation also poses little burden to employers. They are required to provide no days of paid vacation during the first year of employment, six days the second year, and an additional day for each year of service up to a maximum of 20 days. In reality, of course, firms provide something more in the order of eight to 12 days for even the first year of service. There are also as many as 14 national holidays in Japan.

Legally, the employer need not provide any sick leave; but if over three people are employed, the employer is to register them into the expensive government overseen social insurance programs which amount to on average 11.5% of the employee's monthly salary, with this premium payable each month.

The emphasis on guidance rather than on forcing tough rules and penalties on people even shows itself in the way the police deal with the public. When we drive through the United States collecting speeding tickets, my wife is amazed at how the troopers don't say much, walk up to your car, and just write out the ticket and have you sign it. In Japan the emphasis is on giving guidance and cautioning you without necessarily slapping you with a ticket. You do have to put up with some harmless and seemingly irrelevant questions such as the typical pattern of "Where did you come from? Where are you going?" As long as you keep apologizing, they finish up by merely telling you that "Your children are too cute to be involved in an accident, so please take it easy."

Age discrimination issues and retirement age rights take a backseat to economic rationalization

On the average in Japan 50-year-olds make more money than 55-year-olds. This has especially become more prevalent as the workforce has aged, and older workers have proven to be less able to adapt to technological and office automation. Thus, the same man can be working at the same job, and systematized adjustments in salary tables and pay structures provide that his pay will actually start to curve down in real yen terms. I don't believe that would fly too well in the United States. Japanese Rules of Employment also provide that in a systematic fashion over a certain age—depending on the company sometimes this is age 45, 50, or 55, etc.—pay can be cut back for certain selected individuals who have slowed down and ceased to be promotable into higher job grades. Essentially, what we have are individuals being moved back into lower qualification grades essentially for age-driven reasons.

Likewise in Japan when it comes time to carry out a staff reduction, it is possible to announce that only employees over a certain age level-perhaps age 40 or 45—will be entitled to receive the supplemental retirement premium payable to those who are tapped out by management. Years ago there was an employee or two who questioned this practice in court, but the judge ruled that it was by no means an unfair or unreasonable practice on the part of management, for it was based on the rational economic decision that the older workers were less adaptable to new technologies and office automation; and because seniority wages did make them the most expensive workforce, getting them selectively to leave the firm brought about the quickest and most rationally effective way to cut costs.

When President Jimmy Carter signed legislation to the effect that every American had a right to work at least until age 70, Japan was amazed. They are flabbergasted at the current U.S. situation that provides for the possibility for employees to essentially work on as long as they want without a forced retirement age. My understanding is that this has not worked out so badly in the United States. In fact, in spite of this legislation, the average age that employees retire has been decreasing.

The Japanese know, however, that that would not be the case in Japan. In all likelihood virtually all Japanese would prefer to keep working and would cling on to their jobs. That is why in spite of the administrative guidance mentioned above, the Japanese employers associations and chambers of commerce vehemently oppose and will not allow an increase in the retirement age ruling.

Some sophisticated Japanese friends who have worked in the United States have told me that they are worried that U.S. workers may stay and work on into old age. They realize the United States is not a country that would allow discriminatory pay by age, yet as the workers lose mental agility or become stubborn and fixed in their ways, they are afraid that U.S. management might respond by making life tough on those employees to try and get them to resign voluntarily. They tell me it was one thing when you knew Joe Brown had just two or three years left, so you could graciously wait until age 65. But now, with no prospect as to how long old crotchety Joe will stay on, they wonder if there isn't the potential for such friction in the workplace.

Flexibility in employment status, contracts, and transfers are an important strength to business

A senior Japanese executive with one of the most influential banks here once told me that he believed the greatest strength of Japanese management is its ability to assign and station freely employees by both job and work location. If there is litigation, of course, Japanese management would have court restraints imposed upon it, and the judge would inquire as to whether or not the transfer is necessary to business operations and as to availability of a substitute who might face a lower hardship factor. In reality, there is little litigation. At least in the major firms where a progressing career is valued at the prestigious employer (which also provides superior pay and benefits in the context of a closed labor market and lack of alternate job possibility), employees willingly accept transfers in job content and by location. The vast majority of Japanese changing the work location leave their families behind, visiting them only once or twice a month on weekends (the *tanshin-funin* syndrome so prevalent in postwar Japan).

Another cost-saving and rational characteristic of Japanese industry—if not an equally dismal one—is the cost saving inherent in two aspects of the so-called dual structured economy. Pay levels, security, and working conditions for subcontractors are greatly inferior to those of the large parent companies. Many of the employees of subcontractors are themselves on term contracts of maximum one-year duration. Even within the same office or plant of the parent company, it is possible to have various categories of employees with different status. First of all, there are the *seishain* (regular employees) enjoying all benefits and security. Then you have your term contract employees who may not enjoy the same vacation, bonus, or retirement, etc. benefits. They also provide the needed buffer, as the contracts do not need to be renewed in times of economic slump. Although there are court cases where contract employees have won regular employment status, those are generally under circumstances in which the employer did not follow the proper technical procedures in passing new contract paper and securing signatures at the end of each employment term.

Japan is a great egalitarian society in that university is comparatively inexpensive, and anyone who can pass the entrance exams for one of the many national and state universities enjoys essentially a free education. But for those who had to work or, in any case, did not opt to go to college, it is pretty difficult to get out of blue-collar ranks. Salary systems and promotion grids provide for substantial ongoing differences in lifetime earnings and corporate possibilities within the corporation.

Even if an individual goes to night school and gets a degree, few large firms recognize this, and the individual stays in his original category. I think the systems are a bit more bureaucratized than they are in the United States; but after all, all in all, income differentials between rich and poor are less in Japan than they are in the United States. Within a given corporation, the rule of thumb is that the difference in pay level between presidents and entry level people is ten to one in Japan while it is as much as 100 to 1 in the United States.

We should thus not underestimate the savings and cost efficiencies that lower executive pay brings to Japanese corporations. If the Japanese employee puts up with high domestic prices and a low standard of living, so do his superiors and even executive management at the highest levels. The result is that they all work well together, and the team stays together and pulls in the same direction.

Handy efficient mechanisms on the compensation side

Based on company performance, profit and individual performance and contribution, on the average, Japanese companies pay 5.8 months annual bonus to their employees. Generally, slightly over half is paid in mid-December and just under 1/2 of this amount or about 2.5 months payable in mid-June. This is merely a practice; there is no law or requirements on minimum or maximum amount of bonus. During the oil crisis in 1973 to 1974, even a major firm such as Matsushita (National/Panasonic) paid no bonus to its supervisors over section-chief level. This was largely made up for when the economy and sales picked up again.

In a nation where employment security can be so highly protected, essentially precluding termination if there is litigation, the bonus has been a handy practice. On an exceptional basis and for employees who also do not have the support of fellow workers, it becomes possible to hold back on the bonus payment for selected poor performers. This, combined with the practice stipulated in most companies' Rules of Employment (a legal document required to be submitted to the Labor Standards Office when a firm has over ten employees) allows adjusting the job function and making a commensurate pay adjustment. Japanese firms, especially smaller firms which account for the vast majority of Japanese employed labor, have a surprising number of flex points to reward for good performance and contribution and to penalize the poor performer or employee with a poor attitude.

Furthermore, while the perception in the West is that Japanese employees tend to be paid the same based on seniority, that is rather far from true. In some foreign capitalized firms in Japan that were set up improperly, the salary table can sometimes consist almost solely of age-based pay. Actually, however, good Japanese practice provides that the age payline starts and ends at a very low level, often being capped at around age 40. In fact, rather than age pay, the vast majority of the monthly compensation comes from a complex but flexible system of various allowances that can be selectively assigned to employees based on their ability, qualifications, and job functions. Even if employees were litigious, since the system provides legitimization for the practice, the result is that the employer has a free hand without worrying about the kind of litigation that would be a constant source of trouble and expense in the United States.

Paternalistic? In a way. Hardnosed and coldly rational? Definitely yes—Japanese management insists on trading— a positive change in conditions or benefits is generally neutralized with a negative change

Just two or three examples here will suffice. It is only in the last 10 to 15 years that Japanese business has only slowly moved away from Saturday work. In the last three years, the banks have moved to one Saturday off a month, then two Saturdays off a month, and finally this year, all Saturdays are off. Again, only in the last two to three years, government agencies and the post office have moved away from Saturday work. Two Saturdays off at government agencies will soon change to no Saturday work. School children in Japan still go to school every Saturday. They are just beginning to talk about slowly reducing the days of Saturday instruction. In any case, the point I want to make is that as Japanese banks cut back on each day of Saturday labor, they increased the working hours Monday through Friday by that amount, so gradually the employees' workday has become longer.

In a similar sense, as the retirement age has only reluctantly and very incrementally increased beyond the traditional 55 year retirement age, Japanese management always insisted that since the extended retirement age made for a increase in lifetime earnings, the annual pay level of the employees now able to enjoy the extended retirement age should be cut back. Certainly at virtually all firms the years of service beyond 55 were not to be calculated into the years of service going toward the retirement benefit. Pay levels for work beyond 55 (and sometimes even for work done between ages 50 and 55!) were reduced by anywhere from 10 to 40%.

The traditional Japanese lump-sum retirement benefit consisting of a number of months of salary depending on years of service and as determined in a table attachment to Rules of Employment was merely a paper benefit in the sense that it traditionally was not funded with an outside institution. Due to a growing number of "lump-sum retirement benefit caused bankruptcies," in order to provide security to employees (and probably to create a new fast-growth financial instrument for influential trust banks and insurance companies!), in the 1960s the tax-qualified pension legislation was passed. This was not at all compulsory, but companies could opt to get tax benefits by funding in this way. There were a number of Japanese companies that used the positive change of secured funds in the employee's name to compensate for a negative change or adjustment in the quality of the retirement benefit table (number of months of pay for years of service) and/or the basis of the calculation of the weight of monthly compensation calculated into the retirement benefit. Here again, cost-saving rationalization exercises were commonplace. There was little employee-instigated litigation, but even if there were, I believe that the courts would have largely backed up the employer for management efforts were designed to reduce the retirement liability which was a reasonable goal in that funding would now be secured with an outside party. Furthermore, such rationalization moves were required in the face of the rapidly aging workforce, the mushrooming retirement liability, and the need to assure long-term corporate health which, after all, is the only thing that assures job security.

Once again, a flexible response and economic rationality take precedence over binding legislation or jury decisions which can tend to look out unreasonably for the rights of a single or small group of individuals.

Yet in some areas economic rationalization and the greater good are brutally sacrificed in favor of individual human rights

The United States has been pressuring Japan to export less and instead to develop a domestic-demand-driven economy by working on industrial and social infrastructures such as the building of national highway systems, better railroad transportation, and various public works as well as resort and leisure-oriented developments. This is not going to be easy not only because it is prohibitively expensive with the cost of land in Tokyo being worth more than the total land value of the United States, but also because individual human rights are protected to an unbelievable degree. For example, one still has to make a long and time-consuming congested detour at a spot on the Kanpachi Loop road. Apparently there is a single owner or perhaps two who are holding out and will not sell their land to allow the completion of the loop road. I believe this has been going on for 10 or 15 years as this landowner holds out, essentially blackmails the government, while waiting for the bidding price to go up. The cost in time and business opportunities lost to the Tokyo populace is virtually incalculable. Yet the authorities and the public tolerate this.

Even the extension of the Hanzomon subway beyond our station was held up for years for a similar reason. My understanding is that a handful of landowners on the surface must agree to government restrictions on building weight and depth of basement levels above such a subway line. Two or three owners would not accept the compensation offered to secure their agreement, and this held up the subway development for three or four years.

Since its inception there have been struggles at Narita Airport, and even on opening day, in spite of the presence of 14,000 *kidotai* (national riot police), radicals managed to storm and destroy the control tower. I guess this only becomes possible when there is no fear of bullets or of getting one's skull crushed by a police baton.

My impression was that in the United States and most other countries, for the public good such road or other infrastructure public works projects are executed in a routine and efficient way precluding individual "rights" from undermining a greater good. To me that seems the preferred and fair way to do it. We see that even in Japan, economic rationality does not always prevail; but even in these aberrations of human rights, flexible guidelines lacking compulsory teeth seem to prevail. That is to say, just as there is tolerance of unequal retirement ages by sex long after the Supreme Court made its ruling, so can we have a handful of die-hards hanging onto their land and pressing their rights through the court appeals process for many years.

Conclusion

Yes, it's hard to beat the Japanese at their own game because the rules of the game are so different that we inevitably find ourselves not playing the same game.

Essentially Japan lacks many of the inflexible rules, penalties, and forced compliance which may be limiting America's ability to react flexibly and efficiently in certain areas. But adhering to American rules is probably the best way to go for America given our system and pluralistic society.

After all, it really doesn't need to be a question of beating the Japanese, for in many ways they are a force for great good and progress in the world. I think they have finally showed America that the key is to have economic and not military strength and that the world will follow the economic leader and not the military leader, just as America's cultural influence and way of life greatly impacted and continues to exercise influence on the world. We drive better cars and watch crisper televisions thanks to the Japanese.

The iron curtain has melted. The Soviet Union no longer seems to be the threat it was (or was played up to be). For goodness sake, let us not see Japan as a threat but rather as an opportunity to at least become familiar with their rules and make some adjustments to our own society which will allow business to operate more flexibly, efficiently, and perhaps even with fewer rules.

Little and Big Tricks of Any Trade for Japan or Anywhere

This article has virtually nothing to do with
what I've done for a living as an independent businessman
these last 17 years in Tokyo.
It talks about some pet peeves we have probably
all experienced and is aimed at making ourselves
more attractive, more accessible, more pleasant,
more effective, and easier to do business with.
Hopefully, this will make us more successful businessmen.

"He knows my number," is inconsiderate and not even true

The party you have called doesn't "know" your number, unless he has committed it to memory, which is unlikely. While you could routinely get in the habit of spitting it out each time, taking three to five seconds, it will take someone, either your party or the party's secretary, a minimum of 30 seconds to perhaps as long as five minutes to look up your number.

When I return from a two or three hour meeting and face sometimes ten to 15 telephone messages and have only a half-hour before going into the next meeting, only those who leave their numbers get called back (with some exceptions, as they may be reading this article!).

More on making it easy for them to give you their money

If you want to leave an accurate message and be sure to be called back, if you are calling the first time leave only the spelling of your last name, your company name and your phone number. (When dealing in an intercultural and multi-language environment, first names have a way of becoming last names and it all becomes a bit unnecessarily confusing.)

If, however, the other party is supposed to be on a first name basis with you, it would be considerate and avoid embarrassment if you would spell out both your first name and your last name.

First name, not the initials, should go on the business card

Especially if you are from or primarily dealing with Americans, Canadians, Australians, or people who more quickly move to the first name basis, you should make sure that you provide your first name on your business cards for the convenience of the people that have to deal with you. Where you expect to be able to use their first name, you owe them this convenience and courtesy.

Place full address, phone and fax numbers on stationery, fax message sheets, envelopes, business cards and all pieces of a direct mail campaign, etc.

Actually, the Japanese are very good at this. They want to make it easy for you to spend money on their products. It amazes me that although virtually all of our foreign capitalized clients in Japan now have fax availability throughout their international network, still, probably less than 1/3 have the fax number printed on stationery and business cards, and some even fail to provide their return fax number when they are faxing you! This is sloppy, insensitive, and bad business.

I believe that full service and total quality control include looking after these details, watching out to insure that customers or your business parties are not inconvenienced—and it is not just customers—the better you treat your vendors, the more successful they will make you.

When your secretary gets past the secretary of the party you are calling, it is time to get on the line

Even if occasionally you have to talk to the other party's secretary, that won't kill you, and chatting her up for a few seconds could pay out later on. I have always felt that if an executive pushed the buttons himself, he almost might have more control on the whole process and could get more desk work done while waiting, in that he would be better tuned into how the effort to make the connection is unfolding. Also, it must be very difficult for the secretary to get her job done. Think of all the wheel spinning, and the frustration she must feel, combined with the lack of control in getting her own work done, just so that she can push the buttons on her boss's phone calls.

A word of caution! I can only really speak for Japan, but I know that a Japanese executive is severely irritated and miffed if, when he hits the line from his side, in his very best English, assuming that he is talking with you when instead he must start off with your secretary. Even high-ranking Japanese members of the board of directors have no problems pushing the buttons themselves and expect the same courtesy from you.

Make up detailed maps and directions so people can find you

Asian cities tend to be old and crowded, and few of them were planned and laid out. There is nothing more aggravating than the notion that your customer or vendor is sitting tight and getting something done while you are unnecessarily slipping through slush, looking for a phone booth and fogging up your glasses in a frantic search to find his office.

Maps and directions are often not useful unless they are bilingual, appearing also in the local language for the local taxi driver or the guide you buttonhole on the street.

Treat everyone as if he/she is the most important person in your life

Learn the secretary's name and use her name when you call in. She will put you at the top of the call back list and deliver your faxes and mail right underneath her boss's nose for priority reading.

Remember that today's junior support people will be the decision-makers and buyers of tomorrow. In some bottom-up oriented organizations in Asia, their influence even today may be more than you could imagine. Everyone wants self-esteem, and if you give it to them, they will go out of their way to give you their business and their money.

Don't underestimate apology as a social/business lubricant and catalyst toward building sales and reputation

Unlike the Japanese, you don't necessarily have to accept the blame for something you didn't do, but you can explain the actual situation, apologize sincerely, and point out that you will be sure to correct the problem.

You will be best off, however, if you make no excuses, and, in a Japanese context, as a member of the organization, you are the organization and loyalty to the organization, as well as business etiquette, would dictate that you make a categorical apology. After all, the Japanese receiving the apology obviously knows that you are personally not to blame.

Every day ask yourself "How can I increase my service or that of my company and the value of my products to the customer?"

You have to enrich others to gain their riches. People are not interested in product features, but in how the product benefits them. Your personal rewards in life, from the marketplace, or within your company hierarchy in the form of a promotion will always match your service. You must put the oil in the stove before you can get heat.

The Japanese are very good about not worrying about today's income or profits. They just increase their service and the quality of their products. If you fail to give after-service, give shabby service or are less than honest about what your product will do, remember, you will not be able to keep this up for long, and what goes around will come around and hurt your business and career.

You can only get more than your worth for a limited period of time. This is true when it comes to the worth and value of your company's product mix and also to the level of your own salary as an executive, compared to your worth and contribution to the company. Keep adding value to your products; a diamond started from a lump of coal.

Go for the hard ones

The West was incredibly rich when compared with Asia, and so it took the path of the least resistance and got lazy. Maybe it sold technology cheaply when the Asian markets were closed, and that was the only way that business could be done. But even now there are too many Western companies that take the easy way out and set up joint ventures, leave their business solely up to a distributor or go in direct but hire a Japanese executive and leave him alone with the business without checks and balances or further inputs and support from the head office. Few of us are saints, and this is an unhealthy situation that can lead to misfeasance and irregularities and, at best, incredible opportunities lost. At least one such case comes to me per month for appropriate surgery and clean-up.

It is hard for the resident or visiting representative of the foreign capitalized head office to go for the hard ones in Asia. You can't read the language or easily understand the insides of the company, but nonetheless you must do your homework and even ruffle some feathers when necessary. You have a right to. You are responsible for the capital investment. Sometimes you have to ask the tough questions and check the accounts. Certainly, the Japanese do no less with their offshore operations and they would never dream of leaving their valuable capital investment and business potential purely in the hands of local nationals.

Even salaried executives in large multinational organizations are in business for themselves

Develop yourself and see that your stock increases in value. Think of yourself and your career as you think of your business: be sure it is healthy in terms of finances (savings for reentering a home country housing market), productivity (your skills and effectiveness), sales levels (the influence and persuasive power you have with the head office and your own operation) and R&D (your overall knowledge and the specific experience you have gained while working abroad).

Like your company, you as an individual must continue to grow while you are stationed abroad.

A successful posting is a succession of successful single days

Make the most of each and every working day. Be cheery, confident, and expectant. With a flexible but positive "go for it!" attitude you can make a difference even though there are cultural differences and some different rules.

Believe in yourself and what you are selling. Believe that your customer is getting the better end of the bargain. After all, he will probably enjoy your product long after your firm spent the money received from your customer.

A successful life is merely a line of back-to-back successful, single action-oriented days. A mason built with a single brick at a time; if a single brick isn't placed right, the entire tower could crumble and fall. The bricklayer's task looks formidable to the observer. The man with the spatula, however, knows that if he just concentrates on each brick and places it properly, he will finish and succeed.

As an expatriate executive stationed in Asia, you are on the front line in the most competitive and fastest growing region in the world. The obstacles seem enormous, and corporate attention is focused on you. Do not be overwhelmed or discouraged; just take it one day at a time.

Get the little things right, and the big things will fall into place.

3

Managers and
Monday Morning
in Tokyo and New York

*An inside view on why Japanese management
has been winning.*

Alarm clocks measure our motivation

It's 7:00 on a Monday morning with the first rays of spring sunshine fighting to squeeze between the bedroom curtains of a Suzuki-san, sound asleep in a quiet suburb of Tokyo. Suzuki-san is a personnel manager (*kacho*) in his early 40s in a major Japanese manufacturing concern.

On the other side of the world, and about a half day earlier, a New York suburbanite, who is also a personnel manager of about the same age and status, is slowly pulling out of his deepest dreams and getting ready to face the realities of a day at the office. His name is White.

Their alarm clocks buzz off, and this is where our story begins. That momentary and initial reaction and the feelings which gush up within us when we are greeted by our alarm clocks on a Monday morning are probably the best barometer of the way we feel about our lives—the work and play we face each day. It can be the simplest, but perhaps most accurate measure of career and job satisfaction.

—Mr. Suzuki—
Out of bed in 20 seconds, off and running

Suzuki feels good about waking up in the morning. He lets his wife turn off the alarm. But he is on his feet within 20 seconds and goes over to the sink to wash-out his eyes with a splash of cold water. This stimulus reminds him that this morning he wants to get to the office as soon as possible, so that he will have a few minutes to read the newspapers, and browse through some of the newly issued magazines that the company supplies at no charge to the managers and employees. There will be little or no time to do this later on in the day, because from 9:30 a.m. he will enter into wage negotiations with the representatives of the enterprise union at his company.

"There's no telling when they might end, allowing me to get back to my desk," he murmurs to himself.

The big room makes for teamwork, improved communications, rapport, and minimum disruptive status differentials— who needs job descriptions?

As a section chief, or *kacho*, in his firm, Suzuki-san is always careful to set a good example. He never comes to work late. In a Japanese company, it is hard to slip into the office late without being noticed. Everyone works in a large room together. From a department general manager or *bucho*, who may also be on the board of directors, down through multiple management ranks, which include the key middle manager or *kacho*, all operating and line corporate executives, and rank and file in a given department work together in a large room.

The section chief or *kacho* usually sits at the head of a cluster of desks, usually in a double row. Desks are deliberately placed head to head, so that the lower ranking, junior managers, and rank and file office workers face each other. This maximizes communication and allows all members of a section(three to ten people) to grasp intuitively all dimensions of the section's business and their respective jobs. That is why it was never necessary for Suzuki-san and other staff in the personnel department to develop and keep up to date the job descriptions that can be so important to most corporate organizations in the United States.

Suzuki-san's staff somehow seem to know what is expected of them without being told; and since all members of a section work so closely together, almost by necessity, any tasks accomplished become a product of a group effort. This is why it is not necessary to define on paper the areas of responsibility and limits of authority pertaining to each manager and employee. A situation results in which an individual employee may not get full credit for his own idea. Rather the accomplishment will formally be credited to the Section or even the Department. Insiders, however, know who was instrumental and responsible for the accomplishment, and this recognition satisfies the staffer who initiates the achievement.

The carrot is longer than the stick—
hazy accountability encourages risk taking
and makes a manager willing to share the credit

Maybe this is why Suzuki-san can be so cheerful this morning, in spite of the particularly busy day and heavy pressures facing him. He is in the midst of wage negotiations with the union, and although he is the only company representative who is expected to attend virtually all sessions for their entire length, any settlement on wage percentages, or new issues brought-up for bargaining will represent the company's position and not reflect too directly on his own handling of the situation. He certainly does not need to worry about losing his job even if he makes a mistake or two. He also has a comfortable and easy-going relationship with the general manager of *bucho* of his department, and even the higher managing director or *jomu*, who is the top corporate figure with representational responsibility over personnel and general affairs.

Suzuki-san is enjoying his new responsibilities as the key man in negotiations. Although, both the *bucho* and *jomu* are on the board of directors, they exercise their authority as little as possible. They are more concerned with affairs of the wider world of business outside the company. They also maintain good relations between their various counterparts representing other corporate functions on the board of directors, which is comprised almost exclusively of internal directors who grew up with the company. His superiors are deliberately refraining from giving Suzuki-san unnecessary instructions. Occasional attendance at a bargaining session will enable them to guide Suzuki-san should his steering drift off course. Top management is tolerant of this, for Suzuki-san has only had a total of four years in the personnel function: this is his second year, and he had two years much earlier as a young clerk.

Frequent job rotation makes the overall workforce more
well-rounded, seasoned, and adaptable to technological change

Unlike corporate organizations in the United States, Japanese companies place much more confidence in the generalist. After World War II, in particular, large Japanese companies realized the gains in worker commitment which could be had by developing a system of "lifetime employment," or an internalized labor market, which meant that the hiring of regular employees would only take place directly after school graduation on April 1. The employee's position within the enterprise improves with seniority, and there is an economic penalty if one leaves the firm he joined as a new school graduate. This is because there is little mid-career hiring by other high paying large firms.

To make up for this lack of mobility and freedom to change jobs in an open labor market, Japanese management realized that employee restlessness, and "executive burn-out," could be avoided through job rotation every two or three years. A change of working environment and a chance to work with new people can give the manager a new lease on life and inject him with renewed vigor. A manager learning new skills also feels that he will be a better, more well-rounded candidate for a top management position in the future.

All these things were not running through Suzuki-san's mind, but these Japanese management practices meant that he had worked with the personnel *bucho* in the same sales department when he first joined the company; and when Suzuki-san had been in the company for eight or nine years, he worked in the Second Business Development Department with the *jomu*, who was at that time the *kacho* in the section next to Suzuki-san.

As he pushed and shoved to get into his train for the office, Suzuki-san realized how lucky he was to have had those chances in his earlier years to have proven himself to his present superiors.

In Japan, the personnel manager negotiates his own salary increase!

A group of "salaried men" and "office ladies" fought their way at the next station into a train already filled to capacity. As Suzuki-san was rushed up in a corner against the train door on the opposite side from the station platform, he mused that "even if I get shoved into a corner, and have to give away more at the negotiations than we thought we'd have to, my own pay envelope will be the thicker for it."

Unlike in the United States, where blue-collar workers are paid by the hour and according to their job classification, in Japan, even manual workers are paid monthly salaries, and the salary scales of both white and blue-collar are largely uniform and pegged together. Because the annual spring negotiated "base up" applies virtually across the board within the same firm, Suzuki-san really finds himself negotiating his own salary increase!

All newly recruited regular employees enter the company together—the team spirit starts from April 1

Suzuki-san enters the office, taking off his duster and placing it in his locker. He goes out of his way to greet the new recruits who entered the company together just a few days ago on April 1. He took a few of them out on his expense account the night before and is pleased to see that the teamwork and healthy competition between these newly recruited "classmates" are already beginning to shape-up.

Japanese management has mastered the secret of "keeping them scurrying"

One of the great strengths of Japanese management is to treat all employees virtually alike in their most productive years, or for the first 10 to 15 years of employment. With almost no differentiation in promotion speed, and no discrepancies in pay, every young manager feels that he has a chance of getting on the board of directors. They, thus, work and compete with each other very hard, sizing-up each other's strengths and weaknesses from the first day at work. In large companies, Japanese recruiting practices of taking in regular employees only on April 1, mean that from the beginning a young man knows who he is competing with. In contrast to this, in an American company, there is always the apprehension and disincentive effect of bringing in management talent from outside, and having it stuck over your head. A young American manager, therefore, finds it hard to compete because he can never be sure who he is competing with.

The new recruits seem to be enjoying their training program. It is mostly on the job training with some classroom work. It will last several months and expose them to all areas of operations—the office organization, the factory and retail sales. In an American company with higher job turnover, management cannot afford to spend so much money on training, for the manager or worker may soon quit—which will mean low return on investment.

It was January of last year when one of Suzuki-san's sharp subordinates proposed to him that new recruits, and especially all draftsmen and engineers who will be assigned to product design, be given a minimum of two months' experience in a retail outlet. Suzuki-san's subordinate pointed out that this experience, along with two months on the assembly line, would be invaluable to the designers, for it would familiarize them with constraints posed by manufacturing and also show them which designs matched best with consumer tastes, and what parts of a product tended to be returned to retail outlets for servicing.

Superiors are secure in their jobs— not threatened by "he's after my job complex"

This year, this new idea will be fully implemented, and Suzuki-san's subordinate was given the recognition he deserved for coordinating and implementing the program. As the man's boss, Suzuki-san does not feel the least bit threatened by his very impressive subordinate. This is because lifetime employment and seniority securely lock a man like Suzuki-san into his position, and it would be impossible for the younger man in this situation to displace Suzuki-san from his job.

The younger man remains content, however, because he is rewarded by informal recognition-given extra training, a business trip abroad, or a chance to prove himself again on another challenging assignment. Without feeling threatened then, Suzuki-san does not hesitate to train and fully participate in the career development of his subordinates. A Japanese manager, more than an American counterpart, is likely to pass down the hard-won secrets of his trade to the managers under him.

A lack of fixed goals and excessive top-down instructions breeds more initiative from young managers

Furthermore, as illustrated by the young manager's idea of getting the engineer-designers out to retail outlets for training, in the bottom-up *ringi* system of Japan, the comparative absence of American-style top-down management, and structured and fixed goals, means that more young men are taking initiative and feeling like a manager without sitting around and waiting for instructions from supervisors. There is therefore more overall management input in a Japanese company than there would be in a U.S. company.

As Suzuki-san was sitting at his desk a circulating bulletin, or *kairan*, attached to a clip board was passed to him from the section, or *ka*, nearest to him. There are some 60 people working in the big room, and three of the seven sections, or some 25 people, place there wooden name stamp, or *hanko*, on a mimeograph form which is taped to the notice. There is a little box next to each name where the stamp is entered. This particular notice informs all that it has been decided that an assembly plant will be retooled and more fully automated to provide for more efficient production.

Workers don't oppose technological change and job restructuring because it rarely hurts them

A thought crosses Suzuki-san's mind. He knows that as a *kacho* of the personnel department of the head office he will be called upon to help implement the job restructuring by retraining and relocating workers who cannot by laid-off. A Japanese personnel manager is fortunate, however, because his workers' pay and job security are irrelevant to a particular job junction. This means that workers will not oppose technological innovation, as they are confident that job restructuring will not result in a lay-off or a lower job pay rate.

American management should discipline itself to keep men at work—lay-off is an admission of failure

Suzuki-san knows that he cannot take the easy option of laying men off. Lay-off is an admission of failure. The commitment of Japanese management to keep men on the job demands far-sighted management decisions, as well as innovation and diversification into new product areas and fields.

American management treats labor as the most elastic and disposable factor of production. Instead of committing itself to a growth target, an American company merely lays-off workers to maintain profits. Many companies take this easy option. This is a big reason why the U.S. economy has all but stopped growing.

Suzuki-san once sat on the other side of the bargaining table

It is 9:30 a.m., and time for Suzuki-san to enter the negotiating room. The three union representatives are younger men and are already seated at the table and awaiting Suzuki-san's arrival. They stand up quickly, greet him with a "Good morning," and politely bow. Watching them reminds Suzuki-san of the time he was the local elected union bargaining representative while working as a technical advisor at a factory on the outskirts of Osaka. Suzuki-san will be negotiating all day; and since no non-employee outsiders, including union staff from the upper body industrial union in which his enterprise union is affiliated, are allowed to sit in on collective bargaining sessions, we will have to leave Suzuki-san to work things out on his own.

—Mr. White—
He muffles out the alarm clock through his pillow

Across the ocean and a continent away in New York, it is 7:05 a.m. and Mr. White has been aware of a faint alarm clock buzz for some five minutes. He's learned to sleep on his left side, covering his right ear with the pillow. Removing the pillow and tugging on his shoulder, his wife reminds him that it is time to get up and that she wants him to get to the breakfast table the same time the children do. He enjoys being with his family, and this thought gets him on his feet and stumbling towards the bathroom.

Slowly his life and his day come into focus. Like many American managers he does not know what is wrong with him, and why he cannot jump out of bed and go off to work with a spring in his step. His main, underlying problem is that unlike Suzuki-san, he must face his day and his responsibilities very much alone. It does not even matter if he gets into the office a little late—that is unless he is noticed in the parking lot, or his secretary talks. Although he has not conceptualized and recognized it, he does not even like the place where he must park his car. Some younger men who entered the company after he did are higher in rank and allowed to park in the special reserved parking section for executives. Such unnecessary status differentials are more common in Western companies, and they sap the pluck, sense of self-esteem, and initiative out of managers.

There is greater pressure, and not as much fun, when work has to be faced alone

Mr. White greets his secretary with a "Good morning," goes into his private office, and closes the door behind him. He notices that his secretary has organized in his "in-box," the correspondence which must be answered by the end of today. He reviews from his desk memo the key tasks which must be done. White works in a private office, and there is no one else readily available to discuss these matters with. He is an individual manager who stands alone and will be held accountable for what he does that day. Mr. White and millions of Americans like him face-off each morning against only their desk, their responsibilities, and themselves.

An American manager must push himself, and there is not the stimulus of working with others and enjoying a conversational exchange with co-workers, literally working at arms length from you. Mr. White is already getting sleepy headed, and without getting up and walking down the hall to the company snack bar for a cup of coffee, there simply is not enough action and stimulus in his office environment to pull him out of this numbed state of mind. He is having a hard time getting started this morning, and there is not the team effort which tends to draw out action and productivity from staffers in a Japanese company.

Suzuki-san does not work particularly hard, nor does he even turn out as much paperwork as Mr. White does each day. But when it comes to managing a modern, complex manufacturing or other corporate organization, teamwork is the key; while having each manager of any consequence working in his own office, with small isolated pockets of clerical and support staff, cuts down on communications and rapport throughout the company and unnecessarily constructs barriers of disruptive status differentials.

Being made to wait outside the boss's door hurts the ego and stifles communications

When Mr. White wants to have a conference with his boss, he has to first pass through his supervisor's secretary. Even then he is often forced to wait standing by the door, or in front of the boss's desk until the boss looks up from his work. This situation is not particularly good for White's ego, and he subconsciously avoids these situations. It is not, therefore, surprising that there is a comparative lack of esprit de corps, worker commitment, and morale in American and other non-Japanese companies.

Unlike Japanese white collar and young managers, there is no overtime paid in America— this is one reason the Japanese seem to 'work hard'

The Japanese do not work hard, but their great strength is that they work together. It should also be noted that until Suzuki-san was promoted to the *kanri-shoku* rank, or *kacho*—manager level two years ago, he was paid overtime. Even when Mr. White was only 22, having just left college, he was never qualified to receive overtime. In an American company, white-collar university graduates, who are usually considered to be on the managerial course are on a fixed salary from the beginning. It is only blue-collar, production line workers who are paid an overtime allowance.

Certainly young American managers might work longer hours if they were paid for it. And if they handed over their pay checks to their wives the way Japanese workers do, and if the pay envelope were thicker because of working overtime, I am sure that many American housewives would also be happy to have their husbands work late.

The line between work and play is hazy, with the workplace, not family, the center of many Japanese managers' lives

Actually, in recent years since the 1974 oil crisis, in Suzuki-san's company there have been one or two days a week when overtime is not paid on a company-wide basis. This is a measure aimed at cutting costs. Suzuki-san has noticed that on those days, no one lingers around the office and works late. However, many of the men sit around talking and laughing in idle discussion until 7:00 p.m. or 7:30 p.m. This prevents them from spending too much money at the bars to which they are next headed. The line between work and play is a hazy one in Suzuki-san's company.

It is rather the workplace that is the center of a manager's life. Even though since last year Saturday became a holiday, many men come into the office, for Japanese houses are small and often there is no comfortable and quiet place to read at home. Since Suzuki-san became a *kacho* at age 41, he also can receive no overtime, and he found himself leaving the office just at quitting time. His excuse to himself was that since his subordinate team members cannot leave before the captain, as team leader, he had a responsibility to leave the work area promptly, thereby releasing the younger men. He did not go directly home, however.

Unlike a company in the United States, it seems that the more important an executive becomes in a Japanese organization, the less work he does. American top management works very hard and is even involved in implementation of detailed operations.

Mr. White suffers from the disincentive effect of bringing in management talent from the outside—he was left behind

This also explains why Mr. White is not happy with his job. In fact, just this morning, as he was sipping his second cup of coffee between deep sighs, his wife asked if something was troubling him, and then pointed out that "Friday is only five days away."

Mr. White answered that "five days with this new boss is more than I can take. He's looking over my shoulder every time I turn around, and just waiting to pin something on me."

Mr. White has worked for three companies, and he has been with this last one for 13 years since he was 29. He has worked in the personnel area throughout his career. Having learned all the ropes, he needs a fresh challenge badly. Deadening routine has sapped away his motivation, career goals, and self-esteem. He senses that his job is getting him nowhere. To make matters worse, he was expecting to get the position of general manager which was "just filled by a new man from the outside who has some fresh ideas and approaches in the human resource area." That is how it was explained to Mr. White by the Vice-President of Industrial Relations after the last divisional meeting.

Long years of functional specialization can lead to on-the-job burn-out

More cross-functional job rotation in Mr. White's company would make management in general more versatile, competent, and adaptable to technological and organizational change. Mr. White, like Suzuki-san, could experience the satisfactions of self-development and could obtain a better view of his individual role within the total organization. Since American companies tend to pay for experience and specialization, it is difficult for the average manager like Mr. White to break out of this career rut. White had not thought things out this far, but as he switched on the intercom to call his secretary in for some dictation, he found himself wishing that he had a fancy M.B.A. degree from a prestigious school like the younger man who just became his boss.

Rewarding the promising M.B.A. holder may motivate that individual, but American management should give more thought to the demotivating, morale problem that affects the majority who are left behind, Suzuki-san and Japanese management are well aware of this. That is why they are masters at keeping all employees scurrying and competing as long as possible.

Mr. White had been a dedicated and loyal employee in his company for the last 13 years. He was a co-captain of his football team in high school and went on to Colgate College in upstate New York. Always popular with the girls, he met a cheerleader in his second and last year of football at Colgate. They got married in June after graduation and he went off to work in a leading oil company.

"I probably should have stayed with them. This might never have happened to me." He blocked these remorseful thoughts out of his mind, as his secretary pulled up a chair to take dictation.

Another American manager is victim of an executive suite shake-up

There can be too many management shake-ups in an American company. A new president stepped into office at Mr. White's company in October. Mr. White heard something about him having been recruited by an executive search firm. The new president did not know and felt he could not trust some of the key executives under him. He began to bring in some of his friends. One of his first moves was to replace the old Vice-President of Industrial Relations with a guy who he knew was a tough negotiator and would take a tougher stand against the union. And then last month the new V.P. recruited the general manager who stands directly over Mr. White.

As long as White can remember his company has been unionized. The three year collective bargaining contract is up for negotiation this week. For the last nine years, White has been involved in these negotiations and has established a relationship of trust with the union. White has been the guy that the union negotiators turn to behind the scenes. They believe what he says, and since he is a fair negotiator, he has been able to even win some concessions from the union which were exceptions to the industry-wide contracts negotiated with some of the other companies in the industry.

In Japan, blue-collar, and all white-collar managers up to *kanrishoku* level (about age 40) are in the same union together

Unlike Suzuki-san's negotiations, when Mr. White entered the negotiating room, the union and company representatives did not bow to each other, but that represents form more than substance, anyway. In a Japanese union all employees, both white and blue-collar, are in the union until about age 40. Suzuki-san only left the union two years before. Since dues are directly paid to the enterprise union, with only a minor contribution made to an upper body industry-wide union, the power and influence of the outside trade union are very limited. An absence of union imposed seniority and cross-company union hiring hall means that a Japanese worker's allegiance and loyalty is to his company rather than to the union. If he loses his job, he also loses his union affiliation. Since all workers are in the union together, there is a lack of class consciousness, and stronger bonds of trust exist between managers and workers.

Since school graduation, Mr. White, and the other white-collar staff and college-graduate managers, had never been in a union. Unlike Suzuki-san, Mr. White has to negotiate with trade union representatives who are not members of his company. In Japanese companies many top executives have held elected offices in the enterprise union and are aware of the union problems and the need to appeal and convince membership. Likewise, collective bargaining is limited to employees who are knowledgeable and sensitive to the corporate profit picture and the need for management to retain and reinvest profit.

American management should manage better and stop placing the blame on unions

Such a situation could be nothing more than a dream to Mr. White, but in spite of these differences from Japan in industrial and labor relations institutions and climate, he felt he had helped to establish a good record of industrial peace with the union. The company had been committed to sustaining employment, and few strike days had been lost.

"It looks like all that is going to change," thought Mr. White as he exhaled deeply and sadly with a visible expression of concern on his face. His secretary, who was flipping over to a clean page getting ready to begin the next letter, seemed to notice. Her boss asked her what she thought of the shake-up in personnel. Mr. White got along with his secretary better than anyone else in the company.

After a moments hesitation she confided, "the new general manager's secretary told me in the lunch room that he thinks you've been too soft on the union. He says that with union organization rates going down to 20%, the company's plants should be union free."

Mr. White could not help but chuckle aloud for he knew how difficult it would be to win a union decertification election at his company. He went out for an early and long lunch, aware that his job would get tougher and that it was not getting him anywhere.

III

Twenty Questions and Answers on Recruiting, Selecting, Attracting, Rewarding, Managing, Motivating, Controlling Costs of, Disciplining, and Rehabilitating/ "Firing" the Japanese

In this part we cover a whole variety of topics, including employment contracts, the effective use of probation, executive search methods, transfer, the use of temporary workers, the lure of putting an executive on the board of directors as a recruiting tool, compensation structure and the controlling of long-term costs, advice on ways to save money, and coaching on the type of compensation package which should be offered depending on rank and status within the organization.

Then from the tenth section we move to a discussion of corporate rationalization, or how to go about cutting back pay and benefits, talk about payment for performance, and innovative approaches toward commission sales and how these tools can be used to turn a company around.

There is then a chapter encouraging you to give your headhunter the support he needs to do a better search, as well as another on firing and reducing staff as a last resort both in terms of "voluntary" programs and selective action, followed by a discussion of ways to investigate, check references and spot dishonesty and incompetence. We then examine other potential trouble spots or pitfalls to watch out for when hiring, methods and cases studies in persuading reluctant Japanese to join your firm, the situation regarding loan or secondment of personnel, and how to avoid getting stuck with a bad employee loan.

In the last two sections I attempt to give some additional insight into what you should be looking for in the Japanese executives you interview and, finally, present a discussion of some of the advantages of using a good headhunter as well as provide certain guidelines or standards of professional behavior and practice which you should expect from your executive recruiting firm.

Finding the right Japanese to work in your firm and then managing them effectively with suitable compensation and personnel policies is probably the most challenging and unfamiliar task facing the expatriate manager doing business in Japan. Mistakes have been made. I trust this material will provide you with insight, useful information, guidance, and strategic tools to help you successfully recruit, compensate, motivate, manage, and, when necessary, control and discipline the Japanese in your firm.

The strategic employment contract

Can you tell us something about the situation regarding employment contracts. Should they be drawn up? What are the advantages and disadvantages?

Surprisingly in Japan it is the employee without a contract who has job security and is in that sense covered by the so-called "lifetime employment" system. In the United States, for example, such an employee is considered to be an "at-will employee", which means that at his "will" he may resign, or at the "will" of the employer, the employee may be dismissed expeditiously. Given the situation in Japan, if you are not in a position to offer a certain category of employees job security or have serious doubts about a given individual, the employee should be placed on a fixed-term contract stipulating the date of contract termination.

The longest valid legal contract in Japan is one year, and at time of hiring it is legally impossible to have an employee agree to a longer contract period. Any contracts over one year in length are automatically viewed to be one year contracts with the period exceeding one year ruled null and void. It is also illegal for an employer to require an employee to waive termination rights when hired. This is judged to be a violation of Article 5 of the Labor Standards Law and is prohibited by Article 18 of the Constitution, which does not allow involuntary servitude.

When it comes to the breaking of contracts, Article 627 of the Civil Code requires that the employer give two weeks notice. Article 20 of the Labor Standards Law supersedes this requiring 30 days' notice or 30 days' pay, or any combination of the two. Oral notice of termination is sufficient, but a written document hand delivered or by registered mail is recommended.

The role of the employment contract is limited in Japan, for in any company with over ten employees Article 89 of the Labor Standards Law requires the establishment of Rules of Employment and submission to the Labor Standards Office. These work rules have legal precedence over any contract between an individual, and any conditions in that contract are automatically null and void if the Rules of Employment provide for a superior benefit.

In answer to the question "Should they (contracts) be drawn up?", I would answer that when hiring temporary, part-time or *shokutaku* contract employees, it is absolutely essential to write up a contract and a good idea to let an employee have a few days off between contracts when renewing the temporary contract. This respite will tend to remind the employee that his status within the organization is different from that of a regular employee and protects management from claims made otherwise.

In the recruiting side of our business when placing employees we have often had the new hire request that a formal contract be written up. These employees are often not aware that the designation of a term in this contract can legally relegate their status to that of a temporary employee. Frankly, there is no harm for management to go along with this request, for if, in fact, the employee should not work out as expected, the presence of the term contract will obviously be most advantageous to the employer when it comes to dismissal.

The employer will also benefit from having a signed letter of agreement or contract which defines the period of probation and causes employees to acknowledge the future right of management to transfer an employee both in terms of job junction and place of work. Likewise, in any contract, management would not be wise to stipulate the specific job function of an employee because when it comes to transferring later on, the employee could argue that he was hired to do a given job and that any other work assigned represents a breach of contract.

Along with assuring that they are on term contract, you should also have separate Rules of Employment to cover temporary, part-time or *shokutaku* employees. This issue as well as probation and transfer will be described in greater detail in the following installments.

Making the most of probation

What does law and practice say about probation? How should probation be used?

The concept and full implementation of probation is extremely important in Japan where it can be difficult to dismiss a regular employee who was not placed on a term contract at the time of employment. The reality is that many employees are fired everyday in Japan. This is particularly true of certain segments of the labor market, such as female employees in companies of all sizes, employees in small firms, and older male employees even in the very largest, most stable Japanese companies. Among those categories of workers, there is generally more of an expectation that dismissal might take place and that it is the legitimate right of the employer. However, when employees do not have this expectation, it is more likely that they may run off to a Labor Relations Committee or court. If there is such litigation or action taken against the employer, management will not fare well; therefore, it is necessary to maximize the employer's ability to separate the cream from the milk during the probationary period.

Most Rules of Employment will stipulate some sort of a probationary clause. The problem arises when it comes to implementation—management forgets to use this tool effectively. At time of hire the employee should be reminded that the company is serious about its probationary stipulation. This should be detailed in the letter of agreement, contract or confirmation of working conditions, etc. at time of hire.

If it becomes clear that an employee is not going to make the grade successfully, the employer should begin to mention this so that the employee will not be surprised later on and will know where he stands. The employer should give detailed and specific reasons for his dissatisfaction whenever possible. Under these conditions the employee will often decide to leave even before the probationary period has ended. This is to his advantage as well, because there is a consensus in Japan that jobs held for less than three months need not be referred to on one's personal history. Of course the employer can end the employment relationship at any time during probation.

Even when it is difficult to point to specific job-related reasons why an employee does not qualify during probation, in the past employers have been able to argue that the employee was dropped due to the reason of *"shafu ni awanai,"* or "does not fit in with our company atmosphere, culture, or shared values." But in order to cover yourself on this point, it is helpful to have a *maegaki,* or preface, in your Rules of Employment which defines and describes the *shafu,* or corporate philosophy and culture. While judges will reason that specific qualifying skills should have been adequately tested before hire, there's not much they can say on this more intangible and company-specific requirement. If the probationary process is carefully implemented such that the employee expects he may not be accepted for regular employment, chances are there will never be litigation against an employer accusing abuse of his right of dismissal during the probationary period.

It should be noted, however, that the courts have held that the employer has only slightly more freedom of dismissal during probation. Article 21 of the Labor Standards Law also provides that even during the probationary period if the employee has worked more than 14 days', 30 days' notice or 30 days' pay must be provided at the time of dismissal. Be sure that the work rules specifically provide for freedom of dismissal during probation.

When recruiting both executives and lower-ranking managers, we have sometimes come across a situation in which a candidate is hesitant to take a job with an employer who clearly states that employment will be contingent upon successful completion of the probationary period. When our clients inform us of this, we encourage them not to hire an individual who lacks the confidence to get through probation.

You can add meaning to probation and remind all staff that it is taken seriously by sending out a letter of congratulations at the point the employee is officially hired—*honsaiyo*. Note that it is not necessary to include the probationary period in the calculation for years of service. Most companies do include it, however. In the implementation of probation, it is also a good practice to have a slight pay increase perhaps from ¥490,000 to ¥500,000, etc. upon successful completion. This will remind your administrative staff to recognize the end of probation formally, and it will help to make the employee feel pride in making the grade as a valuable member of a carefully screened management team.

Should you hire an employee from April 1 directly out of the university, it will not be as easy to dismiss him or her during probation if that employee takes action against you. In the case of these "new school graduates," the courts have ruled that since the employing company robbed those individuals of their only chance to get a good job with superior pay and benefits and "lifetime employment" in a large firm, the employer had a responsibility to test and screen carefully the employee before bringing him or her in on a probationary basis. This is not as true of mid-career hires, however, as they have already made a decision to leave at least one firm and are considered to be more mature and expected to look out for their own interests as seasoned individuals in the labor market.

It is also easier to dismiss an individual during probation if he is hired to do a specified task, claims to possess the necessary skill, but is found to lack the skills or qualifications required to do that job.

It is legally acceptable to renew probation; and if your probationary period is as little as three months, it would be important to stipulate in the Rules of Employment that it can be renewed for another three months. When dismissing after probation, things can get sticky and most unpleasant in Japan should an employee fight your action. With the proper language in your Rules of Employment, meticulous record keeping, patience, and a dash of cunning, it can be done. But as much as possible make life easier by doing this during the probationary period. Thoughtful and through implementation is of key importance.

How to set-up the most effective business relationship with your headhunter

How do headhunters operate in Japan? How can the client pay only for results, yet assure that the headhunter handles his assignment on a priority basis?

People wonder how we work and why we can be successful. It's true that often we receive an assignment after our client who is knowledgeable of products, companies and people in his field has already used the newspapers and looked directly, with his own company's personnel department giving up on the search. Indeed it takes courage to accept the more difficult assignments focusing in on a senior engineer who has devoted his life to designing molding dyes or heat-resistant graphite rings or a senior technician who in the last few years has become a master of the *kanji* word processor.

We were once asked to find a man in his 20s who was an electrical or mechanical engineer, had printed circuit board manufacturing experience and spoke fluent Japanese, Chinese and English. Guess what? We found him in about three weeks, but it's not always that easy. To fulfill such assignments you've got to be willing to roll up your sleeves, dig in and use methods that a client cannot risk using—including the unabashed use of cold calls, scouting out of trade shows, using inside information sources, working closely with informers and source people and even hunting down people inside company cafeterias and coffee shops, lobbies, and factory gates. We've developed a few more inventive approaches to target in on just the right man, but such proprietary information will not be disclosed in print.

These more interesting methods that a headhunter employs can at times make the difference, but there is also no substitute for complete research of the market and accurate targeting of competitive corporations, along with a knowledge of their organizational structures, and in which *bu* and *ka* the suitable candidate will be situated. A shelf full of various directories can also be of great value, and, with the right approach, it's surprising how helpful a cold call source can be.

Not only is the client unable to employ all these methods, but the search incentive among the employees of any given company is naturally less than it is for an executive recruiter taking generally 35% or more of the candidate's first year's salary. A few recruiting firms of international reputation benefit from searches that are initiated from the home office where these executive search firms are well known. A few of these firms will take the assignment on an up-front contract basis with for example the first 25% of annual income paid within the first month or two and the final 10% (of the 35% of annual income) payable upon successful employment, adjusting for the final salary actually decided upon. Some of these firms charge more than 35%, and a number of them will, in fact, be willing to search on a contingency basis when the client refuses to sign a contract up-front and if the search firm happens to come across a candidate who fits the initial position description presented by the client.

There are a number of different opinions regarding whether or not the search should be done on an up-front contract basis or contingency basis, or perhaps something in between. Obviously it is impossible for any executive recruiting firm to complete all assignments successfully. Sometimes we face a situation where we have a bad client. He can be overly fussy, miss appointments, insult the candidates, offend their pride, act superior, and sometimes appear incompetent, and unattractive to our candidates. Often the candidates know much more about the client's business and growth potential than the client does and there is no way they would enter that market competing against the superior Japanese product or throw themselves in with an obsolete piece of equipment that is doomed to the scrap heap.

I suppose one could say that it is to the client's advantage to have the impossible assignment handled on a contingency basis rather than wasting the first 20% or more of annual income in contracts that tie up up-front money. I'm sure you also know of cases where a candidate could and should have been found, but the client was stuck with up-front charges and perhaps was not even introduced to a candidate anywhere in the ball park.

On the other hand, executive recruiters contracting in advance for up-front money can convincingly argue that the contract forces them to take full responsibility for the search and that if they don't fulfill the search, it is unlikely that they will be asked to perform once again—at least on a contracted up-front basis. Both points are undoubtedly true, and a combination of a total lack of commitment fee from the client, along with the knowledge that the client has asked every headhunter in town to fill his assignment, definitely discourages us from hustling and carrying out an aggressive, well-targeted and effective search. We work much harder when we know a client is giving us an assignment on an exclusive basis and when we know that to this extent he is entrusting the bottom line and his own career to us, fully depending on us. We will work hard for such a client.

We have found that the client/search consultant relationship works best on a semi-contingency basis. We feel that a system which allows for the client to pay only for results yet assures that his search team handles the assignment on a priority basis applying sufficient energy and time toward successful fulfillment is a system in which the candidate is billed an up-front commitment fee, and a fixed fee for each qualified candidate actually interviewed. The judgment of whether or not to interview the candidate is based upon a review of the resume (when possible) or upon a detailed description from the search consultant who has interviewed the candidate in depth. The up-front fee and candidate interview charges will be deducted from the final billing of 35% of annual income.

A good healthy relationship of trust and full cooperation between the client and a headhunter seems to require a mutually acceptable and comfortable balance between payment for results only and encouragement by way of reasonable injections of cash flow to keep the headhunter's spirits up, keep him looking and at least minimally rewarded for his efforts, until a candidate is hired.

The ins and outs of transferring employees

Sometimes there may be options to both hiring new people or dismissing non-performers. What does law and practice have to say about, for example, the employer's right to transfer?

The role of the manager is precisely that—to manage people, directing and guiding them down the path toward business success. Laying-off employees is the easy way out, yet it is an accepted option too easily taken by corporate policy makers in other countries. Lay-off is an admission of failure and so is the firing of an individual when he should be placed into a job he can do effectively or retrained and developed so that he can be a productive and contributing member of the company team.

Management indeed means getting things done through people, and it often should mean getting the job to fit the person rather than the person to fit the job. I would like to talk about transfer of both place of work and job function as an option to hiring and firing.

When a client calls us up and tells us that they want us to carry out a search for them, the first question we ask is "Are you sure the search is really necessary? Don't you have a person already inside the company who can perform that function or would some corporate reorganization allow you to handle the operation in-house?" Sometimes it isn't possible; but more often it's too much trouble, too risky, and the instructions, mandate and budget already came from the head office to look for someone new. Thus we begin our search, but, nevertheless, recommend that the client consider transferring another employee to the slotted position. It is our feeling that before writing off another human being and dismissing him from his job responsibilities, a good manager should also try and save the man through a personnel reshuffle or transfer. This brings us to the question of "What does the law and practice have to say about the employer's right to transfer?"

There's one thing for sure—the employer's right to transfer must be specifically designated in the Rules of Employment. I had a client who staged an effective lock-out for a week (saving one week's payroll costs but losing about half a week's business) because some three years earlier he'd made the mistake of giving up a transfer clause at a bargaining session with the union. Now he was ready to fight and sacrifice to get it back.

Up until 15 or 20 years ago there were virtually no challenges by employees in the courts of the employer's right to transfer. Indeed, the right of transfer is basically viewed as part of the employer's right to give orders. Under the notion of "subordinate labor", the employee's obligation to work is interpreted to mean that he also has an obligation to work in the place or job designated by the employer. With the rise of individualism, however, and an increase in the number of post-war employees who also place value on their private lives and interests, in recent years there has been a number of court cases challenging the right to transfer.

A judge will examine the inevitability or necessity of the transfer. The court will also evaluate the resulting hardship upon the employee and his family, and determine the availability of a qualified substitute who would be exposed to less hardship. Is the hardship on a particular employee too extreme given the degree of necessity to corporate operations? The court may rule that the transfer is an abuse of the employer's right to give orders. The total lack of a qualified substitute, however, will be a factor to management's advantage when arguing that it is impelling that the individual in question be transferred. Obviously, there has been more litigation over change of place of work rather than complaints regarding change of work assignment at the same location.

The job and status at time of hire also influence whether or not the employer's right of transfer will be respected. Generally practice and legal custom dictate that an employee hired through the head office will be expected to work in any branch or operation throughout the country. To the contrary, when an employee is hired regionally to work in a given factory, management will have difficulties in forcing him to work at another plant or at the head office for that matter if he bucks the transfer.

Therefore, I have been advising my clients to hire all new recruits at the head office even if this requires the expense of flying, busing or sending the employee by train from remote areas of the country and putting him up in a Tokyo hotel. Likewise, if an employee is hired to do a specific and limited job, such as driver, keypuncher, computer programmer, etc., it becomes difficult to force an employee suddenly to change his job assignment against his will.

In view of this, I strongly recommend that when writing up the contract, letter of agreement,or letter of confirmation pertaining to the employee's overall working conditions (salary, working hours, place of work, pay day, recess, and work to be engaged in, etc. as stipulated by Article 15 of the Labor Standards Law), the employer specifically state that place of work will be subject to change and that the employee will accept transfer of work location and job function and assignment. The employee should be required to sign this document.

The right of transfer actually represents more than a convenience (and necessity) to management. Particularly in Japan such intra-firm mobility makes up for the lack of inter-firm mobility or job change (especially among large employers with over 1,000 employees). Furthermore, cross training and the mastering of a number of diversified skills allows for greater flexibility in manpower planning and ready adaptability to changes in the production process and new technologies. It should help each man to learn how the company can successfully function; it helps management to find the right job for the man and helps interweave a close knit of healthy personal relationships between staff.

Should the employer go ahead and enforce the transfer, measures can be taken to minimize the possibility that an employee will buck transfer and take action against management. First of all, be sure and check into the hardship factor. If it is too great, chances are you will not fare well in court, so it is best to withdraw your hand and allow the employee to stay where he is. Make sure he knows, however, that his career growth within the company will be jeopardized unless he is willing to accept the inconvenience of transfer like other employees. By giving long advance notice, paying the rent at the new location for a certain period of time, providing various "perks," helping find a tenant to pay rent on the employee's current home, assisting with moving expenses, and a subsidy for commutation on weekends, etc., chances are it will be much easier to transfer your staff.

It is also a good idea to take into consideration school schedules so that students in the very competitive Japanese school systems will not need to leave their school in the middle of the year, yet will be assured of a place in an equally good school elsewhere. The personnel department of your company should also assist with the location of new housing, new schools, and perhaps serve as a guarantor for the enrolling student.

Indeed, transfer should be an option in both hiring new people or dismissing non-performers. Sometimes it is necessary to fire a man before realizing that he never needed to be hired. In the case of one of my clients, we cleverly had to cause an executive to voluntarily resign under the duress of facing a demotion, sizable pay cut, and the possibility of a disciplinary discharge for failure to follow specific instructions and for a serious breach of trust and loyalty. If the man resigned without a fight within ten days, his face would be saved before society and his lump-sum retirement benefit would not have been reduced by the sizable basic salary cut. (Basic salary times the payment coefficient of the lump-sum retirement benefit scale generally determines the size of the retirement benefit.)

We pulled this off successfully, and the employer was about to have us embark on a search for a replacement. As I had had a key role in "dismissing without firing" the individual, I felt a bit like the stockbroker who churns accounts. Instead, I suggested that we reorganize and restructure manpower and functions at the firm. I interviewed each key employee in Japanese, determining in detail the nature of their jobs, what they'd like to do, and what they felt they were capable of doing.

For a fee, which ended up to be only about 1/3 of what our executive recruiting fee would have been, we determined that the "indispensable" man who had "resigned" was not only disloyal and, at times disobedient, but also superfluous. The office ran more smoothly with more effective operating units without this man who alone had accounted for about 15% of the payroll. Think twice before you hire and think transfer.

Using temporary workers so they don't become permanent

Japanese companies hire many temporary staff or non-regular employees. Will this be a useful approach for foreign companies? What are the advantages, differences in legal status, and benefits, etc. that may be possible?

If you are not using part-time, temporary or employees on either weekly, monthly, yearly (or any other period of time less than one year) contracts, take a few minutes to consider how they could effectively work into your organization and save you money. The presence of a buffer zone of temporary employees, who can be readily dismissed without paying costly benefits, has been a key reason why Japan has been able to sustain the peculiar aspects of Japanese labor relations or people management, including so-called "lifetime employment," seniority wages, and the enterprise-based labor union.

According to a study done in 1978 by Hitachi Sogo Keikaku Kenkyujo (Hitachi Research Institute), in the late 1970s as many as 47% of the blue-collar workforce were employees of temporary status. When it came to white-collar ranks, some 18% of those employed were temporary workers on term contracts. These percentages were probably even greater during the prosperous 1960s because the role of the temporary contract employee has always increased when the economy is good; but when sales and production fall off they are the first to go, generally with no retirement benefit cost to management.

For marginal positions and routine jobs or low-skilled manual work where a complete knowledge of the firm and the company way of doing things is not required, temporary employment is something which every foreign as well as Japanese employer should consider. It is not enough, however, to tell an employee at the time of hire that he is a temporary employee. Nor is it sufficient merely to have the new hire sign a term contract.

In recent years there have been several court cases in which "temporary" employees litigated against their employers because they had worked in those companies for a number of years, with the same working hours, doing essentially the same job, and with no distinct procedure of contract renewal. These employees argued that they were covered by the Rules of Employment pertaining to regular employees, and they, therefore, expected to be paid the corporate lump-sum retirement benefit upon dismissal or, in more difficult cases, claimed that they were no longer of a status which would enable the employer to dismiss them on the grounds that they were contract workers.

I encourage my clients to protect themselves by establishing a separate set of Rules of Employment covering part-time, temporary, and contract workers. Furthermore, there should be a clear distinction in the Scope of Applicability clause in the work rules clearly stating that temporary employees are subject to a number of duties and obligations as well as rules and regulations pertaining to disciplinary measures but will be covered by separate lower quality benefits designated in the Rules of Employment covering temporary employees. It is also a good idea to give the employee a few days off in between contract renewal.

When a factory is built in a region with a limited supply of good labor or to have a competitive edge in attracting and keeping the best temporary employees regardless of labor market supply conditions, it can be a good idea to come up with a modest package of benefits for temporary and contract employees. For example, a limited summer and winter bonus might be paid, as could a retirement lump-sum of modest dimensions. This will give your firm better chances to retain the temporary and contract employees who are doing good work for you.

Also you should have a performance range on the bonus paid out to temporaries so that you can make distinctions for performance, attitude, cooperation, and effort, etc. within the confines of the smaller bonus for temporary employees.

When you are considering allowing a staff member to stay on beyond your retirement age for a year or two, I would suggest that you pay out the lump-sum retirement benefit at the normal time of retirement and put that individual on a six-month or one-year renewable temporary contract. Thus, you'll be able to keep the employee as long as he is productive and effective yet have no continuing accumulating retirement benefit liability.

One of my clients had a problem with a labor union which would not permit management to hire temporary or part-time employees. Such demands on the part of a trade union should be given no quarter and rejected. It's interesting that such a demand was made because normally Japanese enterprise unions do not have this reaction against temporary employment.

Rather, they see the presence of temporary, part-time and contract employees with their lower wages, lack of benefits, and job security as an important factor, which allows the regular employees in the enterprise union to maintain their privileged position of superior benefits and lifetime employment. For the same reasons, there is no attempt on the part of a Japanese enterprise union to organize temporary or contract employees, nor to raise their wage levels. Their feeling generally seems to be that less for them means more for us.

During a consultation meeting with another client I learned that they were hiring a number of temporary employees dispatched from a temporary staff agency. The local foreign representative of the company told me that they were concerned that the dispatched temporary employees would join the company's labor union. As a countermeasure, he would only allow a given temporary employee to work at his organization for six months and then would request that the temporary agency send him a different contract worker. He explained that such action was unfortunate because the company would often have to send back an extremely good employee who had become familiar with the organization and work procedures, etc. "A lot of time is wasted in training and orienting the new people coming in from the temporary agencies," he complained.

I was surprised about his concerns and told him that he had nothing to worry about and should be able to keep the temporary agency employees for as long as he wants. First of all, the dispatched employee is on the payroll of another company, and if this has not been clarified in writing with the temporary help agency, it certainly should be. This means that at any point without even a day's notice the employer should be able to send a dispatched worker back to his agency.

Thus, if there's any talk or action toward joining the receiving company's union, that temporary employee is out and the company need only ask for a substitute from the temporary agency. I told the client that his contract with the temporary agency should state that the temporary worker is on the payroll of the temporary employment agency and also need only stipulate the receiving company's intention to hire the temporary employee for a period of six months, nine months, or as long as a year. But there is no way that a temporarily dispatched employee can argue that on legal grounds or by way of local custom he is entitled to become either an employee or a union member of a receiving company's firm.

Actually from the point of view of the temporary help agency, the last thing it wants is the client absorbing their employees. Remuneration for the temporary employee is also exclusively decided upon in the contract between the client and the agency. Furthermore, it makes little sense for the temporary employee to argue that he is a member of the company's labor union in that the enterprise union form generally means a union shop situation in which employee status is a condition for union membership. There may be exceptions to this when a staff is affiliated directly with the upper body trade union organization, but any dispatched temporary employee creating such problems for the receiving company should be instantly sent packing back to his agency. That's one of the purposes and advantages of using such dispatched temporary staff.

In the case of your own directly hired temporary staff, if they are incompetent or creating such troubles for you, you will be able to dismiss them when their term contract expires. (Actually, the contract will be finished automatically when the period expires, but if the contract was already renewed once or more, it's a good idea to give warning.) During the term of the contract, a party can terminate it only for "inevitable reason," which is narrower than "just cause" (required when there is no contract) but broader than "act of God." Remember, however that 30 days' notice or 30 days' pay will be required if the individual has been employed longer than two months.

The *"torishimariyaku* carrot"

Offering a man the title of *torishimariyaku*, or member of board of directors, can be a great incentive for him to join a company. What are some of the issues in terms of job security and differences in benefits for directors, particularly retirement plans?

Unlike most Japanese companies, in the United States where often top, middle and even most of lower management is dominated with Japanese transfers, certainly it is a good idea to make the Japanese working in foreign companies here in Japan feel that they are holding responsible and important jobs and can even have a crack at top positions of authority in their companies.

A couple of years back I knew of a Japanese bank with an agency in a west coast city that had only two Americans out of 17 employees, and one of the two was a naturalized Japanese American. This would not appear to be the way to develop and cultivate good local staff, nor to keep the Equal Employment Opportunity Commission from paying a visit if a complaint is lodged from a disgruntled American employee.

On the other hand, after working closely with over 200 multinational firms here in Japan, I cannot take the position that all the *gaijin* should go home. I've been told, or I have experienced, too many "horror stories." In one case, for example, there were no home office foreigners stationed here in Japan, and the local Japanese president set himself up as one of the distributors for the stateside product. Within two years he made himself the sole distributor, continuing to argue that "This is a very common and usual custom in Japan." That company president's margins were taking larger and larger percentages of total sales dollars, and the office finally began to wonder why it was making no money in Japan. To make matters worse, the president of the American firm used the multinational's local accounting staff to do the books of his sole distributorship before they worked on the multinational's accounting and reporting. Home office filing was often delayed with tax penalties invoiced from the government.

Finally, the head office got wise to what was going on and sent over an international vice president to straighten things out. The Japanese president was given the option to resign voluntarily if he returned ¥100 million—only a portion of what he'd made. The crusty Japanese *shacho* agreed to do so but came back two weeks later with a lawyer. "I've changed my mind on paying back the money, and, furthermore, you owe me ¥50 million in retirement benefit, which is a fair sum considering I worked on the board of directors for over ten years."

The Japanese lawyer representing the home office agreed that under the circumstances this was a fair amount to pay (the only catch was that that lawyer had been brought on board ten years earlier by the same local Japanese president and undoubtedly was going to make at least a half of the ¥50 million tax free!).

At about this point I was called in to shed some light on the mysteries and peculiarities of the Japanese way of doing business. My client was totally bewildered, but I assure you matters were straightened out in short order. The moral of the story is that the vast majority of Japanese are just as honest, dedicated and morally upright as is any equally sized group of Americans, Germans, Turks, Nigerians, or Russians for that matter. But we must not be naive about things, and we must have some checks and balances. You can't leave your business up to someone else to do, but it is tempting with the difficulties of reading Japanese regulations, laws, etc. and understanding business procedures. Many a good red-blooded Yankee trader would also take a Japanese firm located in the United States to the cleaners if he were totally left alone and given the latitude to do so.

Recently it's occurred to me that the ideal solution might be to have a good expatriate, home office financial man or internal auditor backed up by a reasonably strong-willed and tenacious bulldog of a Japanese secretary who speaks a good grade of English and likes to be around foreign things and foreign people. (You know the type.)

We should balance the home office financial man with a foreign "marketing adviser," who is bright, aggressive, persuasive, well connected at the head office but also flexible, sensitive and always willing to listen before he gives his input or begins to guide things in a different direction.

Now we'll focus back on the question of assigning the title of *torishimariyaku* as an incentive and recruiting tool. There is a major difference in the significance of this title between Japan and the West. In the West most members of the board come from outside the company anyway, so the title of *torishimariyaku* doesn't serve as a motivational tool, incentive, or goal for corporate management to work toward. In Japan, on the other hand, there are few outside directors, and a significant proportion of the high caliber management material in any given firm can at least have a realistic hope of getting on the board of directors. Many of them will only achieve the level of *hiratori* employee director, thereby at the same time maintaining a title of *bucho* or general manager as an employee working in a departmental operation. Japanese companies try and hold out the carrot of *torishimariyaku* to as many people as possible; often the *yakuin*, or directors, only keep these positions for two years.

The possibility of becoming a member of the board of directors of a firm and having that title on one's business card is an attraction to any potential candidate and would assist your firm with its recruiting program as well as in maintaining the motivation and morale of your Japanese staff. The nicest part of it is that giving out the title per se really doesn't cost you anything extra.

In Japanese companies the directors are usually subject to a different retirement benefit from other non-director employees. Generally the formula for the lump-sum benefit to members of the board of directors is the last monthly salary times years as director times last director payment status coefficient (which might be 3 for *shacho* and *fukushacho*, 2.5 for *senmu*, 2 for *jomu*, 1.5 for *hiratori*, 1 for full-time auditor and 0.5 for non-regular auditor) times performance evaluation (normally a 40% range as is the case for the performance range on summer and winter bonus for most employees in general).

Of course, the structure or components of the last monthly salary is a factor in determining the quality of the *torishimariyaku* bonus. Keep in mind that in Japan any bonuses paid to directors must come from after-tax profits, so it's generally better to pay directors only their monthly salary. This will comparatively increase the weight of pensionable income of directors because for non-director employees both the weight of the summer and winter bonus as well as additional allowances and perhaps a second salary component are not included in pensionable income.

This difference, of course, should be kept in mind when determining the lump-sum retirement benefit for directors so that their lump-sum retirement benefit is not kept too far out of line from that of non-*torishimariyaku* employees.

If you are surprised to see that in the above formula the number of months of salary for each year of service may be as many as three or more for director presidents and vice presidents, remember that this is in the typical Japanese company where there are many top quality managers qualified to get into these positions. Thus, the average tenure for directors in Japanese companies would probably be much shorter than in a foreign company where an individual might be recruited as director president as young as 50 or even 45 years of age. In the Japanese company, though, there are fewer years of service, so it is economically feasible to pay as many as three months or sometimes more for each year of service as a president or vice president on the board of directors.

Maybe the higher lump-sum retirement benefit paid out to directors can be justified. Being selected or promoted to the board of directors is risky business. Such an individual is no longer an employee and is not in that sense covered by the Labor Standards Law, nor will the courts protect his job security in the same way. At the end of what is generally a two-year term as director, the contract need not be renewed and the *torishimariyaku* can be dismissed more easily than it would be to dismiss a non-director regular employee. I've also worked on cases where we've dismissed a director before his contract expired. Executives in such a position with high pay and presumably able to control the destiny, growth, and profitability of the corporation will not get the same backing and sympathy from the Labor Relations Commission and the courts if they are performing poorly and not getting the job done.

Compensation structure and controlling long-term costs

Can you give us some insight from your labor consulting practice as to how various compensation practices will affect the long-term costs to the company, such as the retirement allowance liability?

Let's assume you're an expatriate executive earning a home country-based salary (independent of expatriate benefits) of $113,333. You've worked in your company 25 years and are about to retire due to having reached the compulsory retirement age. Seems like a fairly realistic and reasonable scenario for a respectable mid-level executive who would be a department head or division general manager (*bucho*) level within the context of the home office hierarchy outside Japan. Is it likely that such a man would be paid $283,333 in a single lump-sum at the time of his retirement in addition to the social security benefit which he is entitled to and will be paid out by the national program? If paid, such a lump-sum retirement benefit would be equivalent to exactly 2.5 X the individual's total annual income. As an American, I will say that I don't believe most American companies are that generous.

What I have just described is the case of what would presumably be a higher level Japanese executive earning ¥17 million and retiring after 25 years of services at a foreign-capitalized firm here in Japan with a "non-Japanized" compensation package. Note, however, that our assumption has included an extremely reasonable payment co-efficient on the lump-sum retirement benefit of 30 months of salary at the 25-years-of-service point. A number of my clients have a much more liberal payment coefficient on the lump-sum retirement benefit, and they would be in even greater trouble having to pay much more than the $283,333 mentioned above (corresponding to ¥42,499,998, assuming a ¥150 per dollar exchange rate). If, for example, the company had a payment coefficient scale providing for 50 months of salary at 25 years of service, we would be talking about a lump-sum retirement benefit of ¥70,833,300, or $472,222.

One of the biggest mistakes made by foreign companies breaking into the Japanese market when they set up their salary regulations and compensation structure is the failure to appreciate that, given that they have adopted the same lump-sum retirement payment coefficient scale as a Japanese competitor, etc., they will forget to make sure that the compensation package is also Japanized or in line with that of the same Japanese competitor or market leader whose benefits they look to as a model. Rather than use the word "Japanization," I would like to make the statement that such a compensation package is used in Japan because it is strategically advantageous to Japanese management. It also makes sense, represents tremendous savings, and is probably the only way a multinational firm here in Japan would be able to survive in the long run and make good on its promise of lump-sum retirement benefit to the Japanese employees.

The lump-sum retirement benefit mentioned above was inordinately high mainly because this company is not paying a bonus, nor are various allowances including a second salary component of non-pensionable income paid out to the Japanese executive making ¥17 million. Among my clients I have found a number of companies in which rank and file or lower management employees are paid a summer and winter bonus amounting to, for example, five months' basic salary, but in those companies an exception is made for high-ranking managers. In some cases the home office got the idea that high-ranking managers should be paid differently. In other cases, the managers themselves must have gotten together and realized that by not taking bonus for themselves they would be able to make a much larger pension, and avoid having any of their pay at risk and subject to performance.

In the case of our ¥17 million earner, by simply dividing out his annual income by 17 (assuming five months' bonus) we can reduce his lump-sum retirement benefit to ¥30 million, or $200,000. However, if for example, we have a properly structured Japanese compensation package, with a ¥20,000 housing allowance, ¥30,000 family allowance, ¥10,000 meal allowance and ¥420,000 second salary component, or job/qualification allowance (which is reasonable and typical at that high-salary level), the lump-sum retirement pension liability after 25 years of service at time of retirement would be ¥19,835,294, or $132,235. This is still a reasonable lump-sum retirement benefit and represents 1.17 X annual income.

According to the most comprehensive and reliable data on lump-sum retirement benefit payments coming from the Central Labor Relations Commission, the average benefit paid out to college graduates with 35 years of service in the cream of the crop firms with over 1,000 employees is about ¥20 million and the figure just above is right on target (with an above average salary compensating for ten years less service).

Note that in the aforementioned example the ¥17 million earner with a proper Japanized compensation package would have a monthly take-home income of ¥1,131,176 which represents a 42% weight of allowances (total monthly allowances being ¥480,000), or a percentage of pensionable monthly income of 58%. The employee in this foreign firm would still be better off than he would be if he were working at, for example, Shin-Nihon Seitetsu, or New Japan Steel, the largest steel maker in the world, or at Hitachi Seisakusho (Hitachi Corp.), the leader of the group where on average the weight of basic monthly salary or pensionable income is only 49.5% at New Japan Steel and 39.9% at the Hitachi maker. This is according to 1981 statistics from the IMFJC entitled "Life of Working Conditions at Labor Unions Affiliated With IMFJC."

Compensation systems that I have developed provide for a second-salary component of non-pensionable income which gradually accelerates as the salary grows. For example in the case of the ¥17 million earner, his monthly second-salary component would be ¥420,000 or 29.2%, whereas at ¥12 million, it would be only ¥220,000, or 21.6% of annual income. This means that a ¥12 million earner on a Western-style compensation package would walk away with ¥30 million in lump-sum retirement benefit, or $200,000; but with a Japanese-style compensation package using the same assumptions of 25 years of service and 30 months' payment coefficient on the lump-sum retirement benefit scale, the same individual would earn ¥15,247,058, which amounts to $101,647 or 1.27 X his annual salary of ¥12 million ($80,000).

Using a proper compensation package for the ¥12 million, we would have monthly take-home pay of ¥788,235 with the weight of monthly allowances being 35.5%, giving a pensionable monthly income factor of 64.5%.

Using all the same assumptions except for a greatly reduced second-salary component of ¥60,000 for a ¥6 million earner, we would have a second-salary component of 11.1%, monthly take-home pay of ¥388,235, which would amount to a 30.9% weight of non-pensionable monthly allowances and pensionable monthly income of 69.1%, or nearly 70%. In this case the individual would retire after 25 years with ¥8,047,059, or $53,647, assuming the same lump-sum retirement benefit payment coefficient of 30 months.

An income of ¥6 million after 25 years of service indicates that we're talking about a high school or perhaps a junior high school graduate. In either case we are still competitive because, according to the same Central Labor Relations Commission data, with 25 years of service the lump-sum retirement paid to high school graduates is ¥8.8 million and that paid to junior high school graduates ¥6.3. (For those who are interested, the figure for college graduates is ¥12.5 million.)

If you, as the expatriate manager in Japan, are not sure of how your firm stacks up in terms of the lump-sum retirement benefit payment coefficient scale and its interrelationship with the structure of your compensation package especially in terms of the weight of pensionable income, I would suggest that you have this area thoroughly reviewed by an expert who can help you analyze the situation and convince the local Japanese staff and the vice president of industrial relations at home if there is the need for restructuring in this critical area, which can either make or break your corporation in the future. With the proper educational campaign and orchestration, Japanese employees will go along with this change, especially when they are convinced that benefits on paper are meaningless if, in fact, the company cannot make good on its obligation.

And until you thoroughly review your system and straighten out any existing problems, I would discourage anyone from funding a lump-sum retirement benefit, which up until now has been only a book reserve. The promise of funding after restructuring compensation and benefits can be used to neutralize the adverse impact inherent in the rationalization process.

Other ways to save money

Other than controlling the weight of pensionable income and the size of the retirement lump-sum through proper compensation restructuring, how else can we save in terms of compensation related practices?

I really get concerned and upset over some of the things I learn when consulting with my clients concerning their compensation practices, benefits and personnel policies. I nearly choked on a cup of coffee when I heard a Japanese personnel manager tell me in the presence of an expatriate superior that the company had been paying full salary for four months of maternity leave and was not even aware that the national insurance programs entitled the company and the pregnant employee to a benefit of 60% of salary during a four-month period of maternity leave (which is basically the period which an employer must let off a female employee according to the Labor Standards Law).

I went on to learn that also at that company and (at a number of other companies) there is not full knowledge of the various coverages and benefits which are available for the asking from the insurance programs that the employer contributes to. Furthermore this company pays 100% of all the insurance contributions, when, in fact, with the exception of workmen's compensation, the employee is expected to make a 50% contribution, and generally does.

I once came across another company that provides its employees with 50 months of guaranteed pay on full salary and an additional 35 months of leave of absence without pay, for long-term non-job related illness, making for a total of 85 months in which the company will make a commitment to an employee by either paying him or leaving his job open for him to return to. Seven years is simply too long to maintain such a commitment to an employee, especially so in a small firm where it would be necessary to replace the man with someone else and presumably impossible to then take the old employee back when the position has already been filled by someone else. What a great company to join for one who is beginning to feel sickly or hoping to become a mother.

At this same company after just ten years of service employees were provided 25 months of full pay with an additional 25 months of leave of absence without pay, making for a 50-month commitment in which action in the area of effective manpower staffing decisions cannot take place or is grossly complicated. Once again, 50 months is over four years, and I would maintain that few foreign capitalized firms here in Japan, due to the scale of operation, etc., can afford to offer such a benefit. (Note that it would also be extremely difficult to find even the largest Japanese employer that would have such a generous but impractical personnel policy.)

Japanese law does not require that an employer make any provisions or have any benefit whatsoever for such cases of non-job-related injury or sickness. One of the most pathetic things about these situations was that at a couple of companies the personnel manager was not even aware that the insurance programs they had been contributing to for years would have helped finance the benefits being provided. We are now trying to assist their companies in getting some of the back insurance payments which they were entitled to. It will not be easy, however, for one common interpretation is that when a company stipulates in its Rules of Employment that, for example, full pay will be available to employees during the four-month maternity period, the company is precluded from applying for the insurance benefit. Therefore, such language should certainly be eliminated from the Rules of Employment.

Certainly a more intelligent, economically rational and fair approach for both the employee and the company would be to provide perhaps only the 40% of pay which the insurance doesn't cover during either maternity leave, or prolonged sickness leave. I don't see how any small employer struggling to make a dent in the Japanese market could consider paying this 40% of salary for more than three months and then allowing the employee an additional three months of leave of absence without pay. After such a six-month period, surely a replacement should be found.

Indeed, very few Japanese companies—even the very largest ones with over 1,000 or even 5,000 employees will pay an employee during the childbirth period. I have also heard from no small number of Japanese personnel managers and labor union activists that even in companies where a generous non-job-related sickness paid and unpaid leave is provided for, there is a tremendous amount of pressure for the employee to resign long before the stated benefit has expired.

I'd like to mention another area where a company can save money. Normally in the retirement regulations of the company there are two separate lump-sum retirement payment coefficient scales—one for voluntary and one for involuntary retirement. Voluntary retirement essentially amounts to the employee voluntarily resigning or leaving the employer, generally to take another job.

Under these circumstances, I would think that the wise management approach would be to penalize severely the employee by having quite a large differential between involuntary retirement (company lay-off, discharge, reaching the retirement age, etc.) and voluntary resignation on the part of the employee.

A look at overall industry practice shows that in general there's about a 20 to 30% gap. However, I would be in favor of a larger gap. This will also help to assure that the employer will lose his employee only when management feels it's better off to do so. But why have a good man voluntarily resign when you might be able to discourage him from doing so by penalizing him in terms of lump-sum benefit.

Other companies make the mistake of paying more than time and a quarter or an overtime percentage factor of more than 25%. It should also be noted that for those companies with a work day shorter than eight working hours, which means nine to six with a one hour lunch, overtime need not be paid until the completion of eight hours of work (not the scheduled work day of eight hours including an hour off for lunch).

Also note that Ordinance Article 22 to Article 32 of the Labor Standards Law stipulates that it is not necessary to pay overtime to salesmen and field staff if it is difficult to calculate their actual working hours. Thus, even if they come back to the office at eight or nine o'clock at night, the employer has no legal obligation to pay them overtime. If, on the other hand, throughout the day the subordinate was accompanied by a supervisor or was given constant detailed assignments, which were easy to keep track of, the situation would be different—when the overtime can be calculated, it must be paid. (Although in realty it is not paid at many firms due to policies and procedure that can be implement at your firm, too.) A holiday change clause, or *kyujitsu-furikae* will also allow a company to have employees work on a holiday without paying them overtime. This was also the only way to get a female to work on a holiday because technically they were prohibited from doing so by the Labor Standards Law. (Until passage of the Equal Opportunity Law from April 1, 1986.) With the *kyujitsu-furikae* clause, you merely switch holidays, and, thus, it is not necessary to pay the overtime allowance on the holiday worked.

A surprising amount of money is probably also wasted on minor points such as absenteeism and tardiness. Japanese law provides for the principle of *genkyu*, or salary cut for disciplinary reasons. Therefore, it is possible, for example, to cut an employee back by ten minutes even though the employee was only four minutes late. At one client company I once ran across an employee with a ¥67,000 commutation fee. He was willing to come in from a very great distance in order to live in a nice country environment—perhaps in the house in which he was born.

Unfortunately, by the time he got to the office, he was dead tired and absolutely worthless; and the company also has a right not to pay this much for a commutation benefit. The maximum tax-deductible amount had been reasonable at ¥26,000 before April 1, 1989 and should have been sufficient to cover most employees. Refusing to pay more than that served to discourage employees from moving too far away. Unfortunately, with a passage of the Consumption Tax from April 1, 1989, this tax deductible limit jumped to ¥50,000. I believe this is too much, and it is creating problems of balance and fairness among employees. Probably paying only up to the old limit, perhaps with an inflationary adjustment built in is the most satisfactory approach. Otherwise, employees who work hard and long hours for you, living in close and paying expensive rent lose out economically to employees who buy land in distant suburbs and benefit from the appreciation.

Great savings can be generated by application of a sensible and practically designed salary table, which will allow for acceleration and promotion at different rates according to ability and performance. Furthermore the summer and winter bonus should not be fixed at a certain number of months but should instead be flexible normally within a 40% range—20% on either side of the company average. This is how most Japanese companies pay. If the firm is "paying six months' bonus," this really means that the worst performer is only making 4.8 months and the top man is making as much as 7.2 months. We'll talk more about performance pay later on in this series. Of course, on an exceptional basis, for poor performers and problem employees it must be possible not to pay any bonus at all, as a strategy to weed them out with job security so well protected here.

At another company a driver was making ¥7.5 million, almost ¥2 million of which came from overtime payments. He was only around 40 years of age with 12 years in the company. The problem was he was taking the expatriate manager out to an office/factory site having to work from 6:00 a.m. until about 8:00 p.m. by the time he got the expatriate back to Roppongi and had the car parked back at the factory site. There was no reason to pay this driver about five hours of overtime per day, however, for most days he had very little to do once out at the office/factory site. He could have been treated as a *danzoku rodosha*, or intermittent laborer, paid only for the hours he actually worked. Thus, he could be considered off during the dead hours each day. If, however, the company wanted to be nice, it could guarantee him eight hours.

Another company was having problems with the expenses involved in keeping on beauty consultants. After a few years the girls were no longer beautiful, but they either wouldn't admit it or wanted to keep working and were looking forward to the lump-sum retirement benefit. In this particular case there was no reason why the company could not have had a separate retirement age for certain special categories of employee. Based on job function these beauty consultants could have been required to leave for example by age 35 or so. Either that or they should have been on temporary employment contracts with separate work rules covering them.

Do you think a review of your compensation and personnel policies would reveal that you are wasting money in these or other ways?

Should the package offered vary depending on rank and status?

To amplify on the preceding questions, what sort of a compensation package should be offered to a new hire? Should the components or allowances and bonus, etc. vary according to rank and status in the organization? What about your opinion of salary administration based on job classification and other Western concepts?

I got a desperate phone call from an expatriate C.E.O. about two weeks ago. It came about two and a half years too late. Within the two weeks before he called me to describe his problems, his company up to the low middle management level had been almost thoroughly organized by a spirited and aggressive trade union backed up by strong feelings on the part of rank and file clerks and office staff that they were suffering at the expense of upper level managers who were feathering their own nests.

If I had been consulted two and a half years ago, I would have never advised this company to go ahead with the idea of taking managers off the summer and winter bonus system, establishing a new system in which their annual income was divided by 12 instead of 17. This move alone naturally had the effect of increasing the lump-sum retirement benefit of the managers by some 40%. At first, this move hadn't been noticed by the employees, but when an employee with a particularly high level of interest in these matters got wind of it, he immediately spread the word around and pointed out to other employees how unfair such a practice was.

Of course, the initial argument made by the now organized employees (and it only took two weeks to organize from the time the initial contact went out to an upper-body trade union) was that all the employees should now benefit from the same change in benefits. However, the employees never seriously expected that the company would go along with that, so their main desire was to have the system changed back to the way it was two and a half years before with the managers also being subject to a five-month summer and winter bonus payment. Because of this change in the compensation package, the amount of the premium paid to the life insurance company (as their lump-sum retirement benefit was being funded) increased from some ¥400,000 per month up to about ¥1.6 million in that these premium payments move in a direct ratio with the assumption on the weight of pensionable income or amount of salary.

This is just one of many reasons why I firmly believe that with the exception of very few specific categories of employees, all employees in a company from the non-director highest level executives to the lowest level rank and file regular employees should be paid basically the same compensation package. In some large Japanese companies with extensive manufacturing facilities there are differences in basic pay salary tables depending upon whether or not an employee is a blue-collar/manual-production worker or a white-collar/office-managerial type employee. (Generally educational level can fairly decisively also be a cut-off here with the tendency for two-year college graduates, four-year college graduates and those with special *senmon* education being on a separate salary scale.)

In the average foreign capitalized employer here in Japan, however, it shouldn't be necessary to have two separate salary scales and salary tables. TMT has designed an innovative approach to compensation, including a salary table which adapts itself extremely well to any small to moderate size organization, Japanese or foreign.

As mentioned in my earlier articles, bonus paid to members of the board of directors in Japan must come from after-tax profits. Therefore, it may make sense to have a different approach toward bonus or performance compensation for members of the board of directors. Furthermore, temporary, part-time and contract employees receive less complete benefits and perhaps should even have slightly different working hours, etc. in order to differentiate them continually from regular employees and prevent them from credibly arguing that they, with the passage of time, enjoy the same status and job security of regular employees. For the rest of the employees in the company, however, I would recommend that any new hire, whether he be a high school or college graduate fresh out of school or a top executive coming out of a major Japanese firm in his 50s, be basically paid the same compensation package. What should this package consist of?

Five to six months' bonus is quite customary in Japanese firms, and, given the same amount of annual income and the same payment coefficient on the lump-sum retirement benefit scale, the payment of bonus in this order will serve to control your firm's pension liability, keeping it in line with local practice.

A family and housing allowance will also serve the purpose of controlling pensionable income and have the added advantage of making your firm seem like a caring or "wet" employer, maximizing the paternalistic psychological appeal of meeting an employee's family needs by providing perhaps a ¥10,000 to ¥20,000 wife allowance when he marries and then smaller, gradually decreasing allowance for additional children born. Likewise, the housing allowance would normally increase from perhaps ¥10,000 or ¥20,000 to ¥20,000 or ¥30,000 when a previously single employee takes on a wife or other family dependents.

Other than this, there would be a meal allowance, and the largest allowance, of all should be a job/qualification allowance, probably more handily labeled as a second-salary component of non-pensionable income. This was discussed in detail in an earlier article and will be covered again at a future date. Note, however, that with the exception of the commutation allowance, tax treatment on these allowances is the same, and if an employer does not want to get involved in these more complicated allowance programs, a solution which at least helps to lesson the retirement benefit burden would be to define simply a percentage of regular monthly cash compensation that is not calculated into the lump-sum payment.

But if these allowances are not now being paid in your company, you should not create them and begin to pay them on top of what are probably already more than adequately high salary levels. Instead, they can be "carved out" from current levels of monthly pay. Orchestration of this process with care toward avoiding complaints of adverse impact will also be discussed in a future article. In general, a meal allowance of ¥10,000 to ¥20,000 would be typical and a second-salary component amounting to 10 to 30% of annual income depending upon salary level seems to be in line with what most Japanese companies are doing. The higher the salary level, the larger becomes the percentage of second-salary component of non-pensionable income.

This is in line with a commonly held Japanese philosophy or way of thinking in personnel circles, which indicates that while a superior performer and productive man of high authority in the organization is working for the company, he should be highly rewarded in terms of his monthly cash compensation (second-salary component or job/qualification pay), but once that man and a much less capable man both reach retirement age, they then become basically equal in that they have severed their relationship with the company and now they are simply individual men standing alone as equals living their own lives. Thus, the tendency is to try and keep their respective lump-sum retirement benefits at least not too far out of line.

Maybe it is this type of thinking that particularly upset the rank-and-file employees who joined the union when suddenly the managers' lump-sum retirement benefits jumped up by some 40% due to compensation package restructuring. The rank-and-file employees couldn't help but believe that such an increase in managers' benefits was at the expense of their own benefit, the long-term health of the company, and perhaps at the sacrifice of their own future job security should the company ever become weighted down with this extra burden of lump-sum retirement benefit.

But actually such inequality in the basis of calculation of the lump-sum retirement benefit runs against both the spirit and the letter of the Tax Qualified Pension Law and Article 159 of Corporation Tax Regulations, which stipulate that there must be no discrimination in favor of officers, supervisors, or the highly compensated in terms of the basis of calculation or quality of the retirement benefit.

At another one of my client companies the expatriate management that I was dealing with was concerned and confused as to why it was so difficult to promote employees up and out of the ranks of union membership to become managers in the company. Even employees who had never taken an interest in the union or union affairs and were extremely dedicated and loyal to the company would not accept a management-level rank if it meant leaving the union. After checking into this and other matters by reviewing the company's total approach to compensation and personnel by going over the Rules of Employment and salary regulations, as well as collective bargaining agreements, I determined that the major reason was that the employees would be much worse off in terms of their accumulated retirement benefit.

For example, if a union member covered by the collective bargaining agreement had 35 years of service, he was to get the inordinately high lump-sum retirement benefit payment coefficient of 70 months' salary. On the other hand, once someone became a manager at 35 years of service the individual would only be entitled to a 31.7 months of salary plus an additional ¥150,000 for each year of service if the individual were a non-manager (but not a member of the labor union) and an additional ¥180,000 for each year of service if the individual was a manager. Under both circumstances, however, the quality of the lump-sum retirement benefit could not possibly compare with the superior conditions of union members.

Obviously once the company allowed itself to be talked into such a ridiculous collective bargaining agreement with the union, this difference in retirement benefit itself was enough explanation for why virtually all rank-and-file employees would immediately join the union and want to stay there. In fact, this was the major explanation and selling point of the union when soliciting new membership.

It is not too late, however, to do something about this situation, and collective bargaining agreements can be changed with 90 days' notice from either party if it is a non-term agreement or if three years has exceeded on a three-year agreement (three years is the longest legal bargaining agreement). This will be discussed in greater detail in later articles.

I've heard the argument that if the structure of compensation is the same for union members and managers, this will create a tendency for the managers to side with the union in that any breakthroughs made by the union in terms of negotiated settlements, etc. will also equally apply to managers. In general, we can say that that is true and that is indeed the way it is in almost all Japanese companies.

On the other hand, however, it is the role of the manager to convince his subordinates (union members), sell the management position and convince the rank-and-file to take the *shunto* Spring Offensive wage settlement or to pull in their belts and accept a rationalization of the wage system so that the weight of pensionable income decreases or the payment coefficient on the lump-sum retirement benefit is adjusted down, etc. Unless these managers are not equally affected by the adverse impact of such measures, they will have no credibility in the eyes of the rank-and-file when it comes to selling, pushing, and implementing these programs.

For the aforementioned reasons I feel that your company will be best off by basically offering the same compensation structure (with the exception of varying weights or percentages of second-salary component) to all employees regardless of rank in the organization. Let me conclude by attempting to answer briefly the second question on "salary administration based on job classification and other Western concepts."

Although some large Japanese companies have very sophisticated allowances or components of pay including those related to working conditions, job pay (but based on appraisal, years of service, and specific ranges of pay), as well as various types of efficiency pay again based on uniform rates and ranges according to position or qualification, these attempts at regimenting pay (and only observable in the largest firms) are not very much related to the work itself but rather to years of service, educational background, contribution, and status within the organization.

Such a system can only work in a regimented way, however, in a large bureaucratic organization, which constantly hires each year a number of employees almost exclusively after school graduation. Since in most of your smaller foreign capitalized firms you need older and experienced people to handle your jobs, and many of your firms have only been established a few years, etc., it is obviously necessary to take in a significant number of mid-career recruits.

You should avoid having different minimum and maximum salary ranges based on job junction because this concept is definitely foreign to the Japanese, and they do not feel comfortable with it. For example, in one client company I discovered that for some reason they placed the greatest importance in terms of remuneration value on financial and accounting jobs. The wisdom of this might also be questioned in that production and marketing are really the entrepreneurial functions which will cause the company to grow and thrive if the right men can be put into the job.

At another foreign company they patterned themselves largely after a huge Japanese trading company in which they thought they could have a satisfactory system where grades would have age ranges so that, for example, between 34 and 37 the minimum monthly salary would be ¥431,000 and the maximum would be ¥469,000. This is fine except they lost an excellent 37-year-old candidate we introduced to them who insisted that, based on his previous remuneration, it was only fair that he be paid at least ¥475,000 per month. On the other hand, their salary grade for executive secretaries (not taken from the trading company) dictated that a 26-year-old must be paid ¥220,000 or more (with five months' bonus). Therefore, their system caused them to pay her ¥3.74 million when she would have been perfectly happy to join the company at ¥3.2 million. There are better alternatives to such job classification and salary grade approaches. I will discuss these in greater detail in later articles.

Corporate rationalization—cutting back pay and benefits

Starting out new hires based on a Japanized or revised compensation package with altered working conditions is one thing, but how can changes be made affecting employees already on the payroll?

If there is something that should be changed in your compensation practices, benefits, Rules of Employment, or other personnel policies to bring you more in line with local practice or to ensure the company's long-term health (thus assuring job security), with the proper approach, orchestration, education and implementation there is virtually no change that can't be made successfully. This is a strong statement, but I stand by it. Even when a company is not losing money, such rationalization measures can be successfully implemented merely based on the argument that the company is out of line with general industry practice or that management has become aware of its long-term responsibilities to assure the survival of the enterprise and the continued guarantee of a job to its employees.

In one stroke we have successfully "carved out" five months of bonus without increasing payroll costs in a company where previously annual income was divided by the 12 monthly salary paychecks. In a number of companies we have thus reduced actual take-home pay, and in all cases we have done this without litigation against us because of the way in which it was done. We've increased seven hour work days to seven hours and 45 minutes, created a new practice in which technical service people and field staff would work on Saturdays without receiving overtime payment, changed regulations such that overtime payment was paid from six o'clock instead of five o'clock maintaining the same work start hours, reduced the weight of pensionable income anywhere from 20 to 55% depending upon what the company started with, cut back the payment coefficient on the lump-sum retirement benefit scale, introduced *kyujitsu-furikae* (or holiday change clauses) so that overtime no longer was paid for holiday work, added detailed disciplinary and job/position adjustment measures which would allow an employer to take legally authorized action against lazy employees with bad attitude and lacking ability in order to protect the great majority of remaining employees who work hard for the company, stopped paying maternity leave and menstruation leave benefits, cut back the days of paid annual leave when out of line with local practice, reduced the number of months allowed for paid leave of absence for non-job-related sickness to 1/3 of the previous benefit, created a bonus performance appraisal system with varying pay-outs where all employees had always been guaranteed a fixed number of months of summer and winter bonus, cut back strange and unusual leaves such as a day off after a business trip of one week or more, etc.

The list is not endless but could be much longer. Let me balance this by saying that we've also done our share of increasing benefits that were below competitive levels at a number of companies. Still, I will admit that a number of years in the labor consulting business has shown us that there are sufficient internal and external forces such that, particularly in foreign capitalized firms, the quality of benefits tend to be as high or higher than would be expected given the size of the firm and ability and clout to do business here successfully in the long run.

It should also be considered that even when a firm has benefits comparable or even superior to the very best Japanese companies, it remains impossible to compete with them for the best Japanese human resources. So why try and beat out the leading employers on all benefits. It's better to concentrate on cash compensation which will not represent a long-term liability that your firm is stuck with.

Let's focus here on how compensation can be restructured or how changes can be made affecting employees already on the payroll. Presumably any such changes would involve an attempt to bring the weight of pensionable income in line with overall industry practice. The result would be that the summer and winter bonus would be "carved out" as would additional allowances be "added" without increasing payroll costs.

At some companies in order to do this it makes sense to set up a task force. On this task force, management should include the most unreasonable and radical member of the labor union, if the company is organized. The task force could consist of about ten members including perhaps 60% from a variety of job functions at the rank-and-file level with approximately an equal number coming from unionized and non-unionized employees. Among the four managers, certainly the general affairs or personnel man should be included, as well as both formal and informal top leaders who can understand the issues and sell them to the employees at large. The same should be said for the representatives of rank-and-file. However, by including on the task force the unreasonable elements, and even the troublesome manager who is likely to be fussy and complain about a number of the new policies, the task force has the advantage of taking a dry run and getting feedback and a preview to the whole array of possible employee criticism and complaints. Task force activity, therefore, allows you to test the waters first.

Before the task force is even set up, however, it is necessary to draft a rather lengthy and detailed document explaining in what ways the company's present compensation benefits and working conditions are superior to general local practice and why the company will be unable to keep up such practices.

Experience with corporate rationalization programs has enabled us to identify which issues are sensitive, and which benefits are not of such concern to employees. We thus approach a cost-cutting program with the aim of generating savings where there is the least resistance, but maximum contribution to the bottom line and corporate health.

Whether or not your company is organized by a union will of course make a difference, because collective bargaining agreements take precedence over the Rules of Employment. Therefore, any considered alteration to either collective bargaining agreements or the Rules of Employment will first undoubtedly be brought forth by the union as an issue for the collective bargaining table. After a certain period of negotiating time, however, management can maintain that impasse has been reached and can then proceed to address the problems, in terms of a Rules of Employment revision. In a unionized firm this would require a signature and written opinion from the head of the labor union, or in a non-unionized situation, the majority representative of the employees.

In non-unionized firms to some extent management should be able to influence or control the selection of this majority representative, for it is not necessary to have a formal election per se by the employees at large. Management should assure, however, that the selection of the individual to draft the *ikensho*, or statement of opinion on the work rules changes for the Labor Standards Office, be a person who has appeal, trust and credibility with the vast majority of his peers— the informal leader, someone who is well liked and respected.

Given that there are two equally forceful and persuasive personalities to choose between, it would be better to be lower in rank and younger as such a person would be recognized by the authorities as being more representative of the rank-and-file. Should the inspector at the Labor Standards Office inquire into the background of the majority representative, the younger individual, clearly up from the lower employee ranks, will have more credibility.

By all means it is a good idea to avoid announcements that are not backed up with detailed information and persuasive documents explaining why changes are being considered or necessary. In Japan sending out trial balloons, leaks or even rumors is preferable to announcements. By definition, an announcement means that the announcer is telling the listener what he doesn't know, and this puts the announcer in a superior position. To the Japanese, the act of announcement tends to be evidence of an air of superiority, smugness, and self-complacency, which they resent.

By preparing detailed documents that compare the company's current practices with national statistics, etc. the company can largely convince employees that the measures being taken are necessary and legitimate. This in itself vastly limits the possibility of complaints out to the Labor Standards Office or a Labor Relations Commission, or that litigation will be sought in a court of law. Nonetheless, the company must be sensitive to protecting itself against possible claims of adverse impact by employees and the possibility that they may be accepted by the authorities.

In the case, for example, when actual take-home pay is going to be reduced due to the "carving out" of summer and winter bonus, the company can protect itself against charges of adverse impact by providing loans to employees, which can be drawn up to the amount of the bonus which is due them in convenient units of perhaps ¥50,000. This method has worked for us at a number of companies.

In other cases we have set up a system of adjustment allowance in which, for purposes of reducing the lump-sum retirement pension liability, on paper a considerably reduced basic salary is instantly determined. Monthly take-home pay, however, will not be reduced. For a number of years all the money made in salary increases will be assigned to the summer and winter bonuses. They will gradually grow, and it's not until they reach their ceiling that the monthly base salary will increase.

At one company we allowed employees to choose between swinging over immediately to the new compensation system taking full summer and winter bonus or switching to the new compensation system but having the escape valve of being able to borrow bonus money in advance if pinched for cash in any given month, and using the more complex approach of adjustment allowance. Experience has shown us that employees who immediately switch over to the new system, tightening their belts for several months and then waiting for the bonus payment are able to save more money each year then other employees and use the forced savings of the bonus to buy high-priced consumer goods. When other employees notice this they tend to quickly opt for the newly revised system with full bonus payment.

Remember the company need not force any employees to accept these newly revised compensation structures, or any altered working conditions for that matter. Rather, the company can give each employee a six-month period (or shorter or longer) to resign from the company under the former compensation package, thereby enjoying the higher lump-sum retirement benefit based on the compensation package before Japanization. If the employees do not resign during that period, however, there could be a document signed which will serve as evidence of their acceptance of the new working conditions. The employer cannot be accused of breach of the initial contract. Verbally informing, perhaps with confirming memo, that staying beyond a certain date will be interpreted to mean acceptance of new conditions should usually be sufficient and is most recommended.

When "Japanizing" the compensation package with the primary intent of reducing the weight of pensionable income and allowing for more flexible pay methods that better reflect performance and contribution, it is a good idea to give a little extra thought to the size and weight of various allowances based upon the specific characteristics of your work force or your special needs. For example, if your firm has a seasoned work force averaging in age over 40, in a stable market where little dynamic growth is expected when Japanizing the compensation and carving out a family and housing allowance, it would be a good idea to have reasonably large allowances. This is because the great majority of your employees have already married, and most of their children have already been born. Thus there is more to be gained from placing the emphasis on cutting back the weight of pensionable income by having larger allowances. On the other hand, if you are a firm with bright prospects for future growth and if your work force is generally young and single, any housing or family allowance which you determine at this time will represent a future liability in that when Tanaka-san marries the extra ¥20,000 will have to be paid to him for his wife's allowance, etc.

I've been disturbed by a number of client companies in which the managers where all in favor of carving out summer and winter bonus and various allowance for rank-and-file employees, but they argued that in the case of managers, this should not be done. There's no justification for this position. In fact, in Japanese firms the higher one goes in the management hierarchy the larger potential for both discretionary second-salary component and for serious implementation of the performance range in the summer and winter bonus. According to 1980 statistics from the Ministry of Labor, the average performance range for managers was 22% and that for rank-and-file 13%. As mentioned earlier, these rationalization programs will be accepted only when the rank-and-file employees realize that the managers are also being adversely affected. Otherwise, managers cannot credibly sell these programs.

If your managers continue to complain and stubbornly refuse to go along with the changes, your appeal should be to rank-and-file employees who often are already on a five- or six-month bonus system. If necessary, you can appeal to these rank-and-file employees who will not be sympathetic toward managers enjoying much larger retirement benefits due to the different structure in the compensation package.

In this way you can isolate and bring around the managers. After all when it comes to the possible threat of unionization or to complaints of adverse impact, if the rank-and-file through proper education, appeals, and persuasion can be brought around, you are well on your way toward implementing the changes. It is the rank-and-file who will receive sympathy from interested upper-body labor unions or the Labor Relations Commission and Courts.

In a number of companies lower ranking employees have been convinced by our legitimate concerns that unless certain sacrifices and belt tightening are required of today's oldest crop of managers (often the first ones facing retirement in foreign capitalized corporations), then in the long run the superior payments to these high-ranking managers will actually be made at the sacrifice of the long-term ability to pay out in the future a reasonable and fair pension to today's young employees as well as future employees.

Paying for performance

After hiring people, it's sometimes difficult to reward performance the way we're accustomed to doing in many other countries. In your labor and personnel consulting work have you developed effective approaches and systems to pay by performance?

For most expatriate managers working in Japan, as well as the academics and researchers who have written a number of books on Japanese management practices, firsthand and empirical experience living and working in Japan is limited. Although there is some truth in the statement that the Japanese do not often work on commission sales systems and are not paid by performance, this is often accepted at face value and creates misunderstanding on the part of many outside observers.

Virtually all Japanese companies have a performance range on the summer and winter bonus, whereas among many of my foreign capitalized corporate clients there is no such range. Thus, if the corporate practice is to pay five months' bonus annually, all employees are uniformly paid five months' bonus. In contrast to this, according to a Ministry of Labor Survey of major firms here taken in 1980, the average performance range on the seasonal bonus for managers is 22% and 13% for non-manager employees. These are average figures, however, and generally the summer and winter bonus performance range is more in the order of 40 to 20% on either side of the average performer.

Thus if a company were paying six months' bonus, a poor performer would only be paid 4.8 months, whereas a top performer would be paid 7.2 months. However, since there is a tendency to evaluate employees on the positive side, the company should make sure that there are also down side ratings such that the average bonus paid each year would come close for example, to the intended six months' bonus.

Although even from the earliest years of employment in a large Japanese firm there will be variation in the summer and winter bonus payment, it is true that the large employers will try and keep regular monthly salary as well as rank and position in the organization as equal as possible until about age 30 or 35. This is one strength of the Japanese organization, for management has mastered the skill of making the vast majority of the young employees feel that they are important contributing members to the corporate team and that they have a good future with the company and will at least have a strong chance of becoming a *bucho* department head, if not perhaps a member of the board of directors.

Thus, employees will maintain a high level of motivation. After age 30 or 35 however the Japanese salary table generally provides for accelerated ranking of high performers. Furthermore, as discussed in earlier articles a job/qualification pay element, or second salary component will increase more rapidly for the high performer. Note, though, that even for these fast-tracking employees the weight of pensionable income will be held under control and not increased too much over the corresponding basic salary of the average performer or the vast majority of employees.

Normally all the figures in the salary table will be increased by only a certain percentage of the targeted base-up. Thus, poor performers frozen in rank will only get that minimal cost of living (COLA) increase. We have developed a compensation system with a salary table which is backed up by performance-related, work adjustment, repositioning, and disciplinary regulations in the Rules of Employment so that if necessary the employer would even be legally backed up to demote the employee in rank, change his job and adjust his pay level. Hence, if a company were contemplating an annual salary increase of 5% on the average, the figures in the salary table might be uniformly increased by three percent, yet an employee moved back a rank would only get a 2% increase. On the other hand, a superior performer might be moved as many as three ranks such that he would win an above-average 6% increase in basic salary.

Additional increase representing either promotion in status, changed job function or superior performance should be rewarded in terms of non-pensionable job/performance-related second salary component. Even if you are not now compensating employees in these ways, it is reasonably easy to make an adjustment to new methods because experience has shown that less competent poor performers who are likely to oppose change are attracted to the concept that most excess reward to high performers is made in terms of non-pensionable income and not at the sacrifice of shrinking retirement benefit to average and below-average performers. Furthermore, they realize that such compensation methods will assure the long-term corporate health of the firm, thus providing job security to employees.

With such a system of job/performance pay or second salary element which can be flexibly altered to meet compensation changes (due to promotion and change in status as well as expansion of responsibilities), it becomes possible to get away from traditional *yakuzuki-teate*, or position allowances. The main rationale for the position allowance is to find a way to reward an employee when he reaches the management level and is no longer subject to overtime payments. Since the employee presumably continues to work late each night, the rationale was that a lump-sum of ¥30,000 or ¥40,000 would help to compensate him for the lack of overtime payment. This, of course, can be done by documenting that an additional increment of non-pensionable income/job-related pay was given to the employee.

Traditional titles such as *kacho, jicho, bucho,* etc. are extremely important in dealing with outside constituencies and in terms of social prestige in ranking. However it should not be necessary to tie a specific monetary figure to a *bucho* title. After all within the same firm there are *buchos* at many different levels with diverse abilities. Thus, the presence of a single *bucho* allowance is not always a satisfactory solution.

In my experience, I have found that it is also preferable to be free to assign newly, change or alter titles without necessarily having to adjust compensation. A flexible job/performance or second salary component provides the kind of latitude and flexibility you need.

I've described in earlier articles why I feel certain systems of job application and job grades can have their drawbacks. In terms of paying by performance as well, a company would want to avoid a situation in which a poor performer is automatically brought up in the ranks simply because the job grade in which he is positioned is increased across the board. If the man really is not working and puling his weight, there's no reason for him to benefit from such an automatic increase. Rather, he could be frozen in rank indefinitely, merely receiving the COLA adjustment on the salary table as is often the case in a Japanese firm.

The important point is to have a system which is recognized as being legitimate in the eyes of the Japanese employees. Many of my multinational clients have had problems here with the simplified approach of increasing annual income by varying, percentages without adequate salary and appraisal systems and procedures.

When it comes to paying for merit and performance, the same thing can be accomplished perhaps even more effectively using Japanese methods that are familiar to the Japanese and are recognized as legitimate. Why not do it their way when it works better? For example, at one of my client companies the area regional vice president told me over breakfast at our initial meeting that "It is time to get these Japanese to realize that they are working in a multinational firm with a head office in the United States, and if we want to pay a $2,000 bonus to managers performing adequately, it is our prerogative to go ahead and do that."

By asking a few questions, I determined that in the last couple of years his company had initiated this new approach toward manager performance compensation and that in one year a manager might be paid the $2,000 but then in the next year he might not. It was an all or nothing approach and, indeed, very unfamiliar to the Japanese. I found that in the very same company there was no performance range on the summer and winter bonus. Rather five months of bonus were paid to all employees regardless of their effort and contribution.

I commented, "Your Japanese management will never stop saying 'We don't do things like this in Japan.' Why expose yourself to this kind of criticism when you can even more effectively reward and penalize by having a 40% or more performance range on the summer and winter bonus? This, in fact, will amount to considerably more than $2,000 for the higher performers. You can make money on the down side by deducting more than $2,000 from those who aren't doing good work for you." He was a good manager, a good listener, and it wasn't hard to convince him of the alternate approach. We took about two months to convince the employees of the need for change, but we were successful in spite of the fact that the firm was already unionized.

In all major Japanese firms to varying degrees the tools which I have mentioned above are in use to assure that there is payment for contribution and that those who work hard are rewarded. Among the candidates that we scout, it is surprising to us how many mention that one reason they were positively disposed to answer our phone call was because at their present employer they felt that no matter how hard they worked, they were not adequately rewarded and they were disturbed that employees around them not working nearly as hard were essentially making the same amount of money.

This signals to me that an employer has not only an obligation to his company to draw out the best efforts possible from his employees, but also to many of the employees themselves who seek special recognition for special efforts.

Two years ago one of my clients hired five young, bright English-speaking females whom he hoped would eventually grow into professional staff positions. When he sat down with supervisors at evaluation time and worked with the numbers, he determined that he would be safest by giving all five females the same percentage increase. This American country manager felt that since this is Japan, all five women would appreciate this approach to salary review.

Very much to the contrary, four out of five of them paid a visit to his office and within one year he had lost three of them to other employers because they felt that not enough effort and substantial review went into salary evaluation. They wanted to go to a company where they could be rewarded for their contribution.

A word should be said about commission sales: Once again there are a lot of misunderstandings on the part of expatriate managers because of inadequate information and lack of empirical experience concerning the orientation of the average Japanese toward commission sales. Maybe in the large Japanese employers where loyalty, esprit de corps, and love of company seem to be quite strong, it is not necessary to have commission sales in order to get good efforts out of the sales force.

But I'm afraid that in many foreign firms, commission sales are an approach that merit careful study and perhaps a second look on the part of firms that are not doing well and have not as yet used commissions as an incentive tool. When changing over to a commission sales base though, careful and thoughtful approaches are required with attention toward avoiding adverse impact and assuring that smooth labor relations are maintained, getting the unions to sign off on these new methods with minimum friction and disturbance to business operations.

Increasing sales and profits with commission incentives

It's often said that commission sales won't work in Japan. What's your experience with this? Can a company switch over to commissions when business is bad?

Some 75% of the 38 million salaried or employed workers in Japan do not work in large firms offering "lifetime employment." Perhaps the minority of Japanese employees working in these largest firms do display considerable loyalty and "love of company" (*aisha seishin*), and thus it is not necessary to get them hustling by use of commission sales tools. (I would argue, however, that it is the closed labor market phenomenon among the large firms rather than blind loyalty which spurs on these employees to work hard for their company. They will have no opportunity to get an equally good, high-paying job in another large firm, so they tend to keep their noses clean and press down on the grindstone realizing that that is the only way they can keep a good thing going and avoid being ostracized or even expelled and dismissed from the group at the comparatively early age of 40 to 50.)

In contrast, however, in small Japanese firms there is an open labor market and considerable turnover. Unfortunately, this situation is also faced by most foreign employers here. Japanese move and change jobs between firms for 15 to 25% salary increases because those jobs are available. The large Japanese firms paying good salaries and benefits simply do not usually offer such mid-career opportunities. Above all, this is probably a reason why the Japanese will not be as dedicated and interested in the success of their multinational employer. They do not necessarily see their destiny tied to that of the firm.

Real and perceived differences in decision making, management style, miscommunications, mutual prejudice, parochialism, irrational emotional responses, and resentment of being managed and dominated by foreign factors also probably contribute to allowing some Japanese employees to rationalize and feel comparatively comfortable with the withholding of effort, enthusiasm, and positive motivation when working in foreign corporations.

A friend of mine who is a partner in a major management consulting firm here states it this way, "when our teams of Japanese management consultants work closely on a project with a multinational client here, they do not show nearly the enthusiasm, energy levels or motivation that excites them when they're working for a major Japanese client. The result is that the ideas, creativity and project outcome of our teams are not nearly as good in foreign firms here in Japan."

This kind of evidence and my own experience have led me to believe that even if commissions are not generally used at the top employers in Japan, in foreign firms where the work habits, motivation, and attitude of Japanese employees probably are more similar to that of employees at home country operations, perhaps creative and thoughtful applications of home country approaches to commission incentives should be seriously considered. And, in fact commissions are widely used in Japan.

For example, one of the first friends I made in Japan has worked in four or five different real estate agencies during the many years that I have known him. He tells me that in many of the firms he's worked for, a young salesman coming into the company has a choice of perhaps three different salary levels with three separate rates of commission. In one company there was an option to receive absolutely no base pay or compensation with an inordinately high commission on real estate sales. A surprising number of employees opt for this approach rather than taking a base salary of ¥175,000 with only somewhat lower commission rate.

Obviously the real estate business is a unique one. However, I have spoken in depth with a number of people working in a whole variety of smaller firms here in Japan. One company selling water purification filters, for example, has some 300 employees with 60 salesman on commissions, which amount to from two to five times monthly fixed salary depending upon level of performance.

Some time ago a client came to our office telling me that it would be necessary to reduce about ten staff in order for this 40-man company to continue to exist in Japan. "Even at that, I'm afraid it's just a matter of time before we'll have to close up the shop completely and move on out of this market," the expatriate representative director said to me. This firm was basically well structured with 15 people involved in assembly of stateside parts, five office personnel, and some 20 salesmen who were to service and encourage distributors as well as do direct sales.

I reviewed the company's compensation data and noted that salary levels were about average. Up until this point there had been no commission system because management bought off on the over-simplified stereotypes pertaining to Japanese business practices (although admittedly there is truth in these stereotypes). When they set up the operation, the first Japanese executive they hired also backed up one of the stereotypes by saying that he didn't think it would be necessary or useful to have commission sales.

"We could reduce staff, but it will only in turn reduce morale and not solve your long-term challenge of pushing your product through this market. If there's any possibility at all, I would rather see us tackle your problem in terms of compensation readjustment and perhaps the introduction of commissions," I told my troubled client.

He replied, "We considered commissions about ten years ago when we started operations here, and the idea was rejected at the time. How could we introduce them at this stage?" I told him that we could have a convincing argument for introducing commission sales as an alternative to staff reduction. But, of course, there would be much greater advantage introducing commission sales if we could also considerably reduce fixed payroll expenses by cutting pay back.

Working closely with the client, we went on to develop a system in which employees could either continue to sell at the same salary without commission or could opt for either one of two additional combinations of monthly salary and commissions. Employees could choose one system in which their salaries were cut back by 20% but with generous commissions, which should easily make up for this, and then another system in which pay would be reduced by 40% with an even more generous commission scale.

Employees were given three months from their initial decision to change their minds as to which system to work under. Then after another six months they could make a "final" decision as to which way they would continue to be compensated.

Just over half of the employees accepted one of the two sales commission systems. They immediately began to make more money than non-commissioned salesmen, particularly for four out of the five or six employees who opted for the higher commission weight. After the first three months, about half again of the non-commissioned employees opted for one of the commission sales systems. The company is doing fine now; and as long as their product is at all salable, you can be sure that this revitalized group of super-salesmen will get the goods out into the marketplace. Who said commission sales don't work in Japan?

By making the commission rates attractive enough, we were able to get employees to swing over to commission sales voluntarily. Thus, there was no complaint lodged of breach of contract or adverse impact, etc. We made sure that the employees signed a document accepting the new conditions and acknowledging that their reduced monthly income with a commensurate reduction in the weight of pensionable income would even reduce the lump-sum retirement pension benefit which they were to receive. The employees reasoned that with the extra money they were making, they could save for their own futures.

Thus we were able to cut back substantially not only short-term payroll costs but also the long-term pension liability faced by the firm. I would encourage multinational firms here to have such creative approaches toward commission systems. There may be variance from head office policy but as in the aforementioned case, we were able to convince the home office sales and marketing people that the use of innovative approaches to commissions made sense in view of the particular problem and challenge we were facing in Japan.

In another company selling high-priced capital goods, at the head office in Germany, salesmen receive the lowest salaries in the company but get 1% commissions on items that are priced anywhere from $750,000 up to about $10 million. Obviously with 1% takes of such sales any salesman worth his salt becomes handsomely rewarded, and the sales force are the most highly compensated people in the company. However, three or four years ago when they set up operations in Japan, they were told that commissions would not work; thus, salesmen were placed on salaries which are higher than salaries paid to salesmen in any other country.

Gradually through sales calls, product recognition increased here in Japan and reached the point where they were beginning to sell some of their highest price-tagged systems. One of the senior Japanese salesmen attended a sales conference at the home office to learn that German salesmen were paid 1% of the sale even on sales as high as $10 million. Word spread back to Japan where sales people began to complain that they also wanted commissions. However, they insisted that they did not want their income reduced—a most unreasonable demand and intolerable mentality.

But with creative and innovative approaches, there is indeed more than one way to skin a cat. We turned the tables around on the employees arguing that "Japan is different. Cooperative incentives are more highly valued here; and since this is a difficult market with more competition, lower name recognition and misgivings on the part of customers, etc. concerning the quality of our after-sales service and so on, we will have to have a commission system which will reward everyone, including the office and technical service people."

We worked out a system with the employees such that 1/2 of the 1% commission proceeds would go into a general corporate fund which would be used to help fund the retirement benefit, make office improvements, move into a new and bigger office or for various employee parties or outings. It was hard for anyone to object to this. Then we used the remaining 1/2% for distribution to all employees in cash. The pay would be distributed proportionate to each employee's monthly salary.

The employee who made the sale would be paid anywhere from two to four times the normal cash incentive paid out based on salary level. If a salesman had made the sale almost exclusively on his own without much additional staff support, he could make as much as four times the overall prorated employee cash incentive. If three salesmen had been considerably involved in the sale, the salesman most directly involved would be given perhaps two and 1/2 X the incentive, with the remaining salesmen getting a 1.25 incentive premium over the overall incentive distributed to each employee based on their individual ratio of the total monthly payroll.

In other words, we devised a system in which a small number of salesmen directly involved in a sale could make larger commissions, while on the other hand all employees also benefited from sales thereby backing up the sales department and cooperating as much as possible with good after-sales service, etc. We devised this system, not only because we felt it would work best in Japan, but also because we felt that unlike in Germany, it would be unhealthy and spoil a salesman to make as much as $60,000 on a big $6 million sale, amounting to some ¥14 million (which would be more than twice the amount that most salesmen were being paid in terms of annual income).

I would think even in Germany such a large commission could be destructive in that it would raise havoc with a salesman's spending habits and lifestyle making it particularly difficult for him to get through dry periods when there were no sales.

There's one more innovation that we introduced at this company in Japan. So that all 40 employees were not rewarded equally simply based upon their salary's proportion of the monthly payroll, we thought it would be best to add a 40% performance range on this "sales bonus." Thus, employees displaying bad attitude, poor attendance, lack of cooperation, contribution, and effort, etc. would be paid 20% less than the amount which would normally be due them, while the top performers would be paid as much as 20% more. The company goes through this exercise every six months when sales are totaled up. However, I recommended that they keep it as a separate issue from the summer and winter bonus. Therefore, the sales bonus is paid out in March and September.

The new approach is working out well for this company, and we recently were visited by people from the firm's head office. They were interested in getting our input on possibly developing such original and innovating approaches there. If your salesmen and staff in general are being paid too much for doing too little, and you need to get them hustling and taking initiative or if staff reduction seems to be the only way to get around low sales and profit figures, how about thinking in terms of restructuring compensation with some innovative applications of sales commissions?

Giving your headhunter the support he needs

How can we work with a headhunter to make him more effective? What kind of information does he need? What turns potential candidates off?

You can make your headhunter more effective by explaining in detail the nature of your business and being sure to supply him with the names of your competitors in the industry. If there is any doubt as to where the potential candidate would be found within those companies, it will be helpful to be sure that your recruiter is supplied with the typical department names and sections, as well as titles (in, of course, the Japanese language) to enable the recruiter further to focus in on your objective.

We have dealt with a number of companies that have actually given us the name of the individual whom they wanted to work for them. This obviously makes our job much easier, although we still have the difficult challenge of establishing trust, negotiating, enticing, persuading, and convincing the executive that the new position can represent a positive development in his career. We feel that the candidate is just as important to us as the client. This is especially true since the difficulty of executive recruitment in Japan is finding candidates. Sometimes a satisfied individual working in a company at our introduction will refer us to a number of other highly qualified individuals in the same or different fields.

In order to assure that we're working on a good match that will last for many years, we like to get as much information as we can on the client company's corporate culture, working environment, and dominant executive style. It's a good idea to be aware of the limitations on authority and degree of initiative and "self start" which will be expected of the new manager. The personality and character of the candidate's supervisor, associates and key subordinates are also factors that should be given consideration. If, for example, the candidate's boss is known to be a particularly abrasive man, it's a good idea to know that. In that case, we would like to find a tolerant and low-key individual who can put up with that personality type.

For the benefit of potential candidates and our own reference, we like to find out why the last man left the company. Was he fired? If so, why? At several companies after discovering that there were unusually high rates of turnover, an initial executive recruitment assignment led to a major labor consulting project in which I discovered a number of problem areas, such as dissatisfaction with systems of reward and punishment, lack of communication between departments resulting in a lack of clearly defined corporate goals and purpose, favoritism on the part of the expatriate boss toward certain English-speaking employees, dissatisfaction with the company's business plan and overall approach to the market, and salary levels that were too low in an industry that is constantly bidding up salaries due to a shortage of skilled technicians.

It was a small company, so I was able to meet with each employee for 30 minutes. We set up what I called *kaizen-kai*, or improvement circles, with cross-departmental representation and combined it with an organizational chart reshuffling, which put the Japanese who was considered to have the "right business plan" in charge. The former Japanese marketing man was really better at administration, anyway, and was better suited for an office administrator position which would also place him in charge of inventory, customer relations, and overall office management.

Executive recruiting can be and often should be more than just a headhunting relationship. It's important to have a trustworthy recruiter who learns a lot about your company and cares about some of the wider potential personnel problems you face than simply having the orientation of finding you a man whom you are willing to hire. It also helps us when a client is frank and honest in the assessment of candidates introduced.

For example, it makes little sense for a client to give us inaccurate impressions concerning the job profile when the main reason for turning down a seemingly well-qualified candidate is because the chemistry is not right. If that's the case, we'd like to hear about it. It should be kept in mind, however, that the expatriate executive may only be in Japan as little as two to four years, so that a certain amount of tolerance and patience may make good sense and end up being to the long-term benefit of the company.

We also feel we have an obligation to give feedback on problems we discover. For example, with one client where we have placed a number of individuals in the past we discovered that in the particular product area in which we were requested to make a major search, there were strong feelings among those candidates we interviewed that the company newly coming into the market would have a surprisingly difficult time in implementing the business plan. This was in terms of the acceptance of the company's product as well as the company's ability to build up the new project as quickly as expected in terms of sales and the number of human resources recruitable in a competitive industry where salaries had already been bid up to levels that were often out of balance with lower salary levels in other divisions of the company.

We discovered other things for the client, such as a commonly held opinion that the machine tools backing up the product were too slow and inferior to those already available in Japan. Thus, even if the imported items were sold at a reduced price, the lower efficiency of the assembling equipment would increase the product price well above the overall cost of doing business with some of the Japanese vendors. By doing our homework and carrying out a very exhaustive search, visiting factories in many companies, etc., we were able to find out such information which actually affected in a very positive way the client's business plan.

I feel this should also be the responsibility of a good executive recruiting firm, but it is important that the client be willing to listen and try to understand why we are having difficulties in fulfilling the assignments. Often the candidates already in Japanese industry are more aware of such potential problem than is the multinational client newly entering the Japanese market or attempting to come in with a new product.

Sometimes we are given an impossible assignment. Clients can make the recruiter's job difficult in additional ways as well. We've had a few clients who have demanded and expected resumes written up by the candidate himself, failing to realize that candidates have a tremendous amount of pride and often prefer to meet with a client and feel him out before they will write up a resume or answer too many detailed questions from the search consultant.

We often have clients who are too inflexible with their schedules and fail to realize that, particularly in the case of young salesmen and technical superiors, it is extremely difficult for them to get away from their jobs during the day. Some clients will try to avoid meeting with candidates after working hours, whereas often a key, hard-working Japanese personnel in his 20s or 30s will find it difficult to break away before 8:00 p.m. or even 9:00 p.m.

It's important for clients to remember that unless a candidate is answering a newspaper advertisement, or perhaps unemployed, he will consider the relationship between himself and the client as equal. They are both doing one another an important service—offering a good job and being a good enough man to take the job.

Candidates whom we've scouted out of top Japanese or foreign firms here—people who enjoy their work and are fully engaged in it yet are smart enough to realize that there are benefits in rubbing shoulders with headhunters and many things to learn from an interesting client in the same field—are not happy when one of the first lines from the client's mouth is "Why do you want to leave your job?" This is about as smooth as a sumo wrestler on a water bed.

We had another case in which a man who was already a *bucho*, or department head was offered by the client company the title of *jicho* (the title that generally comes just before *bucho*). Our search consultant naturally assumed that he would once again be a *bucho* in the new position. Luckily, we heard about this in time and were able to straighten things out without the candidate himself having to get involved and give away a little of his pride by having to squabble over his title. This also must be the role of the executive recruiter.

If a client is going to wine and dine a candidate and spend a good deal of time convincing him to join the company, it is important not to have this process cease after the candidate is on board and has perhaps signed the contract. It will not always be necessary to spend much time with the individual, but in the first month or two the new man will be faced with many challenges in trying to fit in with the fabric of personal relations already established, and it will be helpful to have the moral support of you, the top expatriate manager in the organization.

Our job also becomes difficult when we have to deal with the impatient and over-decisive Western executive who likes to make unilateral decisions without consulting the people around him. We once had two superbly qualified candidates for two different positions at the same company. One position required a bright bilingual individual who had a strong background as a correspondent, translator and interpreter. Specific mention wasn't made on the resume, however, of the fact that the candidate had translated a number of books, several of which were extremely well done and sold well here in Japan. After a two-hour-interview the Japanese manager offered the woman candidate the job.

In the meantime, the expatriate C.E.O. looked over the resume, which made no specific mention of books translated, and somehow assumed that the candidate was exclusively an interpreter and not a translator. Without meeting her himself, he called the Japanese manager saying that the candidate was not qualified. As the Japanese manager was weak, it ended up that he did not go to bat for the candidate, and we were shocked when he backed off and stated that he had never offered the job to her.

The other candidate introduced for a different job was subjected to similar spot decision making without being given an interview by the expatriate boss. A footnote to this story is that since this crusty and incompetent expatriate manager came on the scene a comparatively short time ago, approximately 1/3 of the staff have left the company, with sales volumes steadily shrinking.

As we all know, timing is important in love affairs and romance. The same can be said of executive recruitment matches. When too much time passes, both parties lose interest. Just the fact that a client continues to see additional candidates is evidence to the candidate we introduce that the client is not sufficiently excited about him. This naturally triggers the reaction "I would rather go somewhere I'm appreciated. And in any case, I'm not going to start out in a company where the boss has doubts about me."

About three weeks ago we got an assignment to find "within the next six months or so" a good sales manager handling a certain line of technical products. We came up with an excellent candidate who was so good and so well liked that the client felt they should make a decision soon. Just like the bachelor who keeps searching for the best woman to settle down with and loses all the others in the interim, the client told the candidate that they would run an ad in the *Japan Times* the very next Monday to make sure they could get the best man available.

I think our candidate was extremely understanding and tolerant of their position, but it remains to be seen if he will maintain his interest level and want to join this company after the passage of a few weeks when the company has finally processed newspaper applicants. Timing is important, and if you've got someone that will work out well, why not take him? We perhaps could be faulted by coming up with the ideal candidate in two or three weeks leading the client company to believe that finding someone qualified is easy to do and that there must be someone out there who's even better.

And finally there is much documented evidence that you can't buy a man in this market if the chemistry isn't right. On a search last year I detected that my candidate didn't feel that the foreign boss was a warm and sensitive individual with whom he could communicate openly and through thick and thin. This made the Japanese manager candidate feel insecure and uncomfortable about his future at such a company.

It was a large foreign firm with more than 2,000 employees and considerably larger than the firm he was already in. Nevertheless, he stayed where we was at ¥11 million per year even though he was offered ¥18 million, or a 64% increase.

Firing as a last resort—but, do it right

Sometimes unfortunately the other side of hiring has to be firing, or at least changing the role or status of a high-ranking manager so that he doesn't pose a block to company growth or dynamics. I know you've done a lot of labor consulting work in this area as well as in massive staff reductions for economic reasons, such as when a company is not as profitable as it should be. Could you give us some insight and tips? I suppose that a company's Rules of Employment are a factor here.

What the law says about dismissal in Japan really has very little to do with the realities of this difficult and challenging area of people management. Article 627 of the Civil Code provides that two weeks' notice should be given to an employee. This is superseded, however, by Article 20 of the Labor Standards Law which indicates that 30 days' notice or 30 days' pay, or any combination of the two is required.

It is Article 27, Section I of the Constitution, though, that provides that the right to work is a fundamental right of the Japanese people. Therefore, promotion of job security has come to be considered a matter of public order. The employer is not permitted to abuse his right of dismissal, and the courts have developed a rather strict attitude toward admitting just cause. Frequently unjust or unfair dismissals are ruled null and void, and the employee reinstated in his former position.

The law provides for the immediate firing of an individual on grounds of disciplinary discharge. Under these circumstances the retirement allowance can be forfeited, but the approval of the Labor Standards Office is needed in advance. Substantial documentation, evidence, and extremely strong arguments on the part of management for disciplinary dismissal will be required by the Labor Standards Office before acknowledging a disciplinary dismissal. In short, it's not easy to get a disciplinary dismissal to stick down at the Labor Standards Office.

Generally a poor performer knows in his heart that he is just that—not performing adequately or well. If this is regularly expressed to the individual over a long period of time by verbal and then written warning or coaching and evidence retained in personnel files and is gradually followed by a reduction in responsibilities, suspension of salary increase and then reduction in salary accompanying demotion, it is possible to have an employee go along with a recommended resignation as a substitute for dismissal. It must be done properly, however, and it will take some time and some work. Also, if legally challenged, it is virtually impossible to do these things unless the collective bargaining agreements and/or Rules of Employment back this up.

Even in companies where there is a trade union, experience has shown that the union often has not been involved in negotiating policies in these areas. However, even if they have, it is not impossible to change these policies by simply calling for renegotiation if the longest validly legal collective bargaining contract period of three years has been exceeded, or if 90 days' notice is given to renegotiate a non-term agreement. If an impasse is reached after some two to three months of good-faith negotiations, then management can claim that the impasse status leaves them no other choice than to unilaterally change the Rules of Employment.

Management is free to change the Rules of Employment, although the representative of the trade union has a right to express his opinion regarding the Rules of Employment. This is merely an opinion, however, and when necessary the company should go ahead with the changes. The Labor Standards Office may request that negotiations be continued, and this comes in the form of administrative guidance which should be adhered to, but after another month or so of negotiations the company should go back to the Labor Standards Office and reaffirm its position.

Since comparatively few of your firms are unionized, it should be easier to adjust your Rules of Employment so that they have detailed clauses which will legally permit you to suspend salary increase, suspend attendance, demote, cut back pay, go for recommended resignation and finally disciplinary discharge. You will also need detailed grounds for taking these various disciplinary measures against employees. These grounds can appear in the detailed language of a chapter on duties and obligations which can be tied in with the disciplinary measures and also with specific grounds applying to each disciplinary and job adjustment measure.

In Japan the legal foundation of the employer's power to impose discipline comes essentially from the contractual relationship between the employer and his employees. This means that the employer can only command his right to order based on the employment contract. Therefore, leading legal theories deny the employer's intrinsic power to discipline his employees with the result that the legal foundation to take disciplinary action must be in the contract or in the work rules since in reality most firms have more than ten employees and the Rules of Employment take precedence over a contract between the company and a given individual.

Thus, an employer may only punish his employees when punishments are provided for either in the work rules or in the collective agreement (in the case of a unionized firm). The degree of punishment and reasons for it should always be laid down in precise detail due to the penal nature of disciplinary punishment. It should also be noted that the Rules of Employment will require very detailed grounds to take disciplinary measures against employees or to be grounds for cutting back pay, etc.

If an action you take against a given employee is challenged, the Labor Relations Commission or a judge will look to the specific language in the Rules of Employment. If the grounds for the action you are taking against the employee are not specifically mentioned in the Rules of Employment, the judge may hold that it is not legal for you to take such action. Thus, it is important that virtually all possible scenarios of bad behavior and poor performance be mentioned in the Rules of Employment.

Often when I provide a company newly establishing itself in Japan with detailed disciplinary performance, and job adjustment measures or when I restructure compensation and improve Rules of Employment and other personnel policies, criticism will be voiced against rather detailed regulations in this area. The fact is, however, that none of the worthwhile employees in the company will be concerned that those disciplinary and performance/contribution measures and grounds for action will be personally used against them.

This is not an issue, for they are good employees who are working hard for the company and need never feel threatened by such language, which is merely there as a safety to protect both the company and the vast majority of good employees from the possibility that in the future a couple of bad employees will either damage morale, corporate reputation, or attempt to get a free ride on the coattails of the hard working employees who care about the firm.

Innovative and creative approaches to commission sales incentives may be necessary because the environments in which Japanese work at foreign corporations are not necessarily typically Japanese. In fact, commission sales are widely used as a tool in medium and small Japanese enterprises where there's job turnover, open labor markets, and less "imposed loyalty" due to the absence of closed labor markets experienced by employees in larger firms.

For any foreign firms that need a shot of adrenalin and revitalization of sales forces, etc., I would strongly recommend that they look into the possibility of setting sales targets and keeping good records of which salesmen are meeting the targets and which are consistently failing to do so.

At the same time there should be language introduced into the Rules of Employment providing that management will take action against employees who consistently fail to sell. The details of this mechanism including target figures can be provided on a separate attachment to the Rules of Employment.

A company can attempt to transfer some of its salesmen to different job functions where they may be more successful and productive but certainly not all salesmen. Documenting sales efforts in this way and taking gradual punitive action against consistently poor performers, concomitant with freezes in salary increase and pay cuts is certainly a sensible way to encourage voluntary resignation or to set up management for a successful designated discharge of documented poor performers. With the proper approaches and systems, there is no reason why foreign capitalized firms here in Japan should not be better able to elicit the required effort and activity levels from sales staff.

And as for taking action against a single manager whether high ranking or of lower rank, there are a wide variety of creative approaches. In one case the home office was actually afraid of its Japanese president whom they felt might litigate against them in the case of his discharge and who might turn distributors and customers against the company through bad-mouthing, etc.

After through research and investigation had clearly documented inadequate performance as well as some questionable business and social activities, the president was made aware that the report existed and given the option to sever his relationship with the company in a quiet and gentlemanly fashion. This worked out just fine, but it was necessary to have the guns fully loaded before pointing the barrel.

In another case with a labor home-study buff, we were just sure that the individual would hold back, litigate against us, and fight us tooth and nail. We were able to disarm him and prevent him from going to a lawyer, however, through coordinating our efforts with an inspector at the Labor Standards Office. Essentially we had the Labor Standards Office back us up because it understood in advance why the individual was a divisive and undesirable force in the firm and agreed that the disciplinary action we intended to take against the individual was fair and not overly severe. We were able to tell the problem employee this, by even giving the name of the inspector at the Labor Standards Office.

We did, in fact, "disarm" him, and he too preferred to leave with dignity rather than hang around beyond six days, when the demotion and cut back in responsibilities with accompanying 40% cut in pay would also reduce his lump-sum retirement benefit 40%.

In terms of massive staff reductions for economic reasons a separate book could be written. Let me just give a few random thoughts and guidelines based on my experience. There were two separate companies that were to merge with a requirement for a 50% staff reduction. Both companies were unionized, but one had an extremely unreasonable left-wing labor union. If we carried out a voluntary retirement program, all the best employees would take it, leaving us essentially with the most unproductive and troublesome elements. To try and reduce 50% of the staff of both companies would turn them both against us. It made sense to close down one. (Guess which one?)

A company with two divisions, one profitable and one very unprofitable, was hoping to reduce about a third of the employees in the unprofitable company. They were the worst performers, and inevitably members of the union that had experience with staff reduction in the past. Essentially, it would not have been possible to dismiss those staff on a designated-discharge basis. What should we do?

I recommended that before the word "staff reduction" even be uttered, the rapidly growing and profitable division be made into a separate company. Then we could close down the unsuccessful original company by dismissing all the employees and bringing over the product of the closed down division and only a handful of the best employees on a rehiring basis with no continuation of service years to the lump-sum retirement pension benefit, but instead a special lump-sum bonus to make up for this loss in vested pension rights.

The extra lump-sum bonus paid to employees was still only a fraction of the kind of settlement that would have had to be made, if the company had gone ahead and tried to reduce the union-member poor performers while continuing to operate the limping division under the same organizational status.

Another client had an old and inefficient factory that was losing money in an inconvenient regional location. They came to me asking for advice on reducing 60% of the staff there. Since they already had had experience with staff reduction and were unionized, I knew it wouldn't be easy. Rather than try and reduce over half the work force, I recommended they close the factory and sell the land. Since most of the factory employees owned large farms and could support themselves through farming, it was unlikely that they would demand to be transferred and follow the product. A small modern plant could thus be built near the major metropolitan market.

I'd like to make one brief comment that will assist you in determining the premium formula, which often has to be placed on top of the payment coefficient for the lump-sum retirement benefit pertaining to involuntary retirement. It is frequently a combination of percentage over the number of months which are normally provided for in the work rules times years of service in the company.

Thus young employees (who are usually the radical union members) will gain little benefit from this premium because they have few years of service. For this and other reasons, there is often a fixed number of months of lump-sum, which is the same for all employees. It is this factor that disproportionately rewards the young employees who are usually active union members.

You should, therefore, always look at who you want to discharge on a designated basis and do a comparison in calculation of their years of service factor as well as union membership and the "radical index" (as I have come to call it), then make judgments as to how you can best achieve your goals given the same total premium retirement benefit cost.

Dismissing employees should be a last resort, and it is unfortunate that an entire factory has to be closed down. Unfortunately, overly protective labor legislation and impractical and liberal judges in the court sometimes make it difficult to take remedial and disciplinary action against employees who well deserve it, to the detriment of the vast majority of good hard-working employees. Creative solutions are, therefore, sometimes called for. If you're going to fire, do it right.

Investigate—better to be safe than sorry

Could you tell us something about the necessity to investigate a candidate thoroughly. What kind of horror stories can you give us?

Foreign capitalized firms in Japan have been sloppy in the past and probably still are remiss in adequately investigating and checking references of the people they hire. Very few Japanese are hired by major Japanese companies without a thorough investigation by a *koshinjo*, or private investigative agency. Many years ago I knew a Japanese girl who had just graduated from college and joined a bank.

I was amazed at her description of just how thorough the investigation into her background was, with the investigator going into her neighborhood and speaking with neighbors, the man who runs they dry cleaning shop, a nearby noodle shop, as well as school authorities, local police records, etc. Admittedly, banks may be especially cautious and conservative, but it was after all only a female new school graduate who would probably work there three or four years at the most and unlikely to be in a sensitive position.

A good investigative agency will often put embarrassing and non-job-related information in their report. We learned that one of our star candidates would occasionally beat his wife according to reports of screams which echoed down the hallway of the "mansion" he lived in. Black and blue marks, which gradually darkened over the next day or two, were also telltale evidence according to a busybody housewife two doors down. He'd never punched another fellow employee, however. So after my British client was given assurances that the candidate would continue to take out his frustrations only on his wife at home, he was given the job.

The fact is, however, that many candidates who approach you through newspaper advertising may assume that the foreign employer will not investigate. When I talk with foreign management here and especially with vice presidents of personnel from the head office and mention that they should investigate their candidates, their initial reaction is usually, "I don't think we want to get into that." They're accustomed to Stateside problems with violation of privacy and various discrimination laws. When in Japan, though, you'll be better off doing as the Japanese do—investigate or at least thoroughly check references.

One of my labor consulting clients approached me to get help implementing the salary "base-up," as it was the first year he was using the new system we created for him. At that time he told me about a young Japanese sales engineer who seemed to possess everything. "My sales *bucho* told me I had to meet him and that he had guts, was tough, and was a true Japanese. The guy sounded too good to be true, and I agreed to meet him at Trader Vic's for a luncheon interview. Before that, however, I told my sales manager to check out a couple of references, and the sales manager informed the candidate that a check was being made. The fellow was supposed to have been a graduate of Osaka University (one of the top schools and an original imperial university) and also to have worked five years at Hitachi."

"Phone calls revealed that he'd never studied at Osaka University nor was he known to Hitachi. When I got to Trader Vic's, there was a message waiting for me that Mr. Tanaka got in a taxi smash up on his way to the New Otani and wouldn't be able to make the meeting. We never heard from him again."

So as to avoid this scenario and to make it easier on our clients without them having to look as though they in any way mistrust the candidate, we now generally have the practice of asking for references at the initial interview with the candidate. Although this is not so critical because at least we are scouting into companies, only talking to people in a job, and trying to avoid job hoppers like the plague. It's surprising to us but once in awhile a candidate who seems to be extremely eager to change jobs and shows interest in the job described to him, suddenly disappears and never comes back again after we've indicated we'd check out his background.

There are a number of tricks that can be used to spot a dishonest candidate. You should be sensitive to and observant of certain things. For example, once a client told me about a candidate who had two or three excellent letters of recommendation on the stationery of top-notch companies where he was supposed to have worked. He got suspicious, however, when he noticed that the same word was spelled wrong in all three letters. It's easy enough to collect stationery and it might even be worthwhile for an incompetent executive trying to pass himself off as top-level material to go to the expense of printing up stationery. Be sure and watch out for people applying to you for a job, or for resumes brought in by headhunters you know little about.

There's an easy and quick test which works remarkably well in verifying whether or not someone is being honest or exaggerating on their current salary level. First, you should ask the candidate what his annual income is and then in rapid succession ask him how many months of bonus he is being paid. The next question to fire directly thereafter should be "What is your monthly salary?" Look the individual right in the eye. If he is fudging with the figures, he will get nervous and not be able to give you a monthly salary figure right away. Either that or the numbers won't work out, and I generally have a calculator with me when I ask these questions. It's a good idea to give the candidate any opportunity to explain any discrepancies right on the spot. Actually to avoid this embarrassment it's a good idea to tell him in advance the W-2 form equivalent (statement of earnings) will be required by the next potential employer.

With careful attention for quivering lips, shaking hands, stammering and sometimes a quick flash of color to the face, it is not hard to distinguish between the individual who is deliberately misrepresenting his compensation and the one who is careless and slipshod with numbers. Exaggerating a salary under these circumstances may not be the worst thing in the world, but through investigation or employment of these methods we can get an accurate reading of what present salary really is, or at least what it isn't.

You have to be careful when checking references. Sometimes the party receiving the call may be suspicious as to who is calling and inquiring about a past or present staff (only in the case when you're almost sure you're going to hire the individual and when he gives you approval). To allay these suspicions, it is a good idea for you to allow the other party the courtesy of calling you back, which gives him at least some reassurance that you are who you say you are.

When checking out references, it's probably a good idea to begin with confirming dates of employment and perhaps job functions and management rank, etc.; then after the ice is broken and the party opens up, you can ask more judgmental questions regarding the candidate's performance and ability. Sometimes the referring party is unduly generous or is disinclined to say negative things about the former employee. If that is the case, it might be helpful to tell the referring party that you are thinking of placing the candidate into an extremely difficult and demanding position, which will require top performance and excellence. As it is not to the former employee/candidate's advantage to take on a position he cannot handle, probably the referring party will tend to be more frank and candid about his limitations and management weaknesses.

I once called up the president of a small Japanese company and got a very strong recommendation from him concerning the Japanese we were introducing to our client. After about six months on the new job, the man wasn't working out as well as expected. Upon confronting the individual about his lack of performance, he admitted to me that he had been fired from the small Japanese company but his wife was the daughter of the owner-president!

Along these same lines, you should always be careful when getting a reference from an employee's current employer. In this land of lifetime employment, it can be pretty difficult to get rid easily of an unsatisfactory employee. So if the company was finally successful in persuading an individual to go out and look for a new job, is it likely that they would give him a poor recommendation when he found a strong prospect? That is why it is important to go back and check with the previous employer and ideally the one before that as well.

Be sensitive to gaps in resumes where there is not a continuing flow of dates. Dates should be exact, at least stipulating the month and year, if not date of the hire. (Months are not critical if the candidate has only worked in one company.) You may find that in the job interview the candidate managed to change the subject and dodge around certain subjects. Go back to these areas and watch for signs of anxiety or nervousness on the face or body movements of the candidate.

Special effort should also be directed toward avoiding the hiring of individuals with above-average interest and experience in the trade union movement. Since Japanese firms investigate so thoroughly, it can become virtually impossible for union radicals to get a job in a Japanese company. Especially if they speak a few words of English, guess where they rush to find jobs? That's right, to your firm.

Strong recommendations and introductions from employees already in the company can be good and are definitely advantageous. They're not quite enough, however. One of my labor consulting expatriate clients told me about an accountant who was strongly recommended and introduced by his right-hand Japanese secretary. She'd worked about six months with the Japanese female accountant in another company about two years before. The secretary had said that the accountant was mature, seasoned, pleasant, and very hard working. She was indeed hard working and worked especially hard at embezzling (admittedly small amounts of money) at two of her former employers. Beware of unabashed charm and pleasantries—they're often a camouflage for incompetence, or in this case even dishonesty.

If you've read some of my earlier articles in this series, you've seen that when there are insufficient grounds to take disciplinary discharge actions against an employee, often the employee can be disposed of most readily on the basis of a "recommended resignation," or forced resignation but with avoiding dismissal, shameful litigation and loss of face to the individual. There are quite a few of these people on the labor market. Watch out for them when they write on their resumes that they resigned. Technically speaking, they are not lying, but I don't think you want them in your firm.

And when getting references from a former employer, be sure to ask the million dollar question that tends to focus perspective and get to the bottom of things in a phone conversation, which generally is limited to taking two or three minutes of the other party's time. Ask the candidate's former boss if he was a consistently high performer and if he would reemploy him. Unless he answers with an unqualified yes and goes on to add something like "He was terrific, and I wouldn't hesitate to re-employ him tomorrow." I think you'd better keep checking or perhaps hesitate to hire the man. Unfortunately, in Japan it is sometimes difficult to get such frank and decisive responses from Japanese even when a native Japanese is making the reference check.

Also keep in mind that it is just common sense that no employee except a stupid one or a masochist would offer a potential employer an unfavorable letter of recommendation. You can assume the worst, though, when letters of recommendation come from local politicians or well-known community figures with nothing substantive coming from former supervisors or bosses. Watch out for letters which only praise the personality but don't mention about work performance. If the letter ever says, "He chose to resign." or says anything about "Unfortunate circumstances surrounding the employee's decision to leave us..." or has the phrase "Unfortunate personality clash...," be on your guard.

Also watch out for letters of recommendation coming from former peers or for statements such as, "She was good at detailed work." or "was creative with good ideas." Either of the latter statements might indicate that an individual lacks common sense or a practical orientation toward getting the job done.

Tactics towards successful selection
and avoiding hiring pitfalls

What are some other pitfalls to watch out for when interviewing and hiring employees in Japan?

As in any country, there are a number of personality types that deserve caution when interviewing and when deciding to hire a candidate. In Japan we have the particular issue of English language ability. It definitely does take a lot of work to be able to speak a foreign language fluently, unless there were special circumstances such as living abroad when young or working abroad later in life. When a Japanese speaks English extremely well—especially if he has not lived abroad, it can be expected that there may be some trade off with other skills.

On the other hand, if a conscientious individual spent the time studying English that most other Japanese might spend playing mahjong, drinking with the boys or watching television, it's conceivable that the individual could become extremely fluent and would, nevertheless, be a very solid individual with good work and management experience.

It is important, however, to approach such fine English speakers with some degree of caution. Many of them have learned how to appeal personally to foreigners and have learned to say the type of things the expatriate manager wants to hear. Criticism of the Japanese and their way of doing things, although at times sounding like music to the ears, is probably an undesirable trait. So I would at least ask the candidate some directed questions as to why he feels that way about his own people. In our interviews, particularly among young candidates coming from abroad, we frequently run into this.

It is not a good sign, and it often indicates that the individual takes up this frame of mind to rationalize his own inability to get along with others and work with the group. In the end, you will find that this same individual may not be a cooperative, productive, and effective team player even if he would be on a team exclusively made up of foreigners.

On the other hand, to be suspicious that someone is not competent, results-oriented, and effective just because he speaks good English is also a mistake and not at all fair to the top-notch and high-quality individuals who can fit in and blend in perfectly in terms of both cultures' working environments, societies, and personal relationships.

In any country, people already in an organization will often feel threatened and not be overly receptive to the entry of a new member. This is especially true when the individual is a very sharp and appealing personality. People already in the organization may feel threatened that this individual will make inroads in their area of responsibility and be rewarded with the incumbent's job or a position of supervisory responsibility.

In Japan, especially when the candidate or new employee speaks English particularly well, there is often some (justified) fear on the part of Japanese already in the organization that the good English speaker may be able to better appeal to expatriate management in the organization and perhaps persuade management to adopt his policies or at least elicit stronger friendships. We have seen some cases where the result is that Japanese already in an organization have either blackballed or failed to recommend highly a good candidate or have in other ways thrown a monkey wrench into the works in an attempt to break down the matchmaking process.

Some time ago we introduced an extremely strong and well-qualified candidate. Expatriate management and the personnel department thought highly of the individual. The manager already in the organization, who would essentially be the candidate's boss, was sharp and sophisticated enough not to openly speak ill of the individual. In fact, he gave him quite a strong recommendation. If we hadn't discovered it, however, his boss-to-be would have been successful in causing the candidate to change his mind about the position and the company.

By telling our candidate that he would have very little authority in his new position and that there would be little room to take initiative, offer input, and change policy, etc., the superior turned off our candidate. He lost interest and judged that he would be better off in his current position. We were able to get to the bottom of this matter, however. Then both the Japanese in the personnel department, other Japanese in the organization, and expatriate management convinced our candidate that the description and evaluation of the position from his future boss was inaccurate and distorted.

At the same time, it was pointed out to the organization's boss that management was "surprised" at his description of the position; and, of course, everyone made a mental note that in the future there might be friction and unpleasantness that could be explained by the boss' defensive attitude. On the positive side, however, management realized the importance of making the current boss aware of his strengths, thus allaying his fears and insecurities.

In a rather similar case an employee already in an organization felt threatened and not pleased that a very capable individual was coming in as a mid-career hire, and that this decreased his own chances of winning a top position in the company. He therefore said some rude and rather tasteless things in order either to insult the candidate or make him feel that if the new company were comprised of socially inept staff such as himself, it would turn the candidate off and he would not consider the job offer.

At still another company, without opposing the new entrant in the interview, an incumbent manager spoke ill of the company's business plan and of the quality of the human resources and the foreign management running the organization. This, of course, turned off our candidate until we were able to clear the air.

For reasons such as the above, it is extremely important that for both the client's and the candidate's benefit we stay in close touch with both parties. It's important to ask many questions and try to focus in on any future potential problems. Once there was an extremely competent *kacho* in the leading Japanese competitor. Both the client and we had assumed that the only way we could get him out of his present position was to offer him a substantial increase of some 40% in salary as well as a position at the top of the marketing organization in the receiving company.

Everything seemed to be going well, and the candidate was definitely happy with the offer of increased salary. But then suddenly he began to get cold feet and back out of the new and challenging position. We were finally able to determine that he felt genuinely concerned about being only 41 years and having to go in over a couple of adequate but less promising 50-year-olds already in the marketing organization.

We adjusted the job description, however, creating a *jicho* job for him in "marketing, planning, and execution." He was given the same backing that was originally intended from the top of the organization and was, nevertheless, able to operate effectively by making most key marketing and sales decisions yet having the final implementation orders come from the foreign representative director. This is a typical example of the need to have the job fit the man.

If a Japanese executive speaking in English rambles and says illogical things, which don't always seem to be on the mark, you must be careful not to excuse this for his difficulties with the language and culture. Chances are he may be just as illogical in Japanese. Watch out for someone who can't pursue a discussion to a logical conclusion.

Some of the charming English speakers or non-English speakers when speaking in Japanese with other Japanese, can be just as skillful in capitalizing on the "halo effect," as are charmers and striking personalities in any country. The halo effect would be that situation in which all skills and judgments concerning and individual are rated high because the interviewer and interviewee had established a high degree of rapport.

I would also be careful of someone who compliments you on your suit or your tie or perhaps tells the receptionist jokes. Such unmitigated charm is often a cover-up for lack of competence and ability. Although it is important to be able to get along with others, too strong a desire to be liked and to please is not a characteristic we welcome when we want honest and original input from executives who should be able to think and stand on their own.

You should be suspicious when on paper an executive looks absolutely fantastic, yet his salary expectations are less than what the market would bear. This may be evidence that either his resume is distorted or he may be selling himself short because he is short on ability and proven track record. Also be careful of individuals who have worked several cities with different firms here in Japan. They may be running from themselves, if nothing else. Although advertising, public relations, personnel, and marketing are important jobs, often people attracted to these areas may have less ability to go out and really get things done.

When one of our clients changed a foreign branch into a Japanese corporation, and due to continued growth decided that a personnel manager would be necessary, instead of going to the outside job market, he picked a high-performing and well-liked salesman who had been in the company for years and knew almost everything.

Particularly since the switch over to local corporation was accompanied by some negative adjustments in benefits, restructuring of compensation and cut back in the payment coefficient of the lump-sum retirement benefit, the American president wanted to make sure that he had a man who could "sell" all these programs. When such changes have to be made, there is usually more acceptance when someone already in the organization makes them rather than an outsider brought in.

I'd also like to discuss briefly developing relationships with university professors with the intention of using this liaison as a recruiting tool to get well-qualified fresh college graduates. This is definitely the way to go to build up the right kind of human resources in Japan. Do note, however, that especially while your company is still small and lacks credibility in the eyes of the professor, since in fact you have just begun to come to him for recruiting, etc., it is unlikely that he would give you one of his best students. In this sense, watch out for the first impression you make when it comes to college recruiting. Since first impressions are long-lasting, it's probably better to wait until your operation is bigger hopefully with a couple hundred employees and bricks and mortar.

Also once you accept one of his students, it becomes rather difficult to dismiss him, and there's a tendency to be stuck with these people for years and years while they continue to be unproductive. This down side of the introduction, though, is probably outweighed by the other benefits of developing good relations with university campuses and cultivating your own loyal staff from within.

Persuading reluctant Japanese to sign on

What approaches and tactics can help persuade a reluctant Japanese to join a foreign firm?

If the candidate is sharp and as good a man as you need to help you grow and prosper in this difficult and challenging marketplace, probably the biggest attraction for a man already in your field or one who is familiar with it is to have a good product, a good business plan, and a full commitment to doing business here. In addition to satisfying a candidate that these fundamentals are acceptable, there are a number of other ways in which to persuade a candidate to join your organization.

If you are a huge multinational corporation or a firm with a reputation recognized worldwide, capitalize on this. If you have an organization of considerable size and track record here in Japan, you may be able to argue that while you can undoubtedly provide stability and long-term job security, you can also offer a man more challenge and stimulation than he would normally enjoy at his age in a Japanese organization. The same can be true of salary level. For example, the other day we had lunch with a 39-year-old Japanese vice-president, who had a contract package of ¥21.5 million with ¥18 in cash compensation. This fast-tracker must be the envy of all his college buddies, generally making between ¥8 and ¥12 million at the very most in top Japanese firms.

If you are appealing to highly specialized engineers and technicians, you may be able to attract an individual merely on the basis of the merits of your state-of-the-art technology or the specific project goal in Japan. Your company may be employing new and different technology that is of great interest to the candidate. There definitely are extremely competent people who are impatient with waiting until their 40s and 50s before they can net an executive position in the true sense. Traditionally, this last point has been one of the strongest appeals made by foreign firms to young Japanese.

We've had a number of candidates who haven't been excited about our multinational clients until we mentioned that as part of the new career path there would be anywhere from one month's to one year's training and orientation abroad. This is definitely a psychological enticement, particularly for a young staff member or manager who has spent little time abroad. And from management's point of view, it is a rather economical way to get a good man to sign up with your company. Sometimes the full cost of sending a man to the head office is much less than the cost in management time needed to keep the individual interested and busy.

If the Japanese visitor's English is good enough, however, home office training provides an opportunity for people at the head office to learn about Japan. More importantly, the trainee's experience abroad is of great value to Japanese operations in that his English will be greatly improved and he tends to become more understanding and tolerant of head office policies and needs.

Remember that the appearance of success is as important and critical to most people, as is its reality. Generally the greater the real power of an executive, the less his concern for outward manifestations and symbols of success. Nonetheless, since we're all human, it might be possible to attract a given candidate with the title of *torishimariyaku*, or member of the board of directors (see an earlier article in this series).

We have also known of cases where membership in the American Club was sufficient psychological enticement to nudge a candidate onto the company's side. Many foreign businessmen tend to take that club for granted. But it has become more and more difficult for Japanese to join, and it's a nice place for Japanese to be able to show off to former associates and old friends from school days, who are possibly impressed with the new status of their cosmopolitan friend.

It is true, in general, then that fringe benefits and various perks are extremely important to executives. They may be less important to the Japanese or at least perhaps generally less available so that the size of the office, quality of furnishings, thickness of carpet, etc. are not generally brought into play the way they would be in a decision to change jobs by executives outside Japan.

The corner office with windows facing the park, etc. will often make the difference between acceptance or rejection of a new position in the West. You may recall that in the midst of Chrysler's financial difficulties the president, Lee Iacocca, willingly accepted a salary cut to $1 per year from a former annual salary of $360,000. However, he would not give up any of his perquisites, such as club memberships and use of the company jet, etc.

Probably, however, at the level that Japanese are generally hired to work in foreign capitalized firms here, more relevant factors are the candidate's perception that he will be able to have honest, sincere, and frank dealings with his boss, whether Japanese or foreigner. Often a good man will leave his present company because he feels for various reasons, including that of *habatsu*, or factionalism, school ties, etc., he has been left out of the inner circle of movers and shakers in his firm. If this same individual feels he can be a key man in your organization and break into your inner circle, then he is ready to take a job with you.

We once had a case with a highly skilled scientist/engineer who wasn't concerned very much at all about a salary increase when switching jobs. He was content with the salary he was already making at a Japanese manufacturer as long as he was able to get a written guarantee that he would have a research and development budget of "X" yen in order to pursue research that interested him and that the company wanted him to get under way.

In another case a candidate was disappointed in the salary differential he would receive in making his move. We were able to convince him to join the company, however, because the company did, in fact, intend to put a good deal of money into his training, including giving him his own budget to purchase books and manuals from the United States, sending him to the United States for training, and making up for the comparative lack of salary increase, and title promotion or jump in formal organizational status, with liberally applied doses of informal recognition and ego massaging—both the expatriate representative director and key Japanese in the organization made sure they made the individual feel welcome and important.

This brings us to another point. When considerable time is spent wining and dining a candidate who is considering joining your firm, it is important that this behavior not stop immediately once the man has resigned from his former position and is working for you. There are enough disappointing and disturbing discoveries when taking on a new job, and it doesn't help when one feels that he has been betrayed in that the company's attitude while courting him was considerably different from that displayed after the marriage.

A couple of years back one of our clients had a interesting incentive program, which was designed to attract very good salesmen. The company told young Japanese salesman interested in joining them that if they reached 90% of their sales goals each year, they would be able to go to one of five different countries of their choice, including well-traveled spots such as Korea, Taiwan, and the Philippines.

This appeared to be a very thoughtful and generous approach and definitely had high appeal to aggressive and high-profile salesmen, who were also confident enough to work on that company's commission sales incentive program. For three or four years, this program was seen to be assisting not only recruiting but also sales levels within the organization; not a few of the salesmen would earn as much as 130 or 140% of their sales goals.

At one point, though, a new Asian regional vice president of sales joined the company from the U.S. home office and decided that business was good enough that the company could afford to provide a plane ticket for the wives of salesmen who achieved 100% or more of their sales goals. A personal letter signed by the president was sent home to the wives inviting them to accept the offer with a cash refundable airplane ticket also enclosed.

As a result, sales activity suddenly dipped off when salesmen began to approach the 90% target. They were deliberately holding off below 100% fulfillment of their objective. Not only did the salesmen prefer not to travel with their wives, but also it became virtually impossible for a salesman to go on his own once his wife found out that both tickets could be refunded for cash. This shows the importance of developing the right incentive program, depending on the realistic needs and desires of the targeted party.

I'd like to tell one more anecdote about creative approaches toward persuading people you need to join your firm. One of my clients has a situation where his company has a distinct career path with specific requirements for certain high-level professional staff. Back in the United States they will take promising research staff from the best universities, telling them that they have a chance to move on up the career ladder providing they perform well for two or three years and go on to get an M.B.A. successfully at one of U.S.'s most prestigious business schools.

This system works fine in the United States where an employer could never be troubled by employees digging in their heels and claiming that they were "regular" employees subject to lifetime employment security. In Japan, however, an employee without a specific term employment contract is considered to be a regular employee who cannot easily be dismissed from his job (as has been discussed in detail in earlier articles of this series). The client knew that it would be extremely difficult to persuade top young Japanese graduating from the best universities here to join a firm that insists upon placing the employees on a one-year term contract, since by doing so the employee is being robbed of his one-chance shot at getting a job in a leading firm with superior cash wages and far higher lifetime earnings.

Thus, the company had started out in Japan without hiring such research staff on a temporary contract. The firm began to sense, however, that it might have a potential problem as the first couple of employees hired were moving into their second and third years and were not showing enough promise to move up to the next highest professional slot. In the United States that would normally mean that the person had to get out of the organization. The company began to picture having 10 or 15 only semicompetent female and male "researchers" burned out and pitter-pattering around the office in slippers, primarily drinking tea and watering the plants every day.

We came up with an innovative program which would apply not only to future hires, but also we were successful in getting those already on the payroll to sign off on the scheme. The employees were hired on a one-year temporary contract renewable for a maximum of three years. The company would deduct a certain percentage of their paycheck each month and match that with company funds, plus assist the employees in getting student loans, applying to good stateside business schools, and lending them money as necessary to cover the difference between the loans and tuition costs. One-third the regular salary would also be paid to the employees while they were at the business school.

The company would go on to offer employees a job during the summer between their first and second year at school in the United States and, upon successful completion of business school, would guarantee a job in the United States for six months to one year after graduation. If the business school graduate then went back to Japan and worked satisfactorily for one year, the firm would write off any outstanding tuition costs and pay on behalf of the students. (Note, however, that payroll deductions for a period of two years after graduation from business school were designed to cover about one-half of tuition costs.)

This program was clearly defined for all researcher graduates coming out of Japanese undergraduate schools and had credibility in that minimal payroll deductions were made from the very start of employment. What with the opportunity, guidance, and clear direction toward earning a valuable M.B.A., and the attraction of working in the United States for a summer and six months to a year after graduation, the company was able to neutralize the negative effect from placing these employees on the one-year temporary employment contract. The new employees were willing to go along with the contract in view of the total scheme and package.

This is one example of an innovative way of persuading a certain type of employee to join your firm, although, admittedly, it is based on somewhat special circumstances. However, the lure of special education, training, and work experience should not be underestimated for plucking top-caliber Japanese out of both university and corporate positions.

Problems with employee loan and secondment issues in joint ventures

In Japan particularly at joint ventures and banks as well as at a wide range of employers there seems to be a common practice of loaning personnel, or secondment. Can you talk about this as an alternative method of recruiting? Are there problems to watch out for?

Secondment, or loan of personnel, is quite common in any joint venture or organization that has a close relationship with another organization. Among multinational firms in Japan, often a joint venture will be staffed by the Japanese partner, or a company will either ask for trained staff from a Japanese organization with which it has a close relationship, or, similarly, a closely related Japanese company may at times try to place some of its employees in a foreign capitalized firm.

It is important to be realistic about what is going on here. It is unlikely that any Japanese company will second its very best employees to a foreign operation or a joint venture company. There may be some exceptions in the case of young staff where experience in a joint venture or in a wholly owned foreign subsidiary may be seen as a worthwhile stage in a key employee's career path or perhaps even as an opportunity to gather sensitive or even confidential information. I've had one case in the past in which this was a problem.

To a large extent the loan of middle-aged and older executives is really tantamount to an in-house outplacement service. It is often said that a Japanese company will not second its very best human resources, nor will it send other employers the bottom of the barrel. Seconded employees, therefore, tend to be of average performance and ability. In that sense, it is an interesting option to hiring your own staff; however, it would be a mistake to think that you can get the same quality individual who will really make a difference in your operation in the way that you might if able to identify and pick out your own candidate either directly or through an executive recruiting firm.

Typically, when personnel are loaned the understanding between the receiving company and the dispatched individual should be that the loanee still maintain his official position, or *seki*, with his former employer and that accrual toward his retirement benefit, etc. will take place there with, of course, the assumption that he will return to the lending company. In this scenario, the practice has been that the individual is obligated to obey the Rules of Employment of the receiving company, as they pertain to duties and obligations and disciplinary measures, etc., as well as hours of work, days of paid holiday, and so on. Depending upon the nature of the contract that may exist between the lending and the borrowing firm, however, it may or may not be possible to send the employee immediately back to the firm from which he came.

In my labor consulting practice I have seen some disturbing applications of secondment. In one case, for example, the lending company put off the return of their employee for three or four years. They banked on the good will of the multinational firm, which did indeed have quite a close relationship with the Japanese organization and was, therefore, careful not to queer the relationship over minor issues such as the absorption of an employee who really does not fit in and whom the receiving company would have preferred to send back to the lending firm. Often the lending firm will not clearly state that it has washed their hands of the seconded employee, expecting him to now be an employee of the multinational client.

Behind the scenes, however, it appears that they will often encourage the seconded employee to confuse expatriate managers by arguing that he is covered by the Rules of Employment of the receiving company and, therefore, is an employee on the payroll of the receiving company. If a number of years have elapsed during which time the seconded employee was receiving regular paychecks and pay increases, etc., from the receiving company, you can appreciate why matters can get a bit fuzzy.

In another case, a client had about 50 employees, 20 of whom came from the joint venture partner, which was one of Japan's largest manufacturers. Based on the foreign party's technology, local assembly and, later on, manufacturing were to be carried out in the Tohoku Region of northeast Japan. Technicians and sales engineers, as well as some administrative staff were to be loaned from the local factory operation to the head office. Additional staff from the parent company in Tokyo were also loaned to the Tokyo office of this joint venture operation. Since salary levels were lower in the Tohoku Region, originally there was provision for the employees coming from that outlying area to enjoy a 10% increase in salary so that they could live in Tokyo at their accustomed standard of living.

As the years went by, however, a situation developed where the salary differentials between what the seconded employees would be making at the Japanese parent company and the levels at the joint venture differed by as much as 15 to 80% for seconded employees who had been in the Tokyo joint venture operation anywhere from one to six years. Generally, the longer the employee had been in the joint venture, the greater the differential.

All of this was allowed and tolerated until the joint venture itself began to lose money seriously and siphon off considerable cash from the parent company. At this point, attention was directed to redressing the differences in salaries because the tremendous gap in salary level had begun to impose problems on morale when employees from the joint venture were placed back in the parent company at greatly reduced salary levels. Since the joint venture was also siphoning off cash, the Japanese parent company encouraged the foreign interest in the joint venture to eliminate all bonus payments to the Japanese who were over their own home company's salary levels and, if that wasn't enough, to actually cut back their salaries.

In the meantime, you can imagine that a number of the employees in the joint venture began to put pressure on the foreign representative director, saying that they considered themselves to be employees with the joint venture and did not want to be sent back to the parent company. This was particularly the case for the older employees in their late 40s and early 50s who were hoping that if this argument were swallowed, they would be able to cash in on the higher payment coefficient of lump-sum retirement benefit scale as well as the superior basis of calculation (the weight of pensionable income, or basic salary, was greater at the joint venture due to the absence of various allowances).

The top executive in charge of the joint venture during this period happened to be a foreigner. The Japanese partner expected him to implement this drastic cut back in bonus and salary instantly. The decision was, therefore, made in haste, and it occurred to me at the time that perhaps the Japanese partner would not have been too upset if the foreigner's decision had led to a union organization drive because at that point the Japanese were probably ready to throw in the towel and close down the operation, anyway, and this would be an opportune time to do so and trim back an unneeded 20 employees.

Whether these suspicions were founded in fact or not, I advised that since the seconded employees were dispatched from the Japanese parent company, it was natural that any decisive actions to cut salaries should be implemented by a representative of the Japanese side. I even suggested that meetings be held at the Tokyo head office of the Japanese parent company to put the monkey on their back and to begin to build up circumstantial evidence that the umbilical link to the lent employees had not been severed and they were still the responsibility of the Japanese parent.

When the Japanese side realized that the foreign manager would not do their bidding, they immediately changed their tune and worked together to implement only a minor bonus cut and salary freeze on the seconded employees who were being too highly paid by the Japanese partner's standards.

I then recommended that we change the Rules of Employment of the joint venture to indicate that seconded employees were considered to officially maintain their *seki* with the lending company and that they were only covered by the joint venture's Rules of Employment insofar as stipulations covering hours, scheduling, duties, obligations, and disciplinary measures, etc. We also specifically stated in the Rules of Employment that unless a designated and official procedure and signing of documents took place, the employees would continue to remain on the payroll of the dispatching company.

This may give you some idea of the potential problems, and intricacies of involvement in secondment or personnel loans. As much as possible, I would encourage receiving foreign capitalized firms in Japan to have clear documents defining and controlling the secondment relationship. It would also be best to have the seconded employee paid by the lending company directly through his bank account rather than having paychecks come directly from the receiving company. The Japanese partner could then bill the joint venture. The scope of applicability clause of the Rules of Employment should state that while seconded employees are subject to certain controls regulating behavior and work requirements at the receiving company, they are, nonetheless, considered employees of the lending firm and, therefore, not entitled to the receiving firm's retirement benefits, etc.

Other than a master agreement concerning secondment status with the lending company, it would also make sense to have an individual letter of confirmation or intent, or a contract defining the receiving company's relationship with the lent employee. This letter should require the employee's acknowledgment that he is an employee of the dispatching company and is only at the receiving company at the receiving company's discretion and subject to the relationship as defined in the master agreement.

The documents defining the relationship need not be complicated legal documents. But a written document is useful in that it creates and defines expectations between the parties surrounding the employee loan as well as clarifies status for the benefit of the employee, who is often little more than a pawn between the lender and the borrower.

Interviewing techniques and how to evaluate and measure your candidate

Could you give us some coaching on how to evaluate executives in general and then, if possible, shed some light on the peculiarities of interviewing and appraising Japanese executives. What should we look for in an executive?

Having previously reminded you not to get carried away with a candidate's excellent English-speaking ability, I must add that it is just as important to be sure that you're not overly suspicious of the same individual. Look for a Japanese who can give you logical and reasonable explanations on any and all subjects. Let the candidate know that you're not satisfied with such approaches as "This is the way we do things in Japan," "This is the Japanese way," or "This may be difficult to understand for a foreigner."

Two Japanese talking together cannot win points with such statements, and you want to work with someone who is smart enough to realize that he must persuade and convince you with reason or based on the merits of his position.

I've come to believe that in the United States and in other Western countries it is generally possible to make a reasonably accurate judgment as to how well motivated, ambitious, and hard working an executive will be based upon how successful his father was and whether or not the individual feels he has at least exceeded the social and economic status of his father. Sociological research also validates this idea noting that often a son will slow down, become complacent and satisfied with his position in life when he feels he has achieved as much or more than his father.

Although this rough rule of thumb holds in Japan, I would suggest that it may not be quite as valid in that there is less father identification in this country. Certainly even during World War II, as depicted in vernacular movies, it was true that when the sons of Japan faced imminent danger or death, they screamed "Mother."

I also base my conclusion on many first-hand conversations with Japanese friends during my 18-year residence in this country. Inevitably Japanese speak more of their mothers, and when I ask them about their fathers, they say that they were rarely home and had very little or no relationship with them. (Of course, there are many exceptions to this.)

Anyone you hire should also have a good plausible reason to want to change jobs. When no convincing reason is offered, the truth can be that the person is not doing well in his current job or is moving for mercenary motives—considerably higher salary with you. Although a hefty salary increase is legitimate grounds for wanting to move, I think it is important that a candidate also have a plausible reason for wanting to join your company other than the salary motive. For example, he should be able to articulate that he's willing to leave his present company because your current business plan is attractive to him, he has always been interested in your industry, or perhaps because he feels there is more potential at your company to use his particular skills.

Other than the above, you should attempt to evaluate a Japanese executive just as you would evaluate one in your home country. It is important that you create a non-threatening atmosphere in which the candidate feels free to talk. Some interviewers claim that it is best to avoid taking notes on an initial interview since it often makes the candidate nervous. I've found, however, that note-taking is indispensable and that often a candidate is flattered when you take notes because it indicates to him that you think he is saying something worth recording.

You'll want a Japanese with good work ethic values, a high degree of motivation, high energy level, sensitivity to others, and an ability to maintain good human relations. This last point is especially true in a country where team or group play is especially important.

You'll also want to find someone who is highly resistant to stress and pressure. I would hesitate, for example, to hire a candidate who has a history of problems with ulcers, which is sometimes evidence that an individual has difficulty in handling his job, or his life.

No matter how energetic and accomplished a person may be on the golf course or tennis court, you'll want someone who puts the vast majority of his energy into his work. Responsible personal financial management is important, and frequent job change or other instability in key relationships (marriage, etc.) may be evidence of emotional immaturity or poor judgment. You'll want to look for someone who's compatible with yourself and your current management team, someone who shares common ideals, loyalties and identification to the corporate goal or cause.

To the Japanese it may seem that foreign firms have not been successful in creating their own corporate culture here in Japan, and this is perhaps one reason why Japanese may not thrive and perform as well in the environment of a foreign firm. Just like in your home country, you'll want someone who dresses and acts the part of an executive with your firm. Contrived and cosmetic individuality may be evidence of an inability to get along with others on their terms.

Participative management is a must in Japan. So if you are to have any success with the Japanese executive coming in as a mid-career hire, make sure that a number of key Japanese executives within your firm have an opportunity to meet the new man before a decision is made. This, of course, tends to place ownership where it belongs and prevents your company's executives from having an excuse not to cooperate with the new manager.

It's a good idea to ask questions about specific achievements and reasons for joining and leaving his present firm. Particularly in Japan, the opinion of the wife can be extremely important since in the home Asian women are unexpectedly strong; and, in fact, most Japanese husbands hand over their paychecks to their wives who give them back a modest monthly allowance.

Whether or not the wife opposes her husband's job change can be a significant factor in your success in convincing the man to join your firm. Our other search consultants and I have spent no few hours on the phone with wives explaining about a new position in an attempt to allay some of the better half's doubts and misgivings.

Just as in your home country you'll want to find a Japanese executive who has learned to channel his hostilities and frustrations in a positive and constructive direction. A sense of humor is also helpful. A proven record of perseverance and determination with a desire to finish a task begun are also traits to look for—job hoppers are generally not a good risk. If a candidate avoids answering a reasonable question, there is usually a reason, so further checking of his background is called for.

On an initial interview, sometimes it seems difficult to get a Japanese executive to open up and speak in a frank and free-flowing manner. You must not give up trying, however, and continue to ask both direct and indirect questions. The Japanese language and interpersonal behavioral relations dictate that one should pause more often than he would in the West. It's a good idea, for example, to provide numerous opportunities for a Japanese listener to give his own views and feedback. The give and take or pace in a conversational exchange between two Japanese is much slower. Remember, too, that they will not interrupt as frequently, nor will they be as likely to contradict the other party.

Thus, if an expatriate manager is interested in working with and understanding a candidate, he should slow down, avoid giving away his views and drawing conclusions until he has heard the views of the candidate before him.

Just as in any other country, there are a number of interesting questions that could be asked a candidate. Be sure you ask about job objectives, past and desired future levels of authority, reporting relationships, and the candidate's regular duties and responsibilities in his current job, his occasional duties, and other questions concerning special working conditions, such as how the candidate is disposed toward domestic or foreign travel.

Don't forget the six basic questions about education and job—what, when, where, who, why and how. For example, you might want to ask what skills were needed to accomplish a given task or where were the skills applicable, why was a certain decision made or how did the executive solve a given problem.

Watch out for telegraphing expected answers to the applicant by asking rhetorical questions. If you pose a question to an applicant such as "You have the necessary experience in semi-conductor marketing, don't you?", you are sure to elicit a positive response even if the applicant's experience is inadequate.

Likewise, you should be careful of intimidating the applicant. Using a hostile tone of voice, setting up traps to catch inconsistencies, etc. are used by some interviewers to test the candidate's stamina, but such "stress interviewing" tactics are rarely successful.

Also avoid testing out technical vocabulary on non-technical applicants. Be sure to listen, and beware of doing all the talking (which can be easy to fall into when the candidate's English is weak).

As for interviewing procedures, the "sequential" interview is the situation in which low-ranking managers first interview candidates, and if they seem qualified, they are passed on up to the top. The disadvantage of this is that a lower-level interviewer may mistakenly reject a good candidate due to his own lack of experience or poor judgment.

The "serialized" interview is the scenario in which a number of managers will interview a candidate, each of them filling out an interview form. They will then meet and compare their summary sheets on a final candidate. The advantage of the serialized interview is that the manager to whom the new employee will be reporting can base his decisions on the perspectives and evaluations of many managers, uncovering different facts and perhaps tempering personal biases. The down side is that this is time consuming and can delay the decision, resulting in the loss of a good candidate.

The "panel" interview would be the format in which several related executives would interview the candidate at the same time. There is no need to establish a pattern for asking questions, and the spontaneous interaction will often assure that key questions will not be missed by a single interviewer.

When approaching a candidate in this way, however, it is important that panelists be reminded that even if more senior in rank, it is unwise for a single individual to dominate the interviewing session.

TMT is pleased to provide its executive recruitment clients with helpful guides and forms such as an "interview summary sheet," a "structured interview guide," and an "interviewer's self-evaluation checklist."

Interviewing may seem to be quite straightforward requiring only good intuition and common sense, but there are some basic things that should be kept in mind. Certainly there is nothing wrong with following your intuition and hunches. Frankly speaking, at times even the most professional executive recruiter must fall back on these intuitive skills when selecting between two seemingly equally qualified candidates.

At times after only a half hour or less, it will become quite clear to you that the candidate is not what you're looking for. If that is your gut reaction, there is no sense in wasting more time. Remember, you don't have to drink all the wine to know that it's turned to vinegar.

Other ways an executive recruitment firm can help you

What are some of the advantages of using a good headhunter?

A good executive recruitment firm should assist a client in determining whether a search is really necessary. Some of the first questions we will ask the client are: "Are you sure there's no one in the organization who could handle the job? Is it possible that functions and jobs could be rearranged so that the position can be covered by managers already working with you?"

Sometimes a decision to recruit an individual can serve as a trigger or excuse to implement change or restructuring and streamlining of a corporate organization.

As we focus in on a position description with a client, this process also helps the client to define the job and executive specifications. Sometimes by discussing the assignment and asking questions, the client comes up with a different and more clear perspective of the job and the individual required to do it.

A good executive recruiter also has the responsibility to access accurately and divine the corporate culture. Sometimes the view of an outside consultant can be helpful to the client company since we can more objectively assist our client in understanding the peculiarities and particular needs of his organization.

A good executive search consultant is alert toward taking into consideration differences among various organizations. For example, a candidate presently working in a large and structured organization may not be able to perform as well in a small unstructured organization where he must stand alone without capable and experienced subordinates as back-up staff.

It is important to find someone who is neither over- nor under-qualified to do the job. There's no need to recruit a top-notch executive for an undemanding position. Similarly, if you want to hire a second-rate executive at a lower salary, you may find that he is incapable of getting on top of the task at hand.

You'll find that your executive recruiter will also be able to give you valuable assistance and insight in tailoring the job to the executive, rather than force-fitting the executive into an unsuitable position. In addition, the frank and open dialogue the candidate naturally has with the recruiter provides highly useful information when passed on to the client, allowing him to fully understand what the candidate feels he is capable of doing, as well as how he feels he can personally make the greatest and most effective contribution to your company.

As described in detail in earlier installments of this series, the role of the executive search firm should include more than research of the job market and identification and appraisal of suitable candidates. Most worthwhile executives are fully engaged and active in contributing to their firms and building up their own careers. There is no time or inclination in their lives to look at help wanted ads in newspapers.

Using a variety of methods described earlier in this series, after contacting a prospective candidate, we then face the difficult job of interesting him enough to have an initial meeting with the client. Further, we investigate the candidate not only in terms of past job experience and track record, but also make sure that his chemistry suits your firm.

We are able to do this particularly if we have a chance to meet someone at the client firm who was recently promoted. Generally, such fast-tracking employees within a given organization tend to represent and define the corporate culture at least in terms of executive style, communicative skills, dress, mannerisms, etc. Similarly, by meeting Japanese in the client's organization, we can get a feeling as to what type of executive behavior is rewarded and will potentially succeed within the organization.

Our clients and candidates have found that it is helpful to be able to turn to a third party whose own success hinges on effecting the best union between client and candidate. When required, it is the role of the executive recruiter to do the "dirty work" on salary negotiations so that the involved parties can save face in this delicate bargaining process. Hence, the candidate can maintain his dignity and the client company can avoid the danger of bruising the candidate's ego by offering a too-low salary.

Because of our deep involvement and interest in arranging good employee/employer unions, we naturally accept the responsibility of a continuing role as third-party intermediaries to delicate problem situations between the client company and its new employee.

In one case, for example, a Japanese executive we introduced was finding it difficult to achieve results at the new firm due to a lack of cooperation from two or three key managers at the company. The new executive, however, had a very strong technical background as well as a proven record in marketing the highly technical product. His English was not strong, however, and he was unable to communicate in English his frustration to the expatriate representative director. He asked us to help him, and we felt it was our responsibility to assist him, by gathering full information from him in the Japanese language, which enabled us to convey a clear message to the representative director.

We suspected that since the new executive did not speak English, Japanese executives at the firm felt that they were reasonably safe in failing to cooperate with the new manager in a number of subtle ways, because he would not be able to communicate this directly to the representative director. We were able to communicate on behalf of our candidate, however, and the expatriate manager understood and solved the problem through organizational restructuring and coaching of his staff without ever revealing that he had received negative reports from the new manager.

IV

For a Change of Pace, Other Views on Japan and How It Works

1

What's Wrong with America? What's Right about Japan?— All over Dinner and Drinks

"Mr. Nevins, my name is Harold Edwards. I'm visiting Japan for just a few days. I've got a new assignment with regional responsibilities for Asia. Our local American here in Japan gave me a copy of your book published by the Japan Times, *Labor Pains and the Gaijin Boss*, and suggested I contact you directly. Any chance we could get together for some orientation here at the Imperial Hotel?"

"Fine, is there anything in particular you're interested in?"

"I don't think I want to get too involved with the labor law and with technicalities in setting up work rules and compensation packages, etc. Our man here simply suggested that the additional insight you could provide would be well worth the time and your fee."

"Good. I'll see what I can do. Evenings would be fine with me and probably convenient for you, too."

We agreed to meet two nights later. He had me go directly up to his room.

"What would you like to drink? I can give you a beer or a vodka gimlet with lime juice."

"I'll try the mixed drink."

"Mr. Nevins, just why has Japanese industry been so successful? I kind of hesitate to show my ignorance in front of Rogers, the local head of our Japan operations. I'm in charge of 12 countries now, and I simply don't have the time to read about Japan as I should."

"I think that fundamentally the fact that Japan is a small nation, so lacking in most resources, has convinced the Japanese people that theirs is a poor nation extremely vulnerable to the outside world. Actually Japan is larger than most European nations and is 1/3 larger than both England and West Germany. Unfortunately, the Japanese see themselves on a small island which happens to be sandwiched between the four largest countries in the world—the Soviet Union,

China, Canada, and the U.S. After centuries of isolation, because Japan was so suddenly and forcefully opened up, I think her response to the outside industrialized Western powers was more planned and decisive than that of most countries which moved much more slowly and were often subject to colonial rule."

"When did Perry come to Japan? Wasn't it right around the Civil War?"

"1858, and the *shogun* was overthrown, with the modern Meiji government established in 1867. Before that they carried swords and wore pigtails. Japan was well aware of the way China had been cut up by the West. Some Japanese may not want to admit it but their cultural roots and so much they copied, including the written language, come from China. Korean influence is also great. But the Japanese were indeed a proud people and extremely aware of their unique cultural and national identity. They looked at the West and learned from the West, absorbing all they could."

"Probably the advances made in those earlier days represented quantum leaps in industrialization and productivity that far surpass even Japan's post-war achievements."

"That's a good point. I guess the difference is that the starting point was so low that in terms of non-military, pure economic power; it was only in the last 15 or 20 years that Japan has really been able to pose the sort of challenge that now has us all looking toward Tokyo for answers. It was always Japan that struggled to catch up. In the late 19th century, So many raw materials had to be purchased from abroad that Japan had no choice but to earn the necessary foreign exchange by attempting to sell as much as she bought. Unlike the United States, this has always forced the Japanese to be aware of foreign markets and to become adept at trade."

"I guess by comparison, resources were so cheap and plentiful in the States. that you could just throw up a fence, hire some hands, and stay in business. What's all this I hear about Japanese industry's long term view—something about debt as opposed to equity financing?"

"Although its been slowly changing, most corporate financing comes from bank debt. Whereas American stockholders are interested in a dividend payout or in increasing earnings per share on even a quarterly basis, a Japanese bank is more willing for a company to prosper and grow large in the long run. After all, the bank might prefer continuing interest payments to rapid loan repayment. Banking ties and relationships are also permanent in nature. If a company grows, it will borrow more money for capital outlays in plant and equipment."

"Where does all this money come from?"

"You've probably heard that Japanese savings as a percentage of disposable income are the highest of any major industrial nation. Something in the order of 20%, with France at 15%, West Germany 14%, and the U.K. around 11%. Americans are the biggest spenders with only about 5% savings. While the ratio in Japan has been increasing in recent years, it's been declining in the States."

"Yeah, but what's behind that high figure?"

"The Japanese people are certainly not cheap. I find them more willing to throw their money around than are most Europeans and Americans. When Japanese go out for a meal or drinking, they rarely go dutch. Usually there's a minor struggle, as they all fight to pay the bill. They can also spend a lot of money on brand names and luxuries. Since they don't usually entertain at home; they don't spend much on furnishings and home improvements—a big expense in the U.S. I believe that the payment of the winter and summer bonus twice a year is a big explanation for why they can save so much. It's really a system of forced savings."

"I thought the Japanese managers weren't paid merit bonuses, and this is one reason that they can take a long-term approach, and do what is really in the long run good for their corporations. At least I read this in an article somewhere recently."

Edwards knew he was right. He was so excited that he got out of his armchair and walked around it in a circle. When he realized what he was doing, he asked if I wanted anything from room service. I told him I was fine. "We'll be going down for dinner soon anyway." he reassured.

"You're absolutely right on the absence of that kind of quarterly merit bonuses. The bonus I was talking about is one that is paid out to all employees and managers. Merit evaluation would generally represent no more than about 10 to 20% of this bonus payment; but in cases of exceptional performance much more upside is possible, and little may be paid in exceptional cases of problem employees who also have little support from co-workers. After the war this form of bonus payment became institutionalized. It is negotiated as an averaged fixed number of months of basic salary. In large companies the amount is significant, generally ranging from five to even seven months of pay, distributed to all employees usually in December and June. In smaller companies the payment is more token, perhaps only two to three months throughout the year."

"Wouldn't employees rather have a high monthly salary dividing annual income by 12 instead of say 18?"

"Usually not. The bonus allows the housewife to have a monthly budget geared to the basic salary. When the large cash payment comes on twice a year, consumer durable can be bought; lump-sum repayments on housing loans are made; and probably about half of the bonus can be saved."

"What's all this we hear about Japan Inc.?"

"I think the belief that Japan Inc., or a close, cooperative relationship between government and private sector, is responsible for Japan's economic success, is just as dangerous as some of the earlier theories such as the belief that success is due to cheap wages, or the fact that Japan's factories were leveled during the war and rebuilt anew, while the U.S. continued to use obsolete machinery. American machinery probably averages about ten years older than Japan, but most of the markets, products, and industries taken over by Japan after the war didn't even exist in Japan before the war. This would be true of transistors, color TVs, mass consumer goods, autos, videos and most other sophisticated equipment. More recently it's been easy for Westerners, particularly the Germans, to credit Japan's success to hard work or working long hours. It is not that simple. In fact, while productivity has been increasing, labor force participation rates have been decreasing. People forget that productivity is defined as basic output divided by the basic labor input."

"I get it. What you're saying then is that Japan can't be productive due to hard work alone."

"That's right. New plant and equipment investment, mechanization and automation have allowed the Japanese to work less. The winner, therefore, is the one that reduces the labor input. Hard work alone can be counter-productive."

Edwards remembered that we'd gotten away from the Japan Inc. concept. "But we can always get back to that. On this productivity area, I've heard that the U.S. is still overall the most productive nation in the world."

"I guess that's right. Especially our agriculture seems to be what we do best. In fact, if you stop and think about it, it's almost as though we've become a colony of Japan. They're our biggest customer for our unprocessed foods and raw materials, and we're their best customer for their finished manufactured goods."

"I don't know if I like that." Twitching his neck to the side, Edwards stuck the eraser end of his pencil behind his ear, flicking it away from his head. A tuft of silver hair settled over the top of the upper rim of this ear. He leaned forward, looked me in the eyes and lowered his voice, "Oh, Tom, do you think there's conscious effort to shut out our products by this Japan Inc., or whatever you want to call it?"

"It probably doesn't even have to be a 'conscious effort'. Certainly some NTB, or Non-Tariff Barriers, would include the government bureaucrat who feels it's downright unpatriotic to buy a foreign product, but in general, the average person probably doesn't think that much about where a product is from. Certainly foreign consumer products of high quality can even enjoy an image advantage. The Japanese, however, are very discriminating consumers. I can't blame my Japanese friends' wives for rejecting and turning their noses up at much of the American-made clothing I would bring home from the States. Even expensive brands had uneven stitching, weak buttons, and threads hanging out here and there. We don't see this in Japan. It's sad but true. When it comes to dependability of supply, spare parts, and after service, most U.S. companies can't hold a candle to Japanese competitors. The reality is that these weaknesses have been equally responsible for Japanese wholesaler's and distributor's hesitation to take on U.S. products enthusiastically."

"So the market is no longer protected much by quotas and tariff duties?"

"That's right, but this extent of trade liberalization only came after each Japanese industry was strong enough to out compete most competition. It then came to Japan's advantage to be champions of free trade, as this position discourages and makes it harder for foreign countries to take protectionist measures against highly competitive Japanese products."

"I'd like some more input on how Japan got so competitively strong."

"Well Harold, basically it's the dynamism of the private sector. It's true that the Ministry of International Trade and Industry (MITI) does a considerable amount of coordination by way of 'administrative guidance.' But there are no teeth, and very little that is legally binding. MITI, for example, never really felt that Japan should build up a strong automobile industry, as it would compete head on with the U.S. The government felt that even higher value-added products, requiring less expensive imported raw materials should be developed."

"Obviously Toyota and Datsun didn't listen."

"No, but MITI's role in identifying whole industries to be scraped, and the government subsidies to help these companies switch into higher value-added products is an important part of the kind of industrial policy which America could benefit from. For example, the government is now in the midst of a Seven Year Plan covering from 1979 to 1985. Twelve industries have been singled out as having high-growth potential, and six are labeled as structurally depressed. Government-sponsored research and development is designed to assist these high-growth industries. While the United States continues to support ailing industries, such as shoes and textiles with subsidies which underwrite inefficiency, the Japanese response is to transfer labor and capital out of structurally depressed industries through compensation for scrapping old equipment, retraining programs, and partial payment of personnel costs while companies enter new industries."

"How do Japanese depreciation write-offs compare with the situation in the U.S.?"

"Accelerated depreciation has been an instrument of national policy, encouraging the modernization of plant and equipment. Often more than 50% of these new costs can be written off in the first year. This helps to keep product prices flexible and low. U.S. business has long wanted and now has more liberalized depreciation and investment tax credits. These things alone will not make the difference however."

"Aren't there other ways in which our government's contradictory policies have been pulling U.S. industry in different directions? For example, while the Environmental Protection Agency pushed for stricter air pollution controls, the Energy Department wanted companies to switch to dirty coal from expensive imported oil."

"There are a lot of examples of this foolishness in U.S. government. The National Highway Traffic Safety Administration required weight-adding safety equipment to cars. At the same time the Department of Transportation insisted on lighter, gasoline-conserving vehicles. Americans are also a bit too idealistic and naive when it comes to mixing morals and business."

"What do you mean?"

"Well take something like the Foreign Corrupt Practices Act. This limits U.S. company payments, or kickbacks to secure contracts abroad. The fact is that the companies of other countries are free to do this, and we end up losing out. If someone's going to do it, I'd just as soon see us profit from corruption."

Edwards chuckled. "I quite agree, though. I also think Carter's trade embargoes and human rights policies simply allowed the Russians to get wheat elsewhere at the expense of our farm belt. It kills me to think that over 50% of all machine tools consumed outside the U.S. go to countries of the Communist East bloc. While the Germans and Japanese capitalize on this market, U.S. companies are forbidden to enter due to our self-destructive export policies."

"Really, and I think it's a big mistake that our health, safety, and environmental regulations enforce strict U.S. standards even on the overseas operations of American companies."

"After all, what's wrong with exporting a little U.S. pollution to our neighbors?" Edwards added.

"But seriously, that kind of regulation directly places costs on our U.S. companies which can knock them out of competition with foreign firms unfettered with such restrictions. Or take Export-Import Bank restrictions. They've tended to limit the amount of subsidized credit that we can use in financing our exports."

Mr. Edwards flipped up the piece of white shirt cuff protruding from his suit jacket. He took a peek at his wrist watch. "We're still okay. I made reservations for eight o'clock downstairs in the grill room. We have about 15 more minutes. Can we talk more about the dynamism as you called it, or the strengths of the Japanese corporation?"

"Well obviously the long-term view is a big factor. In contrast to Japan, in the States the Securities and Exchange Commission had always required financial reporting on a quarterly basis. The whole American system is, therefore, geared to look at the short term. Japanese companies realize the importance of technological innovation and continuing research and development. It seems to me that Japanese companies don't diversify as much as U.S. companies. American companies are so busy buying and selling companies that there is no time to run the businesses they're in. There are more hands-on operations in Japan and not so many holding company type operations. In America, because of these diversified holdings, mostly people with legal and financial backgrounds seem to have come into power at the top. Such people don't always know production and marketing. It's expertise in these two areas which makes for corporate growth. Without these skills and experience, a manager is short on entrepreneurial skill."

"On that question of the role of entrepreneurial skill, I read that the U.S. should pay more attention to the potential role of small enterprises. This is the sector which could be cultivated, for the smaller firms represent the most dynamic sector, providing in recent years the most new jobs and new product ideas."

"I think you're making a good point, Harold, and we should look at that for a minute and ask ourselves why it is that the smaller businesses are more dynamic. I suppose that the absence of bureaucracy is a factor. If there are too many financial and reporting controls, a new idea can get smothered. Even the most successful large companies seem to be divided up into a number of small entrepreneurial units. It seems that with the high interest rates we've been having in America, it's mostly the large multinationals that are able to get funds through loans. Loans for these large U.S. mergers are inflationary and in that regard aren't much better than having the same money spent by the government. Worst of all, a mere change of owner-ship doesn't necessarily create growth through investment in plant and equipment. I'd rather see many dynamic, small, high-growth entrepreneurs be able to borrow that money, especially today when there's so little money to go around. Instead, the price of the products we buy will have to increase in order to pay for the interest on those loans."

I could see that I was pitching over Edward's head. He wasn't accustomed to such discussions, and I was making him feel uncomfortable. He avoided making a comment and changed the subject. I was reminded that I can't change the world.

"The word entrepreneur brings an image to my mind of inside holding of capital ownership. Maybe the lessened dependency on the outside public equity financial market, minus the need to pay out dividends and increasing earnings per share is a factor."

"I'm sure it is. But unlike a small American company, from the start a small Japanese company benefits from economies of scale, ability to focus attention on not only the domestic market but also world markets. The *sogo-shosha*, or general trading companies, such as Mitsubishi Corp., Mitsui & Co., Ltd., Marubeni Corp., or Nissho Iwai Corp., have made available to even very small firms the necessary information and export documentation skills that are never present in a U.S. company of equal size. Because of the comparative lack of trading companies in the U.S., small American firms have no place to go, find it more difficult to get export financing, and lack the outwardly looking export orientation of Japanese firms."

"The economies of scale you mention would be the ability for rapidly growing, small Japanese firms to enjoy ever-expanding output and production plans assuming a world-wide market. Unit costs are greatly reduced."

"And don't forget that if domestic sales are sluggish, the Japanese then have the option to pick up the slack in world markets. This allows the Japanese to maintain employment—remember the all important commitment is to keep people in their jobs—even if this means that profits per unit might go into the red."

"In Japan the company is really the people, not the shareholders. I'm beginning to see that they're treated like members of the organization not like mere employees or hired hands. Payment to shareholders is not an object in itself, but something that is a natural by-product if the company performs well enough to keep people in their jobs."

"And good companies in Japan encourage entrepreneurship by allowing as much operational autonomy as possible. The top people in the company make few decisions and pass down few objectives. The main initiator of products are middle and even lower managers. Japanese managers are not tightly held on a leash. Even an inferior idea will be more successfully implemented than a better idea, depending on the self-starting drive and enthusiasm of the implementor. A good rule of thumb is to give as much authorization as possible to the people who come up with the ideas. Then they'll have more guts and act like entrepreneurs."

"In our company there has recently been some recognition of this. Now each division is, within certain loose guidelines, able to reinvest its own earnings into its own operations."

"It makes sense. We'll never develop entrepreneurs if the fruits of a manager's labor go off to the next guy. At Honda Motors there's a 'Dream' contest each year in which any employee can come up with a wild, imaginative plan for a machine or gadget. They apply and get authorization for a certain budget. Employees are totally in control after that, although they can get advice and help from supervisors. Prizes are given for the best entries. This game-like approach, however, is excellent for morale and has actually resulted in useful techniques and insights which are applied to salable products. Of course, with each toy costing several thousand dollars, it gets expensive. But I haven't seen anyone at Honda talk about scraping this annual festival."

"I suppose the Japanese really continue to be mechanics and tinkerers rather than inventors."

"Right. As you know, they're constantly soliciting ideas from their employees by way of suggestion boxes, but more importantly through quality circles and small group activities. Ideas are tested out as soon as possible. They avoid unduly complex procedures for testing out new ideas. Japanese managers, in the good firms, are action oriented. A single objective is articulated, and the best and busiest people are thrown into the project. And always there will be key middle managers from every related department in the company. This assures that no one is left out and means that once the deliberations are over, action or implementation will immediately follow."

"Now, the reason for that would be that everyone involved feels that the decision is his own decision. Therefore each manager pursues and follows up as if he's carrying out his own project, not as though he's merely taking someone else's orders. He really pours his guts and heart into it. Tom, I see what's happening here. It's very good isn't it? But then again, it's all so simple, it's human nature and common sense, isn't it?"

"Absolutely! It just seems to me that U.S. management has forgotten that it's really people that make the difference and that it is human resources that are a company's most valuable asset. Picture the American manager who spends several days on studying, analyzing, and writing up an extensive, many-paged evaluation as to whether or not the company should purchase and install a $600,000 piece of equipment. Let's say it's depreciable over ten years. That's $60,000 per year. But when it comes to evaluating, rewarding, training, or assigning an engineer drawing a salary of $60,000 a year, probably the same executive will only give this decision a few minutes of his time."

"I see what you're saying. Yet the same engineer is capable, if used properly, of even designing a better machine."

"Exactly, Harold! It's the engineer who is responsible for designing the machine. It's people who are a company's most important asset."

"And these two people had better go and get their dinner or they won't be able to carry on much longer."

"What time is it?"

"Just a couple of minutes after 8:00 p.m. Perfect timing."

Edwards started out by ordering a bottle of white wine. He asked the waiter if there was any Japanese wine. "I'd like to try some." His eyes were wide open and blinking at the waiter.

The waiter looked at him in disbelief. "Oh, you mean Japanese lice wine."

"You serve lice wine?" Edwards pronounced each word with a great deliberation and slowness. His jaw dropped and his mouth remained open.

"Yes sir, lice wine, *osake ... sake.*"

"Oh, *saki?*"

"Yes sir, would you like some *saki*, sir?"

I was doing all I could to stop from bursting out and howling in laughter. I fought this impulse because the waiter was standing at attention in his crisp black jacket. He had a perfectly serious and intense look on his face with growing anxiety seeming to pass from a twitch in his eyebrows down to a tightening of the lips.

"No thank you. Actually what I'm after is some Japanese German or French-type wine."

"German and French wine? We have it sir."

The waiter was getting more and more confused, but I try not to come to the rescue, refraining from using my Japanese in such situations. I still remember when I was first learning Japanese years ago, I preferred to struggle through, rather than have a smart guy come forward and help me out with his English.

"No. I'm sorry. Do you have Japanese-made Western-type wine, not *osake?*" I asked in English. Edwards had given up in exasperation. This time the waiter got it. I knew he would. Fortunately, there were no domestic wines on the menu. Edwards ended up ordering a white German wine.

"Welcome to Japan, Edwards-san! Actually it's not usually quite that bad. You forgot about the old American movies where the Orientals couldn't pronounce their r's."

"They really can't, can they?"

"I can only speak for the Japanese. A Japanese 'r,' at least the sound which is reproduced in Romanization using an 'r,' actually is much closer to the English 'l' sound. When I first started studying Japanese in my senior year at college, I was just like the waiter—I couldn't pronounce their 'r.' After an American fellow student told me to think in terms of 'l,' I did much better."

"With all the products that Japan has copied and imitated, and with all the dynamism and energy of the private sector, I'm surprised they don't have a wine industry. Actually the beer is great. I get it sometimes in Milwaukee."

"You get it in Milwaukee?"

"Yeah in Milwaukee. It's not bad." He obviously didn't catch the irony of my question. After my long years out of the States maybe it's no longer the beer capital, I thought.

"And the whiskey has really come a long way I hear."

"Harold, you know there is a pretty good sized wine industry in Japan. It's centered around Yamanashi prefecture, about two or three hours from Tokyo by car—that is, if you leave town around midnight when there's no heavy traffic. I have an old, thatched-roofed, traditional house in that prefecture, and on the way home I always have to buy grapes to give to the women at the office. The domestic wines must be getting better. They're beginning to ask for wine, but I'm afraid they'll make too many mistakes when they type. They're bad enough as it is."

"By the way, what's a prefecture?"

"I'd never heard of it either before I came here. It wasn't in my Funk and Wagnalls Standard Dictionary. That's what the Japanese call the equivalent of their states. I think there are something like 47 prefectures. Tokyo, Osaka, Hokkaido and a few other places aren't called prefectures or *ken*, rather they're classified as metropolitan areas or a territory."

At about $250 per hour (depending on the exchange rate), I was thinking it was about time I cut out the small talk. Then again, maybe Edwards wanted a break. He seemed happy enough making chit-chat."

"Harold, getting back to some of the things which Japanese companies are doing right, it seems to me that management keeps its sights on the basics—service to customers, low-cost manufacturing, constant efforts at productivity improvement and a willingness or recognition that there can be only limited progress unless there are considerable innovation and risk taking. The United States remains ahead in basic research and major break-throughs in the natural sciences. The Japanese excel in innovation and technology, especially when we define technology as the application of basic research to an attractive and salable product that consumers enthusiastically pursue in the marketplace. In terms of economic growth and the prosperity of a nation, basic research alone isn't very helpful. It is the sale of products that generate income, profits, and allow a company and the economy to grow. It is the useful and functional innovation, and the shorter new product cycle of Japanese manufacturers which continues to attract worldwide consumers. Money spent on basic research is largely wasted, unless it is applied to salable products."

"Japanese customer service is really amazing, isn't it? At our company many of the major product ideas and minor improvements on product functions and design have come from input received from customers."

"In general, I would also say that Japanese companies are more aggressive in knowing what their competitors are doing. Unlike American companies that seem to have eyes on internal financial reports, Japanese management has its sights on customers and competitors."

"I suppose achieving success in these areas is easier said than done. Any firm will be successful if it succeeds at low-cost manufacturing, excellent customer service, productivity improvement, and a willingness to identify and take risks, along with constant product innovation."

"I guess we have to ask what gets in the way, what blocks achievement in these areas? My intuition is that above all else, a greater simplicity in managing complicated modern organizations is called for. Unnecessary and detailed procedures and controls overguide an operation and can stifle initiative. The sheer weight of bureaucracy drains the time and energy of managers. Compliance with organizational reporting procedures costs money. In place of dull and dry controls, there should be a unifying major purpose or unifying team goal. Our high school soccer team could overpower stronger opposition when the team was motivitated and working well together. We used to say that the team was psyched. The corporate culture, along with a consistent management philosophy, contributes to psyching up the team. The written word, as distributed in company policy manuals and memorandums, will not instill the necessary motivation."

"The only real motivation that lasts probably has to come from the individual. Therefore, the individual must identify with and share the underlying goals of the organization."

"It is confusing and meaningless to have more than one or two goals. From the top down, IBM always stressed customer service. McDonald hamburger employees are trained to take pride in friendly service and cleanliness. The employees of 3M and a company like Sony are totally devoted to coming out with new, quality products. With every new product they launch, teams are created including designers, manufacturing people, financial specialists as well as people engaged in marketing. Teams stay together from product inception until distribution in the national marketplace. The team has autonomy and is self-sufficient."

"Psyching up a firm's human resources, such that everyone is self-motivated and working toward a unifying goal is no easy task."

"Certainly not. The key to success in Japanese corporations can however be largely borrowed and transplanted to American soil. It's not just a question of beginning a program of quality circles. If an American company's goal is suddenly to become one of people-first management, consistent changes will have to be made from the C.E.O. all the way down to rank and file employees. Merely training and rehiring new people will make little difference. It will also be necessary to develop new systems of reward and punishment, new incentive programs, and new role models with new structures."

"I see what you mean, Tom. In Milwaukee a friend of mine was interested in a new job in which he was told he could maximize his talents. He's a creative and brilliant engineer. He's been working on a new generation of products for them. The pay off is still far down the road, and he's been a drain on company finances. It wasn't too long before he noticed that his raises were much less than the managers in established, profit-generating product lines. Top management's commitment to new product development had been mere lip service. He finally caught on to this and moved to a new company that genuinely was willing to take a long-term view and reward such efforts appropriately."

"There are other areas where Japanese companies do things right, and the savings and efficiencies resulting are tremendous. The Japanese have not only kept plant and equipment up to date by buying the best equipment available, but management and engineers have also always researched the world and bought the best technologies in the marketplace, avoiding the expense of reinventing the wheel. Japanese per capita consumption of energy is the lowest among advanced economies. Japan produces one unit of GNP at a third of the U.S. energy price. Energy audits have aided industry in reducing energy requirements. For example, in the steel industry gas pressure building up at the top of blast furnaces is used to drive turbines and generate electricity."

"I imagine the Japanese are much less wasteful of other resources as well. The savings can be appreciable."

"That's true. Japanese equipment and planning are designed to maximize material yield. Industrial plants also aim for the most efficient use of by-products. For instance, almost all Japanese gypsum is derived as a by-product of phosphate fertilizer production or is precipitated out of the gases escaping from other chemical processes. Since U.S. equipment isn't geared or produced to process out such by-products, it is less attractive to Japanese or European purchasers. For example, the Japanese will continue to buy European food processing equipment because U.S. equipment is wasteful of material and by-products."

"In the quality control area, we all know that there are big differences between Japanese and American performance."

"First of all, just the fact that Americans use the term quality 'control' indicates to me a mistake in our approach to product quality. Quality cannot be controlled but rather must be built into a product from the very beginning. Often in an American company it is found that if the engineering designs were followed as is, a product would barely work at all. Over the years, factory workers have learned to make certain adjustments in either the size of fittings or the materials used. One material may be too hard or brittle. Often engineering specifications cannot even be used as is. In these ways, quality is not being built into a product."

"I've heard there are very few full-time quality assurance personnel in Japan."

"That's right. Assuring quality is becoming the job of every employee. American management assumes that workers know where defects and quality problems are and that only pecuniary rewards will draw out this information. On the other hand, Japanese management's orientation is that no one knows what the problems are and quality problems must be solved together. Through worker participation in shop floor decision-making, there are more self-management and self-innovative capacity down to the rank and file level. In addition to quality circles, much has been done with zero defect programs, and independent targets determined by workers with a direct presentation to management. Attempts to improve the quality of working life by way of job enlargement, job restructuring, and campaigns for brighter and better workshops have also taken place."

"Japanese are doing good things with inventory control, aren't they?"

"Yes, for example in automobile assembly plants they practice *kamban* or 'just in time' system. The goal is to limit vendor parts to no more than a 30-minute supply on a constant basis. Deliveries from vendors take place more often with great savings in storage space, and interest rates on the money normally required to purchase inventory. Factories are also much less cluttered."

"Such practices must make life hard on subcontractors or these parts suppliers. It cost them time and money to constantly make such deliveries."

"There must be something to that. But I suppose the vendors themselves can profit from reduced storage costs, especially if as in theory they are delivered as soon as they are produced. Parts also remain clean and dust free. Your point is, nevertheless, well taken, and it leads to a discussion of the so-called 'dual economy' in Japan."

"What do you mean by that?"

"The expression refers to the lower sector of the economy—the smaller firms engaged as subcontractors largely to accommodate parent companies, or major customers purchasing parts. Actually many Japanese firms are engaged mostly in final assembly with very few component parts produced directly by a well-known parent such as Toyota or Nissan. This is another reason why these Japanese firms hesitated to go into the U.S. market setting up factories. Actually in-house expertise does not include the production of many of the component parts which final assembly relies on. Thus, it was helpful to wait for vendors to first enter the U.S. market, or at least simultaneously enter. The employees in the smaller firms do not enjoy lifetime employment, all of the fringe benefits and equally high lifetime earnings of workers in parent companies."

"You mean there can be lay off in smaller firms in times of recession and these personnel cutbacks won't touch the larger parent companies?"

"That is definitely right. The role of the temporary worker must also be understood, however. Even in the large firm itself there can often be somewhere between 20 to 30% of the manpower on temporary contract employment. Under Japanese labor law, unlike the U.S., it is the workers having no contract whose job security is the most highly protected. American contracts of employment for un-specified terms are considered to be terminable at will with or without cause. Under Japanese law, the contract of maximum duration is one year, and monthly or even daily contracts are common. Lay-off upon termination of the specified contract term is frequent. This provides labor elasticity and flexibility in wage bills, which otherwise would not be possible under a system of lifetime employment, with steadily increasing wages conforming to a seniority pay system."

"Don't the unions object to this kind of exploitation of workers in the lower sector of the dual economy?"

"Unionization rates in small subcontractors are extremely low—in firms with less than 99 workers, organization rates are about 5%, while they're around 65% in larger firms with over 500 employees. Moreover, the temporary workers, sometimes on contracts for years, can work side by side with the regular employee elite, but they will make a much lower wage with even lower annual income. The temporary workers on contract are not asked to join the union. Union membership is restricted to regular employees, and these corporate elites realize that the privileged position they enjoy, and their job security can only be maintained at the expense of the temporary, non-union employees. Understanding the less fortunate status of the subcontract and temporary employee will go far toward grasping the efficiency, economies and rationality of the system of job security enjoyed by the luckier members of the corporate elite. The high wages and standard of living they enjoy are offset by the workers in the lower sector. Nevertheless, income differen-tials nationwide are still less than in the U.S. and in most all industrial countries, except perhaps Sweden."

"That's interesting. It sounds to me there should be a greater disparity in personal income in Japan based upon what you said."

"In a given Japanese corporation income differentials based upon age are greater than they are in the U.S. It's interesting to note, however, that differentials based on educational level obtained are considerable less in Japan than they are in America. The college graduate does not become a management elite, rewarded in disproportion to high school graduate technicians. Since everyone must grow old, rewarding people by age is a more universal and egalitarian approach than the U.S. and European tendency to reward a highly paid, highly educated elite. The consequent reduced class consciousness of Japan may thus explain why the corporate team is stronger, with less resentment, and with everyone pulling together in the same direction."

"In terms of egalitarianism and lack of class consciousness, I'm sure that the homogeneity and comparative lack of racial and ethnic minorities are in many ways in Japan's favor."

"That must be true. The fact is that in America non-white unemployment rates are more than twice as high as those of non-minorities. On the other hand, Japan's incredible homogeneity must make it difficult for the Japanese to assert leadership among the people of the world. It is too easy for outsiders to be suspicious of such a racially pure country. In such a country, however, it's comparatively easy to establish national consensus. I've always said that the role of NHK, the nationwide government television network, is also great in establishing unified goals or all-important shared values on an even broader scale. It enjoys a popularity or viewer ratings far higher than any TV station in the States. The masses of the Japanese public view educational and sophisticated programming that only a comparative few Americans are exposed to. A handful of newspapers also shape public opinion and enjoy massive nationwide circulations that Stateside publishers can only dream about."

"From all that you've said, it seems to me that Japan operates under an overall 'social contract'. The underlying foundation seems to be perhaps a strong identification with being Japanese—and what the role of Japan is vis-á-vis the outside world. Merely calling it patriotism is not enough. It seems that the entire nation, the people, and corporate organizations are willing to take a second row seat, if that will be best for Japan and its position in the world."

"I think that's a good way of putting it—from the individual manager who is content not to receive immediate credit and extra pay for superior efforts, to the company that will at high cost refrain from dumping under-employed workers on the labor market. I've often felt, however, that there's a greater sophistication or higher degree of wisdom operating in Japan. If private industry as a whole cuts back on employment to increase profits, those profits will then be subject to the increasing taxes, which are required to keep the laid-off workers on unemployment roles. Furthermore, in Japan a company's size and, therefore, status are commonly judged by the number of employees. By keeping the underemployed on the payroll, companies can at least look big and fulfill their social obligation to keep men at work. Letting go of workers would also greatly demoralize the remaining workforce."

"I read that Japan also enjoys a built-in incomes policy, with labor unions showing amazing self-restraint."

"Certainly Japan was lucky in that late industrialization meant that there was no entrenched tradition of craft unionism. Workforces were generally right off the farm, and workers had had no heritage of trade union experience. This made them comparatively maleable and perhaps docile. On the other hand, management's approach was more paternalistic than exploitative. Exploitation can only lead to strong antagonistic unions. In Japan there is little class consciousness between union and management because they are really one and the same. Until white-collar—college graduates reach the *kanrishoku* level at about age 40, they are in the same union as blue-collar, junior high school graduates."

"That would go a long way toward enabling union and management to talk to each other and trust each other."

"As a matter of fact, Harold, Japanese labor and management are smoothly working under a system of free collective bargaining. Wage negotiations have been settled within the range of economic rationality without any national incomes policy or other compulsory measures. This means that wage settlements come close to regressional, econometric analysis based upon the supply and demand of labor, the rate of increase of consumer prices and changes in corporate profits."

"I'm sure that lifetime employment also results in substantial savings in orientation and retraining due to the lower turnover rates characteristic of Japanese large firms. Of course, a company also benefits from consequent backlogs of experience and reduced rates of absenteeism, tardiness, slowdowns, and strikes, etc."

"And on the question of 'social contract', the Japanese government at least tries to avoid tripping up the legs of private industry. I believe that as things are now run, the U.S. government policy will continue its failure to develop effective programs aimed at reindustrializing or revitalizing America. The problem is that there are too many political hacks appointed by the executive branch with the change in each administration. In the U.S. government, at, say, the Department of Commerce or Labor, multiple political appointments will be made, with executive changes taking place at even the divisional and bureau level. In Japan, only two appointments are made—the Minister of each ministry and one political Vice-Minister. American government policy, thus, suffers from the same weakness U.S. private industry faces. Shake-ups and incessant personnel changes prevent efficient and consistent long-term planning."

"Gentlemen, would you care for some dessert?"

Our waiter stood stiffly at attention, ready to pass out dessert menus to us. Without looking over the menu, Edwards asked for a ball of vanilla ice cream. I chimed in with, "That's fine with me."

We polished off the ice cream and had another cup of coffee. Mr. Edwards was gracious enough to walk me down to the hotel lobby. I noticed it was raining outside, and there were no taxis lined up at the door. As we said good night, I reached into my attache case and took out my foldable umbrella. As I walked over to the nearest subway on the Ginza, I mentally reviewed the evening's discussion. It went alright. Enough points had been made.

2

Economic Growth Is Fine...
But More Important
the Japanese Must Wake Up
and Join the Human Race

The need for fundamental changes in the "software"
(the Japanese people and their views of the world),
to catch up with "hardware"
(machines, consumer products, and physical economic growth).

This article was inspired by a speech I made in Japanese, and it appeared in Japanese in 1981 *Shukan Diamond* weekly magazine.

I came across this piece in a closet, but believe it has a new relevance after the passage of ten years. The Japanese have improved in this area, thanks to all the foreigners who have learned and are speaking good Japanese. (Now the foreigners have to be careful that they are not *nihongoya*.)

Still, though, a big frustration of the *Gaijin* Boss is that he will typically start-out studying Japanese, but when he uses it, his Japanese staff don't help him and they answer back in English. Until you really get good at Japanese, this is a problem, and you realize you cannot be an imposition on people, and you feel pretty silly too.

Most expatriate executives give up, and should not feel bad about it. It's not a language that can be picked up when you have a *gaijin* wife and full-time job.

Obviously, the comparative ease of reading English and the Japanese businessman's background in English gives him advantages and an ability to manage hands-on, make a difference, and "take charge" in a way not available to many of you.

And finally it's important to realize I aimed the following at a Japanese audience. And I want to say that most good, solid and sharp business people have become laudably flexible, responsive and truly international, willing enough to deal in Japanese if the foreigner's Japanese is fully functional. In fact given Japan's history and racial and cultural situation, most Japanese are surprisingly good on this point.

Introduction

First of all, my position is that economic growth, which crosses the borders of the countries of the globe, may be multinational and international, but in order for Japan to be truly international, Japan and the Japanese people will have to identify more with other people of other countries, not as unique or interesting foreigners, but more as people.

I will try to describe to you through my own experiences and personal life, what I have observed about some Japanese, and why I believe that a country with people as economically and technologically sophisticated as the Japanese must now work on changing the perceptions of the common people and business and government leaders, so that they begin to identify more with the rest of the world and its problems. I would hope that the Japanese national government and business leaders would become less selfish, not always thinking of Japan's interests, but rather of spreading wealth through the giving of untied foreign aid, and the selling of Japanese technology etc. at reasonable prices.

I would hope that the Japanese would become more able to think of themselves not as Japanese, but rather as members of the human race. Through personal experience, I will try and show what and where this problem lies, and make a connection to where it may even affect the way Japanese businesses and government policy operate.

And finally, I will mention some concrete areas where Japan can make not only an economic contribution, but can also help the world in an even broader sense.

Frustrations and headaches of a foreigner
trying to be accepted into Japanese society

In my opinion, if Japan is to have a respected role in the world and is to be loved and looked up to as a leader by the other countries of this globe, it must begin to think in other than purely economic terms.

I think it is necessary that you understand the perspective from which I speak to you. Although I am very much an American, I have spent most all of my adult life in Japan, and feel that Japan is also—perhaps almost equally with America— very much my country, and I feel that the Japanese language is my language and it is the language which I use, and must use, everyday in my work and play, just as you do. This is because I feel that I am a member of this society. So I want, even insist, that the Japanese I deal with treat me not just in the way some Japanese are so accustomed to treating non-Japanese, especially white *gaijin*, but rather as a working and functioning member of Japanese society.

One of my largest and most painful frustrations in Japan has not come from my inability to adapt to Japanese food or customs. Rather, I used to bang my head constantly against the almost insurmountable barrier of not being accepted as just another functioning member of Japanese society. When I was a researcher with the Japan Institute of Labor and Cornell University, when I first came to Japan over eight years ago (my first visit was a short one to do research on labor relations for Cornell U. in 1970), I soon came to like all Japanese foods (yes, even *sashimi*, and *natto*!!), and learned to read Japanese newspapers and books (yes, even 2,000 or so *kanji*!) within two years.

Many foreigners can and do live in the same world as you do—they watch and understand the same TV., and read the same newspapers. And, most importantly, they want to. When I was studying Japanese with all my might, I was surprised when a Japanese asked me, "Why do you want to learn Japanese?" Another Japanese once was making me very frustrated, because he insisted on speaking English to me, when I was speaking to him in Japanese. I finally told him that this was Japan, and even though his English was very good, for my own psychological peace of mind and in order to preserve my identity as a member of Japanese society I had no choice but to speak in Japanese.

You're still a guest after eight years in the country

He replied that he stubbornly insisted on speaking English, because, he sees me as a guest in Japan (even though he knows I've been here eight years) and feels that it is more polite to speak the language of the foreign guest. Do you think I should believe his explanation? A Japanese friend I trust told me that that Japanese was lying and didn't see me as another human being struggling in this world, but merely as a tool to practice his English on. I would also like to ask you if it is acceptable for Japan in this age of internationalization to treat someone like me as a "guest" even after I have been here over eight years?

Recently I was at a very high level cocktail party and reception made up of about 95% Japanese. Most of them were quite elderly, and people such as former Prime Minister Kishi, former Ambassador to U.S. and Trade Minister Ushiba, and U.S. Ambassador Mansfield were also in attendance. Two very senior and dignified Japanese came up to me (one being a former ambassador) and began to ask me some questions in English. I answered of course in Japanese, as I have a responsibility, I feel, to internationalize Japan in the true sense, but they continued (for two or three minutes!!) to answer and comment in English.

Are former ambassadors mere *eigoya*?
(someone whose main claim to fame is English
and he shows it whenever possible—
Eigo is English and the *ya of sushiya*).

I very patiently spoke with them only in Japanese; then I finally began my lecture, which fortunately is not often necessary these days. I told them that as former ambassadors and the so-called elite leaders of Japan, they were a disgrace to their nation. I said that just because they spoke English did not make them international at all, and that to me the definition of the so-called *kokusaijin* or international person should be someone who is sensitive, perceptive, and most importantly, someone who sees the other people of the world as members of the same human race.

Unfortunately, these two Japanese gentlemen and a number of Japanese like them still think in terms of Japanese and non-Japanese. And worse yet, I'm sure that the strange blend of Japanese superiority, mixed with perhaps feelings of inferiority, causes them to look down on other Asians (*sangokujin*) and look, if not up to at least very differently at white American or European types.

"*Jinshu sabetsu izen no dankai ni aru*"—
still no understanding or grasp of racial discrimination

I think Japan must realize that many of the Japanese people have not yet even come to sense or understand what racial discrimination really is (*Jinshu sabetsu izen no dankai.*) I notice that there may be an exception or two to this—in the case of the Koreans, voices will lower when the subject comes up, and I think many Japanese realize that Japan's treatment of Koreans is discriminatory.

In the case of white foreigners, however, it seems that most Japanese fundamentally think of them as being so different and living in such a different world that different treatment of them is only natural, and that the foreigner always wants to be treated differently. This must be why the former ambassador at the party was so shocked and surprised when I told him that "it makes me mad" when a Japanese like him insists upon ignoring my Japanese responses and not allowing me to relax and feel comfortable as a member of Japanese society, even though I have worked and struggled so hard and so long for this recognition.

I am sure that he had never seen his words and actions as symbolic of behavior that would never be tolerated in the United States. His mind-set and attitudes are examples of classic racial discrimination and an inability to perceive me and other foreigners as the same type of animal (human being). That former ambassador can only accept a non-Japanese as a foreigner or *gaijin*. When he sees our faces, "English" registers in his mind, and he does not even want to spend time with us if it means he will have to speak Japanese with us. Such a man is happy to practice his English on us, however.

But the Japanese cannot be blamed
because they often don't realize what they are doing

I would not have learned Japanese if I also, like the former Japanese Ambassador, had not practiced. However, at least I was in the right country (Japan), and I have, I believe, followed a basic code of rules and fair play and have the flexibility to adjust my behavior. We really can't blame the former ambassador, because I'm sure he doesn't act the way he does consciously or intentionally. But his great tragedy, and perhaps the great tragedy of Japan, is that it doesn't even realize that it is terribly closed-minded and that its actions can be racist, insular, parochial and totally unacceptable in the present *kokusai-jidai*.

And this brings us directly to our topic. It seems to me that Japan's "hardware" or economic development, has raced far ahead and is far more advanced than her "software," or the Japanese people, their actions, and the people-planned policies of her businesses and government.

Japan is not the only insular nation in the world, that as Professor (and former Ambassador) Reischauer says must join the human race. I'm sure that I could be just as frustrated in a struggle to become accepted by Tibetan society, or a tribal nation of Africa. The problem is that unlike these other countries, Japan's economic power has now become so great that it is influencing nations throughout the world, and often these can be negative influences, such as the generation of unemployment or destruction of local industries (like radios, color TVs and now autos in the United States). Other people of the world can come to feel threatened by Japan, jealous and even resentful.

On the other hand, Japanese people and leaders are not sufficiently developed to perform on this international arena. They are not always internationalized to the point that they know the proper rules of behavior, have a sense of fair play, know when to stop and how to control Japan's great economic machine.

Would the Japanese tolerate the type of unemployment U.S. auto workers are having?

When Americans grow up, they are told by their mothers, "Do unto others as you would have others do unto you?" or, "Put yourself in the other person's shoes." The former ambassador failed to be sensitive enough to do this when he would speak to me only in English.

I get a feeling that the Japanese automobile industry is also failing to live up to these two fundamental rules of behavior for both individuals and nations. Would Japanese workers and the Japanese government tolerate the massive unemployment (estimated at one million) taking place in the U.S. auto industry? Would Japan allow foreign companies to take over so rapidly, such large shares of key and fundamental industries here in Japan?

The answer is clearly "no," and when Japan was industrially weaker, she did indeed heavily protect her economy. I would hope that the managers and workers in the automobile factories here in Japan would be a little bit more sensitive and able to "put themselves in the shoes of the laid-off American worker," seeing him as the head of a family with small children to feed and having to face the shame and frustration of not being able to get a job.

6,000 people lined up at 8:30 a.m. for 18 jobs

Recently at an automobile factory in America, a newspaper ad appeared, announcing that 18 job positions were open. Six Thousand workers rushed to the factory to be first in line that morning. Picture yourself as one of those workers.

I am not suggesting that Japan should pull back, and that the Japanese people and policies should shoot for anything less than excellence. Rather, it is necessary for America to openly accept Japan's challenge, and I think America wants to do that. To protect the U.S. market would only make the U.S. less competitive and weaken her industrial structure.

In the short run, however, there should be limits to unduly harsh export deluges. And these should come voluntarily (as they are to some extent). After all

America has been a very generous and considerate big brother to Japan, and Japan must realize that those days are over.

Democratic and capitalistic nations must prosper together

For Japanese exports to contribute to unemployment and a recession in America and Europe is in the long run self-defeating, because a crippled U.S. economy will mean that this huge American market for Japanese products will begin to dry up. Above all Japan and the United States, along with the free, capitalistic European countries, must stick together and cooperate. There could be nothing more tragic than to have bickering and in-fighting among a family of siblings, making it possible for less friendly neighbors of disturbing ideology to gain inroads which might even threaten the economic and individual freedom that our societies value above all else.

Japan's role in an internationalizing world

Japan is the first major world power in history to achieve this status through non-military economic strength. Japan should work with other friendly free nations, encouraging them to develop the economic and industrial base and strength that win the quiet respect of all people in the world. By trading with virtually all nations, participating in development projects across national, and ideological boundaries, there is an exchange of people and mutual economic dependence between nations, which should serve to defuse tensions. While the U.S. faces off in confrontation with its near neighbor Cuba, Japan goes quietly about establishing a constructive relationship of mutual dependence in which both nations prosper. Behind the Soviet Union, Japan is Cuba's second most important trading partner.

Japan then should honestly admit to the U.S. that these are Japan's policies, and that the U.S. is foolish and will end up the loser with policies of confrontation. Japan should take the aggressive lead, not apologizing for these policies, but rather encouraging America also to adopt a "business first" approach to national and diplomatic policy. It is a safer and more constructive way to forward national interest.

I would also encourage Japan to have a more reasonable export policy, although I admit that the shock of massive loss of market share may be essential to impress American industry with the need to get its own house in order. As a substitute for export, investment in foreign countries will make the Japanese economy truly multinational and can also contribute to absorbing some of the unemployment caused by export alone.

Japan can also now have a useful role in transplanting some of the practical and useful Japanese management techniques of improving work motivation and product quality. Guidance could also be given to the United States in pointing out some of the weaknesses in business practices and economic policy planning. Of course, the formation of a reindustrialization policy in the U.S., and a break away from such management practices as "profits first," and the short-term perspective must come from within the U.S., and there are signs that this is already happening.

Participating in joint ventures with firms of other nations, engaging in licensing agreements and sales of Japanese technology will also contribute to mutual prosperity among Japan's trading and business partners.

The most important theme—the Japanese people must wake up and join the human race

All these activities will mean that the Japanese people will be having more and more contact with people of the world, and more people will be learning about Japan and the Japanese language. The number of people who speak a second language (foreign language to them) is directly proportional to the power and influence of that nation in the world. For example, before the victory of Sir Francis Drake over the Spanish Armada in 1588, almost no one spoke English except the people on a tiny island much smaller than Japan.

While the Japanese people should learn English to communicate with foreigners who live outside Japan, or foreigners in Japan who are unable (or find it easier to make the Japanese speak English) to speak Japanese, the Japanese people must also learn that they must have the consideration, sophistication, and also have the responsibility not to treat a foreigner like myself the same as one living in the U.S.

Recently I was at a television studio recording a TV show. I had had two in-depth preparatory meetings with the director in Japanese, of course, and the TV show was to be recorded in Japanese. We were having a *bento* lunch in a conference room near the studio just before taping. Although this director knew all about my background, and that I lived in Japan for over eight years, he asked me if I could use chopsticks as we were about to eat.

Probably he and many Japanese still sincerely and seriously ask foreigners like me such stupid questions, and I think this is perhaps the greatest tragedy of the Japanese people. Correcting this, or developing human "software" is in my opinion the greatest challenge facing Japan, as it moves into an age of further internationalization.

3

The *Gaijin* Boss
and Japanese Women—
New Opportunities

A big day on Tuesday, April 1

April 1 is the day the Equal Opportunity Law takes effect. It was passed by the Diet on May 17, 1985, in this final year of the United Nations Decade for Women and completes Japanese responsibilities toward the UN Convention on the Elimination of All Forms of Discrimination Against Women. This is probably one of the most important laws passed in modern Japanese history in that it will end up personally affecting our working, private and family lives. Provisions concern such areas as training, job assignment, promotion, welfare benefits, retirement age, discharge and, of course, remuneration. It can be expected that a period of defining and testing will ensue when the Ministry of Labor will provide guidelines to employers, and employers receiving complaints from the female workers should settle them through grievance machinery, advice from the Director of Prefectural Women and Young Workers Offices and through the establishment of an Equal Opportunity Mediation Commission set up in each of the prefectural Women and Young Workers Offices.

Past and present discrimination

In 1984, the number of salaried female workers topped the 15 million mark for the first time, out-numbering those women exclusively engaged in housekeeping. According to a Ministry of Labor survey released in September, 1985, 40% of the nation's workforce is composed of women (as compared to 48% in Sweden, 44% in the United States and 39% in West Germany). Unfortunately, the wage gap between men and women has been steadily expanding since 1978. Women part-timers account for 22% of the total female workforce, and their working conditions are indeed poor. The average hourly wage for some 3.28 million female part-timers stood at only ¥572 per hour in 1984 or about 75% of the pay of regular female employees broken down on an hourly basis. Such part-timers, of course, can be summarily dismissed, and this has been a key to productivity and profits in certain sectors.

A survey released Wednesday, August 7, 1985 by a private labor research institute surveying 300 major Japanese firms employing female part-time workers reveals that 30% of these Japanese companies do not give them paid holidays, and 80% make the women work overtime at low hourly wages. 51% of these firms increased their number of part-time employees. On the average, female part-time workers are 41 years old and are employed for 3.5 years at average hourly pay of ¥603. Even when these part-timers work the same number of hours as full-time staff, their monthly income did not reach 90% of the salary given to full-time employees below the age of 20.

According to a Home Affairs Ministry survey covering 47 prefectures and 11 major municipal governments, 1/3 of these governments are discriminating against women in recruiting practices. The survey released on Monday, May 20, 1985, has government personnel officials admitting that women's scores on entrance exams are too high. Based simply on the score, the full quota of new employees would be met by female hires unless some discriminatory measures were taken against women. They are indeed taken, and because of this only 21.6% of the employees at local governments were women at the end of fiscal 1983. It will be interesting to see if the implementation of April 1, 1986, law will change these practices.

Nonetheless, some progress is being made, and starting salaries of university graduates starting employment from April 1, 1985 reveal that the differences between sexes are decreasing. According to survey findings of the Institute of Labor Administration announced on Friday, June 21, 1985, based on a survey of 447 companies listed on the first section of the Tokyo Stock Exchange, the starting salary for male university graduates was ¥143,600, an increase of ¥4,900 or 3.5%. As for female university graduates, the monthly salary was ¥136,600 with the same ¥4,900 increase for a 3.7% increase. Of the corporations surveyed, 49% had equal pay scales for both men and women with university degrees in 1985. In 1984, however, only 43.4% of the same companies paid men and women equally. When it came to high school graduates, as many as 62% of the companies paid equally for both sexes. The impending Equal Employment Opportunity Law has been having a large influence in bringing about this trend.

The law until now—protection vs. equality

Due to the almost total segregation of occupations by sex, men and women rarely do the same work, and, consequently, there are few opportunities to compare equal pay for equal or even comparable work. While some argue that the protective legislation inhibits the women from reaching equality, others argue that these protections have to compensate women for the many disadvantages and generally discriminatory treatment they receive on the job.

For example, the Labor Standards Law guarantees equal pay for equal work (Art. 4); prevents women from working during the hours from 10:00 a.m. to 5:00 p.m. (Art. 62); controls the maximum amount of overtime allowed per day (two hours), per week (six hours), and per year (150 hours) (Art. 61); prohibits women from doing dangerous work five meters above the ground and from lifting heavy weights (Art. 63): nor may women work underground (Art. 64). They may request menstruation leave when it interferes with their ability to work (Art 67); there is a maternity leave of six weeks before and after childbirth and the Health Insurance Law (Art, 50 para. 2) provides for paying insured women workers 60% of their standard daily remuneration for six weeks before and after childbirth. Furthermore, women may not be dismissed during maternity leave nor for 30 days thereafter (Art. 19). Should a pregnant woman require it, she may be placed on a lighter job (Art. 65). It is legal for a woman to request nursing of an infant under one year of age and to receive at least 30 minutes twice a day during working hours (Art. 66). Note that menstrual leave and maternity leave do not have to be paid by the employer, however.

The new Equal Opportunity Law will strengthen Article 3 of the Labor Standards Law, which limits equality affecting conditions of work to questions of creed, national origin and social status, without mentioning any thing about sex. Indeed, from April 1, things will change, and in some respects there is even more protection. For example, pre-natal leave in case of multiple pregnancy is being extended to ten weeks instead of the present six weeks, post-natal leave is extended to eight weeks (six weeks in the existing law) out of which six weeks instead of the present five weeks will become compulsory.

Attitudes and interests— competition less welcomed by young men

A Prime Minister's Office survey, announced on February 24, 1985, reveals, that among 3,000 women polled only 26.3%t of them knew that the Equal Employment Opportunity Law had been presented to the Diet. Some 54.7% of the respondents had jobs, whereas among the unmarrieds 77.8%were working. As many as 73.1%

felt that women's status had improved in recent years, and 41.3% rejected the traditional concept that the women's place is in the home. And they are not so eager to be in the home, as only 5.4% replied that the most worthwhile thing to them were their husbands.

More recently, the Japan Recruit Center conducted a survey of 1,000 women between 20 and 34 years of age in October and November of 1985. A surprising 70% of these women polled in the Tokyo area think that they are equal or superior to male workers in terms of their ability to perform on the job (11.1% of them felt that they were superior). Only 31.5% felt that they were inferior to male workers. Furthermore, the survey revealed that as many as 55.9% of the female workers wanted to have an equal relationship with male workers such that they could compete with them in terms of job performance. Among the graduates of four year universities, 77.5% felt this way. It appears that more and more women are wanting to become partners of men in the workplace.

According to another survey published on April 25, 1985 by the Japan Recruit Center, out of 498 women of *kacho* and above level, 70% feel that they have advantages as women executives. Apparently, they do not see being a female as being a handicap to them in the workplace. Nonetheless, 53% of them felt that the difficulty of going out and drinking with colleagues was disadvantageous, while 31.1% felt they had an advantage in that they could be more outspoken than their male associates, in that they were more able to disregard office politics.

As for how the masculine side of the business is reacting to all this, according to the December 23, 1985 report of the Nikkei Industry Research Institute (affiliated with Nihon Keizai Shimbun, Inc.) out of 1,000 households sampled, it was the young men in their 20s who showed the most reluctance to opening up the workplace to competition by women. Perhaps they are the ones with the most to lose in that older established male managers have a healthy lead in terms of experience and seniority over female counterparts that largely does not exist at comparable age and experience levels. As many as 52.4% of the males answering the questionnaire revealed that they look for "attention to detail" (support for male workers) as the most important characteristic of women. Only 10.6% of the men responded that they would look for "organizational ability and leadership" from business women. One-third of the men felt women would be undesirable as superiors, and 40% of the respondents did not want to see a woman president at their firm.

New opportunities—multinationals in Japan can compete on this one

Perhaps due to administrative guidance and to the impending Equal Employment Opportunity Law, a Ministry of Education report issued on November 8, 1985 shows us that a record 72.4% of the 92,370 women university graduates in 1985 have successfully entered the workforce. This represents the highest percentage in 30 years. Multinationals in Japan stand a good chance of competing for some of the best female human resources among these graduates. In less structured and bureaucratized foreign firms, Japanese women have already been successful in enjoying more responsibility and higher pay than would be possible in more traditional Japanese environments. Many foreign firms, due to their smaller size and potential for growth, are in a position to hire good female staff with less threat to male-dominated sanctuaries not yet established.

Thus, many foreign firms have already displayed a greater receptivity to utilizing the untapped female labor resource. Now with the implementation of the Equal Opportunity Law, society will gradually change, and the greater acceptance of the female marketing and sales representative can perhaps provide greater benefits to multinationals in Japan in a shorter period of time. As Japanese firms have been doing, foreign firms in Japan must also learn about the new law and about the changes which will have to take place. A Kyodo News Service poll carried out in October, 1985 and covering 200 firms revealed that 35% of them were planning to introduce equality in male/female recruitment, employment opportunities, promotion, and loan financing. Another 33.8% of the firms answered that their workplaces were already "liberated" and they had no plan to carry out additional reforms. The remaining 31.2% replied that they were not sure of future policies.

I strongly recommend that foreign firms make a conscious, planned, rapid, and strategic transition so that they can more rapidly get access to and take advantage of the still largely unleashed woman power lying dormant in this society. Foreign firms can more rapidly make this transition, and word will spread that changing attitudes and perceptions can match the reality of a more interesting and fulfilling working environment in multinational firms here.

What to do in your firm—problem areas to look at

First of all, recruitment and advertising in newspapers for new staff should be based on job function without stipulating sex. That's certainly something you are used to if you come from the States or from many other Western countries. You should begin to think about recruiting employees by job functions such that there would be a legitimate rationale, for example, hiring the necessary number of engineers, where the number of male engineering graduates are still larger than female. Likewise, training programs can be set up by job function rather than sex-based groupings. Of course, the goal should be to attain maximum participation and productivity from fully utilizing female resources rather that finding clever ways of being able to maintain current practices.

In the firms where there are still unequal retirement ages such as 60 for males and 55 for females, this should be changed. It doesn't have to happen over night, and I would strongly recommend that as Japanese firms would do, there would be some adjustment or trade-off such as, a scenario in which the company would agree to provide employment security to all females until age 60 in return for the freedom and flexibility of placing all employees, both male and female, on one year contracts after age 55. Pay could, thus, be frozen or even adjusted up or down based on performance and continuing contribution. It is certainly not a Western concept that the pay of more senior employees is reduced in real terms, but, unfortunately, in order to compete in Japan with Japanese companies that follow such practices, foreign firms here will have to find the proper blend between a Western management concept of kind-hearted, fair play and the Japanese business necessity to fight for survival in a competitive environment.

Obviously, any sexually differentiated pay scales will have to end in exchange for employee groupings based on job content or performance rating.

Foreign firms starting up in Japan need not design their compensation using the traditional family, housing or other sex based allowances. In fact, in terms of assuring that the lump-sum retirement benefit liability is not too great, a firm will be better off rather introducing a second salary component or *daini-kyuyo* approach toward reducing the weight of pensionable income. In a number of foreign firms, TMT has already assisted by cashing out family and housing allowances into a non-sex-based component.

The problem is that, especially in terms of the spouse allowance, many Japanese and foreign firms have had a practice of paying the allowance to men regardless of whether or not their wives were wage earners, whereas, the same companies would not pay the allowance to women if their spouses worked and earned on the job market. In fact, on Thursday, March 28, 1985, the Morioka District Court ordered a bank to pay a female employee family allowance, which it had refused to pay her because of her sex. Your firm can avoid the extra expense of paying family allowance out to all female employees by instead giving up the family (and perhaps housing) allowances in return for a more rational approach to compensation. This is just one of the many things Japanese companies will be doing in the next few months.

V

Case Studies and More
from Behind
the Bamboo Board Room

1

Absolutely Required Reading for the Serious Businessman —the ¥ and $ Lifeblood and Guts of Your Company

Rules of Employment, salary and retirement regulations —the traditional no-touch area for the expatriate executive, but one that is too important to be left to subordinates.

You need built in Application Software—giving you your own on-file personnel expert who won't allow a strategic mistake on the important issues facing you.

The right policy language, programs and application techniques (which are basically little more than the best of good Japanese personnel practice and the tools that make Japanese companies so strong), adapted to your Rules of Employment, compensation, and retirement plan, along with the establishment of a few simple appraisal, motivational, and reward techniques can lead to significant cost savings, sales, and profit gains.

Introductory comments

No single product or service can favorably affect your operation more. You will gain the effect of having a built- in, on-file, personnel manager assuring that you always execute the right policy in every key strategic area.

With strategically improved Rules of Employment, in a direct sense you can immediately cut back costs of staff leaving and drastically reduce turnover. You can have more control over performance and staffing problems. Why loose the good performers to competitors? Instead, reward and energize your staff with rich performance pay systems. You will be able to "rehabilitate" problem employees and poor performers at salary levels in line with their contribution and bring equity and balance to the pay levels of other employees at similar contribution and performance levels (even when their initially determined salary levels were inappropriate, or over the years have proved to be out of line with corporate contribution.)

Coasting will no longer be rewarded. Corporate culture can change, assuring a union is never organized. And if it is, it will make no inroads and will dry up and whither away, because you become confident and know how to manage your employees in a union/collective action free environment.

Supervisors, up to the highest expatriate executives, should have the tools they need to manage effectively and with the control and power, critical to good corporate management.

You'll be able to attract, hire, reward, and keep top management talent and key performers.

As an introductory and integral part of your new Rules of Employment, you should have these and your other corporate philosophies explained for all employees to see, creating a dynamic corporate culture. There should be guidance and policy rules already written in to prevent top management, either expatriate or local Japanese management, from making serious strategic mistakes, even in the distant future and long after the current management leaves Japan or retires.

A company is only as good as its people. Whether it's manufacturing a product or getting it to the market, your human resources are the key. Direct payroll cost can represent 50 to 70% of total costs, and the difference that good strategic Rules of Employment, compensation, retirement, and implementation policies can have has been misunderstood and greatly underestimated. In terms of yen-based cost and gain, these indeed can only be rough estimates, and assumptions can be made in a number of ways.

1. A single performance problem is handled properly and quickly bringing total savings and gains to your firm of ¥160,000,000 or $1,100,000.

His salary is ¥20,000,000 per year. Instead of putting off the unpleasant and difficult termination for one more year (an optimistic number—often the problem isn't faced for years) you move immediately and save ¥20,000,000. Instead of paying him 1/2 year's salary as a settlement, such a settlement becomes unnecessary saving ¥10,000,000. You save legal expenses (conservative estimate) of ¥1,000,000.

Because he was a poor leader and manager, ten employees performed at half their potential; three quit with replacement costs (including recruitment fees); your firm's reputation in the market was hurt; and there were the opportunities lost if all this had been avoided and the right man had been in the job sooner. We calculate this waste and potential gains of ¥130,000,000 for a total waste of corporate resources amounting to ¥160,000,000 or $1,100,000*.

[* Surveys and studies confirm that in any company about 10% are poor performers. In a company of only 100 staff the aforementioned problem could be magnified perhaps five times (doesn't have to be ten X since it will also involve manager/staff at lower salary/authority levels). In money terms, then we could be talking about a net cost saving gain difference of ¥800,000,000 or $5,500,000 difference per year!]

2. Retirement benefit wasn't properly set up and lacked a strategically sound design. (Only involuntary retirement or *kaisha-tsugo* is considered here.) This alone could create unnecessary costs of ¥720,000,000 or $5,000,000 with just 50 employees.

Your compensation design is wrong in terms of the number of months of summer and winter bonus payable, the percentage of non-pensionable allowances, and perhaps the increments payable in the retirement benefit tables (months of salary for years of service).

When calculating for as few as 50 staff (assuming ¥10,000,000 salary per staff) with as little as 20 years of service, your practice versus proper practice could result in such cost differences.

3. Retirement benefit design mistakes subsidize and encourage turnover, making it easy for headhunters and competitors to attack your firm and take your people, for direct costs in wasted retirement benefit of ¥220,000,000 or $1,500,000 in a firm of 50 employees.

For 50 staff at ¥10,000,000 average salary, who quit your firm with ten years of service, your current retirement benefit practices could very likely be costing you such an amount.

4. If you also look at how this (immediately above) largely unnecessary turnover/talent drain weakens your firm with opportunity lost, replacement/recruiting costs and harm to your reputation, one possible calculation places the costs at ¥1,140,000,000 or $8,000,000.

5. If we total these retirement benefits/compensation design issues and their effect on turnover and influence on building a strong loyal organization, they could be costing a multinational of some 100 staff a conservative (but rough) estimate of ¥2,000,000,000 or $15,000,000 over a ten year time frame.

6. You need to get rid of 20 salesmen who aren't selling, but your firm doesn't have the proper policy language/practices to handle this in a strategic cost effective way. Your direct payout in retirement premiums could be ¥50,000,000, but long-term costs to the organization could be more like ¥1,500,000,000 or $10,000,000*.

Given your current policies and practices it will likely cost you ¥50,000,000 more than it should, and this is not even taking into account the fact that you may allow the performance/contribution problem to continue longer than it should due to your lack of knowledge and absence of the tools in your Rules of Employment to handle the problem strategically and decisively. Considering this, and that if handled wrong, there could be moral/motivation problems among remaining salesmen and staff or drawn-out expensive litigation. The actual realistic costs could be more like ¥1,500,000,000 or $10,000,000.

(* This assumes a larger firm where non-strategic handling could demoralize/demotivate and create problems and costs affecting 100 salesmen or staff at average ¥7,000,000 annual salary. These salesmen would not be on their toes and never reach their potential.)

7. As your firm's retirement age is increased from the traditional age of 55 on up to 60 and beyond in the future, make sure you avoid escalating payroll and retirement liability costs along with the loss of corporate vitality by making the adjustments that Japanese firms made and will continue to be making. (Currently the government social security pension is paid out at 60 but this will move to 65. There will be increasing pressures/guidance to increase corporate retirement ages.) Failure to implement properly these routine policies that are so widespread in Japanese firms could cost you ¥1,000,000,000 or $7,000,000.

Such a waste of scarce corporate resources could take place in the typical foreign capitalized firm with as few as 100 headcount and 30 people over 40 years of age. This is without even considering the greater problems in costs in terms of demotivated younger managers, turnover in their ranks, and excessive pressure/health problems faced by older managers kept too long on the line in this especially tough and competitive market place.

8. Over a ten year period, a company of some 100 headcount loses and has to replace some 50 of its stronger performers (including key marketing/sales people) because the company fails to recognize and reward their extra efforts and merely pays out at about the same level of average and even below-average performers. One of the simplest and most powerful ways to reward for performance is to utilize fully the leverage of the typical five to seven months of summer and winter bonus paid at your firm. Nine foreign firms out of ten are not effectively and adequately doing this now. Our estimate of possible lost sales and opportunities is ¥12,000,000,000 to ¥24,000,000,000 or $84,000,000 to $168,000,000 based on our assumptions.

You can make your own estimate of what these costs are. We have experienced it can mean the difference between just being in the market and being successful as well as a major player in the market. Sales of ¥2,400,000,000 or $16,600,000 could have been at least doubled and on just the last five years; that's the difference of ¥12,000,000,000 or $84,000,000; if tripled, it's ¥24,000,000,000 or $168,000,000 potential gain (or loss).

Questionable calculations? Maybe.

But how are companies, especially sales/marketing organizations built? By attracting, keeping, motivating, managing, and richly rewarding a good team of people.

9. Mistaken and poor strategies (yet 97 X out of 100 they're applied!) toward corporate rationalization/"voluntary" staff reduction exercises can cost your firm US$ millions in direct out of pocket costs, not to mention the loss of irreplaceable managers/staff and setbacks which may lead to bankruptcy/Japan market withdrawal.

In a company needing to reduce 40 staff at an average salary of ¥10,000,000 per year with ten years of service, the wrong approach could cost an extra ¥250,000,000 or $1,800,000, just based on the plus alpha of the "voluntary" retirement benefit premium.

But this does not take into account the opportunities not lost but rather gained because the company insisted on not letting good performers retire with the extra premium. Over a ten year period this will amount to many times the aforementioned savings in retirement benefit payout—perhaps to $10,000,000 to even $20,000,000.

10. Policy language, corporate culture, and supervisors' orientation toward overtime allowance payment are wrong with burdensome overtime, also triggering some turnover among female clerical and perhaps other categories of staff. Improved policy language and practices could be 1/5 as costly.

If 15 employees at annual salaries of ¥6,000,000 work ten hours of overtime per week, the extra cost is ¥100,000,000 per year or $700,000. An acceptable allowance program should/could cost 1/5 of that at about ¥20,000,000 or $140,000 per year.

11. There are any number of other Rules of Employment determined/driven policy areas that will have significant impacts, such as,

a) Long term disability policies where money is routinely wasted, yet the benefit to the employee can essentially remain the same or even increase. (With the government insurances picking up the difference as should have been the practice from the beginning!)

b) You might be a company that has an unusually short working day of 9:00 a.m. to 5:00 p.m. or 5:15 p.m. Increasing this will help you serve customers better and keep staff support people around longer each day making managers and key producers more effective. Even such "negative" changes CAN be done if deemed appropriate and if properly communicated and implemented.

c) Many companies fail to adhere to "no work, no pay" practices, failing to cut a day's pay and instead keeping pay levels the same between employees who work rain or shine and those with aberrant attendance—certainly no way to build a strong organization of committed people who want to be justly rewarded for their extra efforts.

d) Providing legally required non-paid menstrual leave on a paid basis is an unusual practice, costly and has even caused rifts between women who take advantage of it and the more dedicated women who work for you, instead. Bad feelings and tension result. Once a union organization drive was started by the dedicated women who were angered because management ignored their request to change to the more common unpaid leave basis.

Effective management is not about providing rich and liberal pay and benefits if they go to the wrong people for the wrong reasons—The same is true of the uniform pay increases and fixed non-performance summer and winter bonuses that only the below average employees, and perhaps union members want to protect themselves so that they can maintain their level of mediocre effort and performance.

More on why improved policies and the right "application technology" can work for you in Japan

1. On misunderstandings of Japanese style performance pay, and rich (but sensible) reward systems that work.

There is actually more room for flexible performance pay and a rich and varied reward system at well managed Japanese firms than there is in your home country firm. You can install these policies and practices at your Japan operation too.

2. On the "hire-fire" alternative that works in Japan.

The "hire and fire" approach does not work in Japan and is not the powerful Strategic Tool that you need to succeed here. There are other options as used by the Japanese that must be available to the foreign capitalized firm to keep the playing field even and enable you to compete effectively, at reasonable fixed cost levels, and free of debilitating litigation.

3. On transfers and reorganizing/restructuring work.

One of the great strengths of a Japanese business is the ability to transfer pretty much freely any man to any position (or even location!) Without wreaking unnecessary hardship on your staff. This can be your strength, too.

Summary statement

Your Rules of Employment and other personnel documentation should assist you in anticipating, identifying, reacting to, and fixing all of the biggest people problems and challenges you and your firm will ever face in Japan. The necessity and reasons justifying any changes you make or will have to make should be at your fingertips.

Your employees and supervisors should have built-in guidance and instructions on what is expected of them, allowing them to do their jobs better, work better together, always with a sensible and strategic application of the carrot and the stick (if unavoidable).

Kindly understand that we are talking about much more then merely replacing or changing conventional Rules of Employment. For many clients even that would be enough, and they would benefit in ¥ and $'s as shown above.

But good policies and documentation—definition and guidelines of a dynamic corporate culture with detailed personnel and management policies should be the indispensable basis of defining any program of corporate revitalization and giving the effort direction and permanence.

One-off training or even constant non-focused training without vision and consistency will not do that, and nothing will get the needed attention and focus better than permanent policy changes.

The implementation process and orchestration, (perhaps by employee task force if recommendable) backed up by an internal educational campaign leading to new "strategic tools" in the hands of managers and supervisors, and a new confidence and mandate given to them may be just what your firm is lacking and most needs.

This can be particularly true in well established firms of several hundred (or thousands) of employees that need to become energized and adapt a brighter, more vibrant and more positive, forward looking, "can-do" corporate culture.

The right solution gives the required permanence and this new way of thinking, behaving, and managing will permeate throughout your organization as each old and new employee gets his own copy of the Rules of Employment, "Application Software," and your vision.

Supervisors and employees can understand, accept, and own intellectually and more importantly, emotionally what is expected of them, what is the standard, how they will be managed and rewarded and what will happen when they do not or cannot make the grade.

2

Headhunting the Samurai

In today's newspaper I saw the boldest and blackest headline in weeks. Mr. Ezoe, chairman and founder of Recruit Inc., and two executives cooperating with him, formerly of NTT, were arrested and taken away on bribery charges—another chapter in perhaps the largest postwar scandal rattling this island nation. Just as big as, if not bigger than, the Lockheed scandal, which brought down Prime Minister Tanaka.

What is Recruit, Inc., and why has the scandal reached such proportions? While Ezoe was a student at Tokyo University, he started up an advertising publication to help place students into companies and meet the part-time employment needs of employers in the area. He perfected this formula of matching applicants for jobs, but in the format primarily of being a publishing and advertising firm more than being involved in recruiting and headhunting per se.

He was probably too successful and too rich, rapidly diversifying into similar publications in real estate and other areas. Although he wasn't scouting per se, he shook up the establishment by providing options or alternatives to the Japanese employee who had primarily worked within a closed labor market environment. Mr. Ezoe was not the first to commit such bribes; it's quite common here. But he was a rebel, so no one protected him. The model of lifetime employment was never characteristic of medium and small enterprises or any start-up company which had to establish critical mass quickly. They had been running advertisements in newspapers and magazines for years; for, after all, you cannot run a company purely with new school graduates. Nor are you able to attract new school graduates the way the large firms can when you are still small and are a company of no social prestige.

In fact, the Japanese model of lifetime employment, seniority wages, and enterprise unions really only applies to the largest firms, generally with well over a thousand employees. In such firms the high school and university placement officials take the employment request seriously. Most employment, other than for a small percentage of specialists or part-time contract workers, has traditionally taken place from April 1, as the school year ends. Smaller firms, however, have had to get their personnel through advertising, word of mouth, introductions, direct raiding and scouting, and from about 1965 executive search or recruiting firms that set up shop in Japan, working on a standard fee basis of generally 35% in this marketplace.

With the exception of the *jinzai-haken*, or, temporary placement firms which employ the staff and continue to take about a 1/3 percentage of the fee (firms such as Man Power or Kelly Girls in the U.S. or Blue Arrow in Britain), it is impossible for an executive search firm or headhunter to achieve anywhere near the scale of business that Mr. Ezoe masterminded at Recruit. Actually, the largest search firms in the world with a multinational network rarely have total gross billings of over $30 to $60 million. In Japan such firms are also here generally with a team of two to three or four consultants.

Here at TMT we have been able to support a team of some 25 employees, with 15 executive search consultants. This has only been possible through the labor and personnel consulting side of our business, which brings in good clients and allows us to establish a special relationship from the start.

Executive search is tough business out here in Japan. Six or seven years ago most candidates did not even know what we were doing when we cold-called them out of the blue. Nowadays "headhunter" has become a household word, and one out of 10 to 20 people called (depending on the skills and tone of voice of the recruiter, as well as the message, of course) will come and meet us at our office. It is from there that the fight begins, however.

Generally, the younger the candidate, the less willing he is to move; especially if he is in one of the large Japanese firms with social prestige and well known to his potential marriage mates, family, and relatives, etcetera. Such a man is still subject to the dissuasion of his parents, family, peers, and above all else, his boss. It is not unknown for a man to come in and resign, submitting his resignation and even giving the date when he will leave, including very crisp and cogent reasons why the new opportunity is better for him. In spite of that, a boss will often just say, "You can't go." He takes the resignation letter, rips it up, and throws it away.

This shouldn't be acceptable, but why is it accepted? It surprisingly is, and that tells you something about how different Japan can be. What the boss doesn't tell his subordinate is that "if you quit, it makes me look bad because I'm judged on my retention rating of good subordinates (although I have also heard of cases where that is the reason the boss gives, and the subordinate, because of that, feels obligated to stick around and serve!).

Are the Japanese candidates we scout really different from managers in other countries?

After 17 years in Japan, having studied the language at university before I came, and having a Japanese wife who avoids speaking English like the plague, I think I know the ins and outs here pretty well. I don't want any readers to walk away with the impression that everything an executive learned outside won't work here, and that the *nihonjin* is always a puzzle.

That is not the case. Working within their rules, in their language, and in that context, there is very little that surprises me. For every American I know, I know a Japanese just like him. For every Hong Kong Chinese or Singaporean you know, believe me, there is a Japanese just like him, too. On second thought, I would have to say that it is very different working with the Japanese, and perhaps I am just too used to it. Indeed, every foreign executive or expatriate I have lunch with constantly points out the differences—even the Swiss who speaks five languages and has worked on all the continents.

But still, if something is wrong or inefficient, it's got to be fixed and there is a way to do it. If you need to upscale the quality of your Japanese managers at a multinational firm in Japan, it must be done, and it can be done. You can, in fact, scout out the very best and the brightest Japanese from the top employers in Japan.

It helps if you are representing a world-class firm, have an excellent business plan, stroke the candidate's ego, convince him that he will get new experiences that will further develop his career, and it often requires paying through the nose. But this should be smart money with performance-based components. That kind of package in itself is perhaps even a better screen than a probationary period to test the confidence and determination of the candidate you are considering to hire.

3

The Japanese (Asian?)
Executive Search Trap

Recently within the same week, two particularly glaring but actually rather typical hiring mistakes were made by our clients, as our firm tried to save them from themselves and effectively and successfully meet their executive search needs. These were both extremely bright and sophisticated clients who clearly, in their home country and in many other countries around the world, have made the right hiring decisions. The mistakes made this time, however, were so big, costly, and unnecessary that I vowed to put pen to paper the very next weekend.

In one company's case, several of our executive search consultants had put up as many as 11 experienced and talented managers from other major hi-tech firms. Most of these candidates had never changed jobs. Two of them changed once, and one was admittedly a job-hopper (he was put up after the first round because our consultants were so discouraged and demotivated because they knew that their candidates were the best available for that particular general manager slot, and there was not much more they wanted to or could do for that client). Sure enough, bingo, the job-hopper with the excellent English and ability to display his vision creatively and energetically and sell himself was given the nod and whisked off to the home country for orientation.

I should have stopped it, but we did have a good reference from that candidate's last employer. Also he was free and the only one readily available because he headed a division which closed for reasons beyond his control, as we had confirmed through our sources. I knew the other slate of candidates we put up were excellent, and I asked the client why he picked that man. He replied, "He was the only one I could see representing my firm as my general manager in Japan."

Within a month the honeymoon was over, and the client was back for a replacement (which we probably shouldn't have to do free of charge)! Three of the candidates we originally slated were from a major computer company in Japan, and we had a consultant who worked with them for three years. He testified that on a scale of one to ten they were "definitely number one." To no avail. A good line in English, the right chemistry, and over-emphasis on the interview itself, rather than the background and track record of the candidate had won the day.

The other case could have been potentially even a greater tragedy. A well-established multinational with over 1,000 employees in Japan was looking for two or three top level executives. I had heard off and on that a very senior executive had been hired through another headhunter and had been engaged in training abroad for a few months. Luckily, the day they flew into Tokyo to interview our candidates, I heard through the grapevine who had been hired. I was absolutely startled and amazed. A classic con man who had flitted about the multinational foreign capitalized labor market in Tokyo for years, stealing money, using aliases, and getting fired any number of times had been picked up by them. He was introduced from a "prominent and reputable Japanese headhunter." Evidence against the con man was readily available, and the problem was solved that week.

Once again, this second client made its mistake because they were looking for the wrong things. Track record and background in terms of the person's position and social/business standing of his firm took a back seat to silver-tongued oratorical skills in English, chemistry, and the interviewing process. In Japan, often the doers are not the talkers (at least, they often can't talk well in English). Good, solid candidates, who had their arm twisted to come to the interview because they were targeted and scouted after careful research by a good, ethical headhunter, have never thought about changing jobs, are not good at the employment interview and do not try as hard to sell themselves, even when their English is adequate.

When a Western business executive hires someone in Europe or the United States, he is looking at chemistry and fit, as he should. The difference is that this is after the other more important things are already in place. For example, the companies in the industry are known, as well as the relative standing of the candidate's company. Even if the candidate is not from a leading and well known firm, that may be all right in the home country, but certainly will place the candidate at a severe, if not disqualifying, disadvantage in a country like Japan. (Actually, the client that slipped up and hired the con man admitted that they only hire Western executives from leading firms, yet a simple lack of knowledge or interest in the background of the candidate, including size of firm, resulted that they were hiring a man whose last position was with a Japanese firm of only some 200 employees.)

Unfortunately, it also becomes much easier to lie to someone from a different race and culture, while it becomes difficult for a Japanese to lie or pull the wool over the eyes of a fellow Japanese. Even the big lie can become believable to foreigners who don't know much about local companies, the local industry and who have proven time and time again that they can't easily check up on background and references and often don't bother to.

Indeed, it is not easy for the expatriate or visiting Western executive to make a culturally and socially sound hire in Japan. For example, if you are hiring someone to go into an established, major firm, with several thousand or even several hundred indigenous Japanese employees, you will almost always fail unless you bring in a candidate of sufficient caliber from a Japanese context which would, as prerequisites, include having come from the right university and from a yet larger firm within that or another industry. When it comes to the world of work in a country like Japan, there is indeed a pecking order. The ministries get top people primarily from the national imperial universities. Beyond that, each year most serious businesspeople in Japan know exactly which companies rank at which number in terms of their popularity with graduating seniors. The new school graduates join on April 1, and it is only a unique and exceptional case that someone will make a decision to join a lesser firm if he is capable of getting into one of the universally recognized top employers.

IBM, for example, is the only foreign capitalized firm, which has consistently been at the top and which will impress Japanese virtually as much as any indigenous firm. The big blue is head and shoulders above the others with 24,000 employees in Japan alone and some $9 billion in sales.

There are tens of foreign capitalized firms in Japan now with a thousand or more employees. It is often said foreign firms cannot attract the best Japanese human resources. While that is true at entry level on April 1 as new university graduates, with proper scouting and handling, it is possible to bring in top mid-career hires. In fact, a foreign based multinational with only 50 employees in Japan is probably three or four times more attractive to a key performer from a leading Japanese employer than would be an indigenous firm of 50 or even 500 employees.

There are a number of good, reputable, executive search firms in Tokyo, specializing in serving the foreign capitalized corporate community. I would like to think your chances of hiring a classic con man would be less using them, for the multinational expatriate community is largely governed by reputation and the rules of the village. A recruiting firm whose client base is comprised primarily of indigenous Japanese firms may occasionally be able to get by with pawning off a weak or even dishonest candidate on a foreign capitalized firm. This is also because the candidate himself realizes that the Japanese headhunter is not plugged into the tightly knit community of foreign capitalized firms and will not know about the candidate's many failures and job-hopping at foreign capitalized firms.

Asian businessmen are aggressive. It can be a rough and tumble market. You are a babe in the woods. Make sure you ask tough and direct questions of both the candidate sitting in front of you and of your executive search firm. If the candidate is a job-hopper and there is any room for doubt that he is not now employed as indicated in his resume, ask him for his company phone number, assuring him that you will be careful. Be sure to get references and phone numbers at all the companies where the individual worked in the past. Obviously, this kind of reference check would jeopardize the individual's position at his current employer, but there is no reason not to get names and phone numbers at previous employers. Often this is enough. If the candidate calls in and says he is not interested or doesn't show up for the next interview, you will have a pretty good idea why.

Most importantly, remember that the basics of your decision must not be the interview and the way the individual comes across. Chemistry, charisma, ability to communicate in an interesting way in English or even to answer logically in English questions posed become largely cultural exercises, yet the culture in which the individual is expected to establish or make a company grow is not your culture.

It matters less what a man says or how he sells himself. Look at what he did and what he is doing. You will be largely there and more than halfway on the path toward a successful hire, which will also be greeted with an acceptable level of credibility and respect of the existing Japanese organization, if you focus on what must be the true basics.

And this is what the man did and accomplished—his track record and the record should include no more than one to three companies at the most. In Japan it is also helpful if the candidate should have at least started his career in a leading, well-recognized Japanese or major foreign capitalized employer.

Certainly, you will and should occasionally hire candidates that are an exception to these rules. But at least you must know the rules and under which circumstances the exceptions may or may not work. There is less room for exception when bringing a senior, outside mid-career hire into a firm that is already well-established here, with several thousand or even several hundred employees.

If you are an outsider interviewing Japanese (and candidates of other very different cultures), please learn to discount the interview, and avoid being impressed by good chemistry and presentation skills unless the more essential track record and corporate background (status) is in place.

4

Gaijin Boss Beware! of the $400 Commuter Allowance

Along with myself, I am sure many expatriate managers in Japan read with interest the January 13, 1989, article in the *Japan Times* concerning changes in the new tax law taking place from April 1 of this year. There is one minor change which is worth taking a minute to focus on. Have you noticed it? And are you aware of its implications?

It read, "The ruling party decided to exempt from income tax commuting allowances of up to ¥50,000 a month, compared with the nontaxable ceiling of ¥26,000 at present."

Fair enough. A good, reasonable attempt to reduce taxable income of salaried workers in a country where the high land price is causing people to live further and further outside the center of city and their place of work.

Because Japan has always provided a tax deduction to employees for their commutation allowance and for whatever other reasons, there is an unusual practice in Japan of having the employer pay the employee's commutation allowance at cost. This, of course, always greatly surprises human resource types from the home office. Their initial reaction is that the place where an employee lives has nothing to do with the job; and there is no reason why compensation should vary in this way—depending on the distance between home and office.

Nevertheless, I have always recommended to clients that they provide the commutation allowance at cost, as it is such an ingrained practice here, and the employees you hire certainly expect it.

In most employment contracts, letters of offer, or in the Rules of Employment, it generally states that "the commutation allowance will be paid up to the maximum tax-deductible amount." This has generally meant that should the employee have a commutation cost beyond the tax-deductible (currently ¥26,000), the employee would have to pay the difference out of his or her own pocket.

In my company, for example, we had similar language in both our letters of employment and our Rules of Employment. Such language was acceptable when the tax-deductible limit was at the more reasonable level and when it only went up gradually and incrementally every year or two.

Now, however, in one quick shot, the limit moves from ¥26,000 up to ¥50,000. This could represent a significant extra and unacceptable cost to many firms.

While employees and unions may hope that the current widespread policy language prevails, allowing the potential for a not insignificant number of employees to enjoy a commutation allowance of as high as ¥50,000 per month ($400), I believe companies should move quickly and should point out that assumptions have drastically changed and that it will be necessary to change policy language, such that, for example, "commutation allowance will be paid at cost but up to the maximum level of ¥26,000."

More generous firms may be willing to set in an inflationary escalator, such that the ¥26,000 limit will gradually move up by 1% or 2% each year.

In my opinion, this is not just a question of unacceptable, rapidly increasing cost to firms. It also gets into a question of fairness and equity between employees. Frankly, it is not in either the employee's or the employer's interest to have employees commuting as much as one-and-a half, two, or even three hours one way per day! Such employees will be tired and their health could be endangered. If they have to work late and take a taxi home, it will cost their employer a fortune.

Although it is a pity that an employee must commute so far in order to own his own home or apartment, there will be employees who will give up their dream or hope of owning their own place and enjoying the tremendous growth in personal assets and will sacrifice themselves for their jobs in order that they can be fresh, rested, and able to do their jobs better.

That is another aspect of this problem. Is it fair to subsidize and encourage a small number of employees by paying as much as ¥50,000 per month, which may amount to 1/3 of lower-level employees' monthly pay, while other employees live in close so they can avoid the travel and do a better job for their employers?

I believe that few Japanese companies will continue to pay at cost as much as ¥50,000 for an employee's monthly commutation pass. I also don't think that increasing the tax deductible amount to ¥50,000 is really an answer to the problem. It is more important to bring down the land price, make better utilization of land and buildings, accompanied by improving and speeding up train services to outlying areas.

But in the short term this spring, this particular change in the tax law is going to cause a lot of headaches for employers. Make sure you are one of the employers who quickly and clearly makes the distinction between the amount you will pay as an employer and the amount which the employee will be free to declare as a tax deduction to himself.

I also hope that the Ministry of Labor and local Labor Standards offices will be sensitive to this problem affecting employers and provide fair and reasonable administrative guidance and support to employers in their need to adjust their policy language and achieve a fair reconciliation between this change in the tax code and the financial constraints and difficulties of running a business in this tough and competitive marketplace.

5

A Neck Cutting Leads to Revolt — West Clashes with East

It was just another business luncheon featuring a big name speaker stopping off in Tokyo on his way to somewhere else. These things usually take two hours and irreparably cut into the working day. If you join the right places, it's easy enough to get on the mailing lists.

As I was walking out the door of the Tokyo American Club, crossing the parking lot toward my car, I heard my name called out from behind me. I spun around and visually checked out my pursuer until we met up with each other. All within a second, we instinctively moved together under the awning hanging out over the club entrance.

"You would be Mr. Nevins, the labor consultant, wouldn't you?" he said extending his hand with a small nervous smile. I greeted it with a firm handshake. It was a thick European accent, which I'm only beginning to be able to label as French, thanks to my five years of lackluster effort in junior high and high school language class.

"If you have a minute, I may have some business for you, which may be of interest to you." He was reaching into his suitcoat pocket. Before he could draw his hand out, I passed him a calling card, which I normally transfer to the breast pocket of my shirt before such luncheons. Even if the speech content isn't worth the two hours, I attend in hopes of just such an opportunity.

"How do you do Mr. Devereaux. I don't know if you plan on telling me about it now, but if there is any confidentiality at all, may I suggest we step away from this entranceway?"

"Do you have a minute?"

"Yes, indeed."

"Do you have transportation here today?"

"Yes, but I'll walk you over to your driver."

"Well Mr. Nevins, to get to the point, we have made a Japanese gentleman, our C.E.O., as I wanted to step down, leaving our local operation for the Japanese to

240

run. I was also looking forward to getting back to the head office in France. He has only been in position for six weeks, but all hell is breaking loose. The man appears to have a little Hitler complex, and he works the six *bucho*s (general managers) over with a bull whip at each staff meeting. My Japanese is still not so good, but I can clearly know that his way of giving orders, and even the Japanese words he uses for "you" are totally unacceptable in this culture."

"Sorry, but which form does he use?"

"People tell me and I have heard that he overuses *kimi* and he has said *omae* on multiple occasions."

"Okay, I get a feeling for what you're saying. Doesn't sound too good."

"I have also seen him drive his index finger into some *bucho*'s breast bone, when he strongly lectures them. He has also upbraided and scolded non-management people in front of their peers. In your experience, what do you think of such a man? Is this some new effective style of Japanese management?" he asked somewhat sardonically with an obvious twinkle of enjoyment in his eyes.

I grinned along with him asking if the man had ever been thoroughly investigated before being hired.

"I'm glad that you are already one step ahead of me. And that is the step I was about to make. Where can such an investigation be done? Do you get involved in this kind of work?"

"Of course, it's best done before the man is hired. How are you thinking of using such information?... to answer the question, in the executive recruitment side of our business we will never place a man of questionable or job-hopping background without undergoing a through investigation, often, by an outside, objective, third-party detective and research company known as a *koshinjo*. My firm, TMT, would, therefore, not directly conduct the check. Obviously it is by no means the main thrust of our business, but it is a necessary and critical service which we will provide."

"Can you say this word again, this *kochinjo*, is it?"

"*Koshinjo.*"

"And what may I ask can I expect these services to cost?"

"Our direct out-of-pocket expense to the agency will run you anywhere from ¥80,000 to ¥150,000."

"That seems quite dear for a couple of critical phone calls."

"Mr. Devereaux, they will visit rather than phone. People in personnel departments, etcetera, or even neighbors, and local shop keepers will be met face to face. Actually a lot of man hours are involved. They do quite a thorough job."

"Is this common local practice? I have been here three years and have never heard of such a thing."

"Most large, established companies with over 1,000 employees and certainly almost all financial institutions would never think of hiring even a clerk fresh from school without having first completed a check of character, family background, and claimed credentials. Japan's own watered down version of the equal employment opportunity movement is to some extent placing restrictions on how this information is used, however. But they still have a long way to go."

"You mean Japanese companies will go to such expense even before hiring someone? I knew that they invested in training, but...."

"Your company has a problem now with the president. Money spent before hiring would have been money well spent."

"Mr. Nevins, would you recommend that we proceed with such an investigation?"

"Have you sat down and had a few frank words with this man? Maybe he can take it. Maybe he will respond and come around. Just be sure and base all your thinking and actions on the assumption that it will not be easy or pleasant to fire and replace such a man."

"In any case I want your input and this information to help me grasp the situation. More importantly, it was really a boss several rungs up in Paris who pushed through with the Motoyama appointment. Motoyama's English is unusually good, and he sold himself well to two of my superiors at the head office. I'll therefore need documentation to cover myself on all fronts."

"We'll do it for you. Is there anything else I should know?"

"Four of my *bucho*s say that if Motoyama doesn't go, they will."

"I didn't realize the situation is so serious. I'll get right on it but give me about ten days."

"At the latest, please. I'm scheduled to return to France by November 20 and before that and in about three weeks we have scheduled a big distributors' meeting at which Motoyama was supposed to be introduced and presented as the new president and formally and ceremoniously inaugurated as the C.E.O."

"Too bad you have these constraints pressing in on you."

"I was looking forward to going home, but I cannot with any peace of mind leave the company to this man under these conditions. I hope to hear that he uses his 'whip of love'—that is what he calls it—only in the beginning, and that he is a warm and balanced man of compassion once he has molded the organization to suit his tastes."

"Is this guy at all competent? Does he have strong points in his favor?"

"Motoyama has studied and worked very hard. He stays on late into the night. He has good analytical skills. His strong leadership seems to be welcome by some of the rank and file. I will even frankly admit that because he is Japanese and can speak and use the language, he has already grasped elements of our business here that I might never master. Motoyama can implement and deal with the entire organization, not just the bilingual *bucho*s. He has an effective, hands-on approach that I could only dream about in this country."

"Well let's move cautiously. I'll let you be off and will report as soon as possible."

I got back to the office and within an hour personally contacted the man I normally deal with at the *koshinjo* agency.

Actually over a week had passed, and the investigator still had not been successful in persuading key managers at two of Motoyama's known former employers to make time for the investigation interviews. I resolved that with the time constraints we faced: our own staff had better begin some independent research of our own. This is, fortunately, an infrequent necessity and a chore we were not looking forward to.

Two days earlier in the search for a Japanese female executive secretary by our ABA clerical division for a close personal friend, we had come across, through sheer and unusual coincidence, a letter of recommendation signed by Motoyama. It was stapled to the young lady's resume.

I didn't think she was adequately qualified to work as my friend's secretary but thought two birds could be killed with one interview. She was very forthcoming with information on Motoyama. She was young, and he had been her first boss. He took a fatherly interest in her almost attempting to pass on to her all his business experience and skills. She admitted that he was tough and intolerant of incompetence. I was told a long story about how he was done-in through dirty tricks.

At his former employer, Motoyama had also been president. It was a smaller company with only about 20 employees. Apparently, his abrasive and forceful management style over a five-year period had culminated in another case of him or us. In particular, two or three subordinate managers used the telex terminals and phones to communicate directly with the head office. They would undermine Motoyama at every available opportunity. Finally, he either voluntarily quit or was essentially forced out. The effect was the same. Even today, I'm not sure whether he was, in fact, technically fired.

In any case, the Japanese woman I interviewed was extremely dedicated to her former boss during the first two years of her short career. It was six months ago that they both left the company at about the same time. They continued to see each other at least once a month, however. Motoyama would give her heartfelt advice on how to handle her job interviews and how and where to train herself best to become a first-class bilingual executive secretary in a foreign capitalized firm.

This young lady felt that Motoyama would accept and favorably respond to frank advice cautioning him on his abrasive management style. In that this was his downfall when he was her boss; she was convinced that this time he would correct himself and behave better. I immediately conveyed her input to the client, Mr. Devereaux. He was encouraged by the news and still in hopes of being able to get back to France by November 20 as scheduled.

Meanwhile, it had occurred to me that the parent company of Motoyama's former employer was one of our clients in the executive search side of our business. I knew that one of our consultants was in charge of that account and that he'd been dealing with the American with overall responsibility and authority over the main company as well as three or four joint venture operations. Motoyama's former employer was one of those joint ventures.

I phoned up Motoyama's former boss. He was very accommodating, stating that he thought that Motoyama was all in all quite an effective manager. Although they never worked in the same office and only saw each other a few times a month, he was willing to give Motoyama a fairly strong recommendation. He confirmed, however, that Motoyama had got himself into hot water with subordinate Japanese managers and that they had maneuvered to force him out. Like Motoyama's former secretary, he also thought that a good frank discussion would go far toward alleviating the problem.

Mr. Devereaux was quite encouraged with these two reports. The investigation agency was just finishing off their report, and the next day, after it was formally typed up into Japanese, I submitted the report without a translation. Devereaux had remarried to a Japanese woman the year before. "I'll depend on her to translate the report at least verbally for me. Her opinion will be valuable for she knows him," he concluded.

I summarized my opinion with "If I were you, I'd try to work with Motoyama. He should respond to a good talking to, and wringing him out too precipitously may open a can of worms."

Four days later I got a frantic phone call at 9:15 in the morning from Devereaux.

"How are things going?" I asked.

"Absolutely awful." he bellowed out frantically. "I conveyed the results of our findings by phone to our Executive Vice President in charge of worldwide sales. He listened for about 20 minutes, and apparently had heard enough. He said that he recognized a pattern of managerial style which was totally against corporate policy, and said that he's never known a 50-year-old man who could change his personality and character. At the distributors' meeting coming up early next week he didn't want to have to introduce a local Japan president who would soon be fired."

"Motoyama has been fired, hasn't he?" I cut in.

"Yes, I wanted to check with you first. I've heard its impossible to fire in Japan, and I didn't expect that a firing would result from a single phone conversation."

"If he's been fired, he's been fired. Don't worry about that. Since he was the president and was a member of the Board of Directors, he's not legally considered to be an employee covered by the Labor Standards Law. You can probably legally get away with it. Your settlement costs will depend on the length of his director's term—it can be worked-out. But what was Motoyama's reaction? I'll bet he was surprised."

"He was indeed. It's the only time I've ever seen him short of words. His jaw dropped, and his hand trembled as he signed the resignation papers."

"Do the other employees and managers know yet?"

"Yesterday afternoon, just after I called Motoyama in and gave him the news, I went around and told five of the six general manager *bucho*s. Even the four who opposed him the most were a little surprised with the speed at which it was executed. One of them said with some temerity, but nervously 'In your country neck-cutting is too easy.' What was he saying?"

"*Kubi-kiri* is the common word for being fired in Japanese. It literally means 'neck-cutting'. Although those four *bucho*s had told you that they wanted Motoyama out, I don't think they really expected it to happen, at least not so quickly. Now they see their own necks on the chopping block. A single firing always seems to create a wave of insecurity throughout a foreign company in Japan."

"I think I'm going to have some trouble with the sales manager. Yesterday afternoon he was tied up in a number of meetings. I probably should have made more of an effort to see him. In any case it seems that he's quite miffed and upset over Motoyama's forced resignation. I just had my secretary call him to have him come to my office. He refused to come saying something like, 'Tell Mr. Devereaux that it was yesterday when we should have talked. I have nothing to say to him."

"Sounds like a classic case of the left-out and ignored Japanese manager. Participative management is serious business in Japan. If a Japanese is satisfied that he's been given a chance to put in his two yen, you'll usually have no problems. My golden rule as a consultant is always to let the Japanese opposition think that the ideas or actions I work out with the client originated by them."

"That sounds easier said than done."

"It requires patience, restraint, and a full dose of humility. Rather than presenting programs, you must rather seek opinions and open up the floor to discussion. Careful orchestration in a non-directive atmosphere is essential. By jabbing and only giving half a hint, you can be successful in getting the Japanese to come up 'on their own' with almost the exact same proposal or program. Sometimes I even get the feeling that they really know what you're trying to do. I guess they're willing to give you credit and points for the way in which the ceremony is conducted. Sincerity and the time taken seem to be all important."

"I wish I could have put you on an extension when I spoke with my boss. Anyway, Motoyama has been fired, in the tradition of our French guillotine. The Executive Vice President of sales, Mr. Rouseaux, will be in Tokyo for the distributors' meeting on Monday. He's flying in on Saturday afternoon. I told him about your input and your work. He's hoping to meet with us on Saturday night. Maybe you will laugh, but he's wondering if you can present him with a few candidates to take over as president while he is in Tokyo until Tuesday of next week."

"Our executive recruitment business does not work quite that way, especially in Japan."

"I know this will not be easy, but as long as the executives you present do not have running noses and can sit straight in a chair, it will be alright. We won't expect too much."

"I'll see what we can drum up."

"Is Saturday at six o'clock at the New Otani alright for dinner? That's where Mr. Rouseaux will be staying."

"Fine. I have a social commitment, but it can be easily broken. In the meantime, I suggest that you personally announce the resignation decision to all employees, at least at departmental meetings."

"Any advice on what I should say?"

"In any case it's going to be weak, but how about something like 'As of this morning, Mr. Motoyama will no longer be with us due to a significant disagreement in management style and philosophy'. Add that 'In view of the distributors' meeting coming up on Monday, it was felt that rapid action was necessary. It would not have been good for our key distributors to meet and become friendly with the president, only to find that he is soon no longer with the company.'"

"Anything else I might do to improve the situation?"

"Make yourself available for questions and discussions with all employees. Tell them your office door will be open all day. It's most important that you allay their fears and doubts. I'd also go over and see the sales manager who refused to come to your office. No sense in playing a game of hide and seek."

About an hour later Devereaux called me again. "Watanabe, the troublesome sales manager, has been holding a meeting all morning with his 14 subordinates in the sales department. They've been distributing fliers demanding that Mr. Rouseaux and the head office join me in reinstating Motoyama. The sales department says that until that happens, they will not work, and they are going to boycott the distributors meeting on Monday. Maybe they are even planning to go out on strike."

"Mr. devereaux, they are already on strike. You are lucky that a *bucho* manager like Watanabe is in charge of the rebellion. He is probably fighting more for his pecking order among the other managers. I doubt that he would want anyone to go off to a labor union for he would lose his power and control over the revolt. I have a feeling that Watanabe has a lot of guts and is a potential leader for you. How old is he?"

"He's only 39 and is our second youngest *bucho*."

"Does he have any personal animosity or resentment against any of the four *bucho*s who were trying to pull the rug out from under Motoyama?"

"Yes, he feels that his department is limited by the utter incompetence of the distribution *bucho*, Tanaka. Also last year a 30-year-old fellow was hired. He was a graduate of Columbia, one of your Ivy League schools. His English has no accent.

Perhaps Watanabe resents that this fellow, Yoshioka, became a *bucho*. This means that Watanabe is no longer the youngest general manager."

"Can you tell me more about Watanabe?"

"Actually I respect him and am rather fond of him. He has guts. One day late last month he got so mad at Motoyama he nearly pushed him through a wall partition. Since then, it seems they've had a healthy respect for one another. None of the other *bucho*s have had the guts to stand up against Motoyama. Instead, they just complained to me behind his back."

"What triggered the fight?"

"Motoyama criticized Watanabe once too often in front of his subordinates. The sales manager flew into a rage and attacked Motoyama. underneath that thin veneer of patience and restraint, I guess there's a good deal of samurai within them. By the way, what can I expect from this samurai strike?"

"Don't be surprised if the sales department never goes out on strike. It is more likely that they will stay on the premise. It is in the company where Japanese feel that they can create the most trouble and post the largest embarrassment to management, as well as score political points by converting other employees to the cause. In a union situation, due to the absence of a strong strike fund, because of the small dues base limited to a single enterprise, a typical Japanese union cannot attempt a Western style sustained economic strike where all services are withheld."

"In this case, Mr. Nevins, you say it is unlikely a union will become involved. How can I allow the sales department to strike if they're not even a union?"

"It's true that unless the rebels write up a constitution and register themselves with the Labor Relations Commission they will not enjoy protection under the Trade Union Law, but I wouldn't push them too hard. Watanabe, the sales *bucho*, doesn't want a union, but should even a single employee be fired, I guarantee that within 24 hours an outside union will become involved. Then you would have to contend with Unfair Labor Practice charges as well."

"What should we do? I'd like to give you a carte blanche in getting the company through this crisis smoothly."

"A carte blanche, hey? Coming from a Frenchman, that really means something. I'll cancel my lunch at the Hilton. How about calling a meeting of all employees for 11:00 a.m.? They must be confused about the sales department's actions and the fliers they've been sending to all employees. Let's have a *shojiki-kai* or honesty party, in which all employees can ask questions and be heard. We'll also find out if they're willing to let Watanabe, the rebelling sales manager, be their spokesman. I also want to get a better idea of sentiments for or against Motoyama."

"What is this thing you call an honesty party?"

"Honesty means *shojiki* in Japanese. An honesty party is simply one of my own techniques. I've invented it to put a stop to all rumors and to defuse building sentiments in just such situations. Let me run this meeting. Let's also allow Motoyama to show up and attend. I'll run the meeting in a very autocratic style, telling the employees that I'm in charge. I'll talk and act in Japanese in the way Motoyama has been handling himself. I'll then make an analogy between the way I'm acting and the way Motoyama carried himself. I'm sure that at some point and certainly within half an hour, your employees will reject me and demand that you run the meeting. This is exactly what I want. You will be returned with your full authority and with a mandate to assert leadership and see the company through the crisis. In the meantime, as a scapegoat, I can play the valuable role of directly telling and actually demonstrating to the employees why Motoyama was subject to the forced resignation."

"About me asserting my leadership and returning as the unscarred hero, I think what this company needs most is a strong but benevolent Japanese president and we should find this man as soon as possible."

"I know, but even assuming that we could identify and scout out the ideal Japanese executive in time for the Monday distributors' meeting or shortly thereafter, your employees would be convinced that any man found in such short order could not possibly be any good. They would feel that it was just one more example of rapid and rushed Western-style hiring and firing."

"I see. If we are going to get the 11:00 a.m. meeting of all managers and employees organized, I'd better start moving. You can make it by 11:00 a.m.?"

"I'll jump in a taxi and be there. One more thing. Have a high-quality *bento* box lunch ordered for each employee. After feelings have peaked at about 12:30 p.m. or 1:00 p.m., bring out the lunches for everyone to enjoy at company expense. It may seem like an unnecessary and troublesome expense, but the psychological pay off will be great. A more relaxed atmosphere of trust and loyalty to the company can also be created."

"I can see that you've done this before Mr. Nevins."

"Actually it's all very simple. Just listen, stay away from legalisms, avoid showing anger, avoid surprises, get everybody involved, and above all, be sincere."

The meeting was moved up until 11:30 a.m. because Devereaux was unable to get either Watanabe of the sales department or Motoyama to agree to come. Watanabe would only come if Motoyama were going to be present. The former president turned Devereaux down, saying that he would only talk to the big boss, Rouseaux, if Rouseaux called him. Devereaux asked me to speak with both Motoyama and Watanabe. I called them up in that order, speaking Japanese. I was able to persuade them both to attend.

Watanabe's first question to me over the phone was what is my relationship to Devereaux and to the current problem at the company. I had to think fast and knew that Watanabe would only come to the meeting if he trusted and respected me. In the back of my mind I already had a couple of candidates to take over immediately as president, and the employees should believe that a search for any new president had been conducted for at least a month.

"I carried out the investigation with the *koshinjo* and did research on my own, looking into Motoyama's management style, and the abrasive way he has handled staff at other companies in the past. My report and input was therefore partially responsible for the Motoyama firing. Furthermore, should I find a new Japanese president to replace Motoyama, my company will make 35% of the next president's annual income."

Watanabe was silent for what seemed to be 40 or 50 seconds. "Alright, we'll be there." he said in a voice full of conviction.

The meeting went pretty much as expected. When the floor was opened up one of the questions from a young female employee was who are you and what is your role in all this. Without blinking an eye I told her my part in the Motoyama investigation and that I stood to make 35% of the new president's annual income. I was vehemently shouted down, and they screamed for Devereaux to run the meeting—so far all was going as planned.

Devereaux didn't understand what I had been saying to the employees. I merely signaled for him to take over and he spoke mostly in English through his secretary or in his broken Japanese. Compared with me, he came out smelling like a rose.

After I was satisfied that I had a good grasp of the situation, I left the meeting early. There were more important things to do. I got back to my office, and we tried to come up with two or three of the most qualified people we could produce. During the day and by Friday afternoon we had screened out about 15 executives and narrowed down the field to an excellent man who was currently on the Board of Directors of a U.S. computer manufacturer with several thousand employees. It was also rumored that he was restless and interested in getting into a new field with new challenges. He'd been with his current employer for 27 years.

I called him late Friday afternoon—of course, in Japanese, which is the language I do all business in.

"Mr. Ohtsuka, do you remember me? My name is Nevins. Over a year ago I wanted to make you president of that European computer manufacturer."

"Oh, sorry, at first I thought you were a Japanese. I remember you well. You're the young American who would only speak to me in Japanese. At first, it took me a minute to get used to that, but it was very convenient." he said with a chuckle.

Getting right to the point I asked him three or four questions. I confirmed that he was now ready to consider other opportunities, mainly because he disagreed with the head office's lack of emphasis and commitment to the Japanese market. When asked what kind of industry he wanted to work in he answered anything but computers. I asked if he wanted the security of a large, established organization. The answer was a clear no. If anything he wanted to build from scratch, and unlike computers in Japan, he wanted a company with rapid growth potential. So far so good.

I arranged for him to spend three hours with me at my apartment on Saturday from 10:00 a.m. Nothing he heard about Devereaux's company and the situation fazed him. I told him everything, presenting all the warts, and all the weaknesses in company management and the manager's themselves. He was definitely interested. He trusted me.

In the meantime I had received a few phone calls from Devereaux. Watanabe the sales manager had on his own initiative suggested that instead of boycotting the Monday distributors' meeting, it should instead be postponed. He had his people work with the distribution department in personally calling the same 40 distributors who had been invited. Fortunately, in Japan it's not necessary to give a reason even for such a last-minute cancellation. A mere hesitation in the voice will prevent virtually any Japanese from pushing and asking why a second time.

I told Devereaux about my great find in the form of Ohtsuka-san. He was extremely pleased and said he would arrange to meet with him from 11 o'clock at the New Otani on Monday. Following that, Devereaux, his superior, Rouseaux, Ohtsuka and myself would get together for lunch at the New Otani.

As scheduled, I met with Rouseaux for dinner at six o'clock at his hotel on Saturday, the day of his arrival in Japan. I think we both had quite a favorable impression of each other. Devereaux was really depending on me to explain what was behind the tremendous fuss surrounding the forced resignation of Motoyama. As usual, I pulled no punches and told Rouseaux that it was a grave mistake to have hired Motoyama without a thorough investigation. I also said that my advice on first giving him a good frank talking to should have been followed.

When I told the two French executives that I had gone ahead and ordered a ¥150,000 investigation of Ohtsuka, Devereaux chimed in with "That Mr. Nevins has not been authorized and will come out of your 35% fee."

"Unfortunately in a crisis we don't always have time to discuss things as we'd like to," I said.

Devereaux looked down at his plate, and Rouseaux cleared his throat, "Our company believes in paying whatever is necessary for timely and the right services."

I knew I had a top man in Ohtsuka. I had also been working behind the scenes late Saturday afternoon. By making a phone call to the rebel sales manager, Watanabe, I was able to establish a bit more rapport. I was trying to encourage him to give up on Motoyama and to call in his subordinates and get them all to work for the company on Monday.

A few phone calls helped me to focus in on where I could outplace Motoyama. I came up with a client that needed just his abilities and personality. After honestly telling the client everything about Motoyama, as well as the situation and the investigation report findings, the client was still interested in meeting him. This time Motoyama wouldn't be the president but would be the number two Japanese under a firmly entrenched and strong, charismatic (but quite unanalytical) Japanese president. Motoyama's pay would jump by four or five million yen. From the start this time we all would remind him to control his 'whip of love.'

I discussed all of this frankly with Motoyama. I think we were coming to have a mutual respect for each other. He admitted that his autocratic and abrasive style would only be his downfall again. He said that he probably wouldn't go back to the French company even if they asked him back. I asked him if he had anything more to say to Devereaux or Rouseaux.

"If Mr. Rouseaux calls me at home on Sunday or Monday morning and if he wants to talk with me, I will be willing to see him."

Motoyama's attitude clearly indicated to me that he was looking on to a new career opportunity. After being fired and openly ridiculed by me at the *shojiki-kai*, the loss of face would make it difficult to continue at the French company.

Our dinner meeting Saturday night ended well. Rouseaux stated strongly that he was willing to spend at least an hour on Monday with both the rebel sales *bucho*, Watanabe, and with Motoyama, the fired president. I agreed that it would be useful to defuse Watanabe by being a listening board and giving him a chance to say his peace. From the nature of commitment etc., and the tone of the Japanese language fliers, I knew from experience that no matter how convincing or charming Rouseaux tried to be, he could never persuade Watanabe from retracting the strong statements he had already gone public with. Watanabe had committed his entire sales department (15 employees) to quit the company unless Motoyama was reinstated as president. Perhaps it could only happen in Japan. The most amazing thing is that Watanabe himself as well as most of the employees didn't even like Motoyama.

I had explained to Devereaux and Rouseaux that this issue involved much more than whether or not the employees felt that Motoyama had been qualified to be their president. I pointed out that it was the common problem of Japanese subsidiary autonomy versus the use of power and authority by the head office. In a large Japanese company, operating at its best, the Japanese can be some of the most docile, maleable, and manageable employees in the world. This is because they see their superiors, the goals, the lines of authority, and the entire organization as being Japanese and, therefore, legitimate.

The challenge facing foreign companies in Japan is indeed a great one, however. Even the most generous and well-meaning initiatives can be subject to misinterpretation. Comparatively speaking, the Japanese are not a nation of complainers. They grin and bear it, accepting realities as they are. In the foreign company context, however, the un-Japaneseness itself can become totally unacceptable. And the conviction held by Japanese that their language, people, thinking, and even their feelings are totally incomprehensible to foreigners provides fertile ground to breed complaints, misunderstandings, and a racist indifference on the part of the Japanese to finding any common ground at all.

At the honesty meeting a comment by one on the young employees is illustrative of this. Devereaux commented that "Motoyama was fired based on a pattern of incorrigible personality and nature identified by Rouseaux, and on Rouseaux's 20 years of management experience with many foreign subsidiaries in different countries." The young employee retorted with "Rouseaux's 20 years of management experience means nothing. He was not born as a Japanese and has not lived a single day as a Japanese. A foreigner is not qualified to judge a Japanese."

For these reasons I didn't dissuade Rouseaux from meeting with Watanabe, but suggested that he give him a maximum of one hour. I told him that he should schedule something else one hour later to provide a natural cut-off time. "How about the Motoyama meeting to follow one hour later, say at 11:30 a.m.? Then you can get a good sleep, meet Watanabe at the hotel at 10:30 a.m., Motoyama at 11:30 a.m. with our lunch with Ohtsuka to follow at noon."

Actually I was confident that dealing in Japanese with Watanabe, I would be able to convince him to call off the threat that the entire sales department would quit. I would play upon his feelings of responsibility for his subordinates. He had the power to either bring them back to rally behind the company flag, or to force them all to resign. He knew that some of them would be unemployed for months. Since Rouseaux and the head office represented the direct enemy and the blue-eyed devils who ran in and made monkeys out of the local Japanese employees, no compromise could be reached. The insult from France could only be met with a sacrificial suicide. This time it was the 15 *ronin* (masterless samurai) against the foreign head office instead of the historical 47 who killed themselves to preserve their honor.

Because my Japanese ability and the way I come across comes so close to the Japanese model, it becomes impossible for the Japanese to say 'things cannot be done that way because this is Japan' or 'you cannot understand because you are not a Japanese.' Obviously, when arguing among themselves the Japanese cannot score points by saying such things. Nor can they avoid the issues and make the miserable and meaningless excuses and rationalizations that they so often pawn off on foreigners.

Devereaux and Rouseaux walked me over to the lobby exit of the New Otani after dinner. I had assumed that they would follow my advice. When he was first informed of the sales department's demand to rehire Motoyama, Rouseaux had sent back a telex stating that 'under no circumstances will the rehiring of Motoyama be considered.' Now under the pressure of crisis, the mass resignation of the sales force, and perhaps their perceived threat of unionization, it seemed that Rouseaux (not Devereaux) might even be toying with the idea of rehiring

Motoyama. Why else had he suggested that he would meet with Motoyama for one or two hours?

As we parted at the hotel entrance, I reconfirmed that a ten-minute meeting between Rouseaux and Motoyama would be most appropriate. I also told them that two or three hours with Watanabe, the sales *bucho*, would enable me to persuade him to call off the revolt. I thought that Rouseaux was with me on these points—so much for my understanding of a proud and self-important French executive. "I'll then bring the candidate, Ohtsuka, over to the hotel at 11:00 a.m. on Monday." These were my last words.

When I met Devereaux at 11:00 a.m., I was, nonetheless, surprised to hear that Rouseaux had been dealing with Watanabe, head of sales, since 8:00 a.m. at a breakfast meeting. They were still going at it in Rouseaux's hotel suite. Finally at about 12:10 p.m., and after Devereaux, Ohtsuka and I had already been together for over an hour, Rouseaux came up to the restaurant on the top floor where we were waiting for him.

He looked a little indignant and a little weary. Rouseaux, by spending all that time with an angry Watanabe, had clearly swallowed his pride, and it was not sitting well in his stomach. "He just keeps saying the same things. I haven't changed him the least little bit. I would only do this in Japan," Rouseaux complained.

I found out that at 2:00 p.m. Rouseaux was to meet in his hotel suite with the fired president, Motoyama. "I will listen and give him time if he wants to talk. I feel bad about what has happened to him." As Rouseaux was getting to know Ohtsuka, and as they felt each other out, I had some time to ponder the reasons why Rouseaux was not following my advice. Did he actually think that Motoyama could function effectively and happily as a once fired and rehired president? Was he even reconsidering the possibility of taking Motoyama back? I couldn't believe this.

Had I stated my case too strongly? Are objective, outside consultants in France more careful about the way in which they word their opinions and views? I have always prided myself on never accepting a regular retainer fee from a client. By doing so, I would lose my objectivity. As soon as a consultant is on a retainer, he can come to depend on such fees, building up his overhead around them. Soon he is no longer an outside consultant. He ceases to say the things which a client may not want to hear. The client is done a disservice. Perhaps Rouseaux does not appreciate or understand this. I was not about to explain it all to him. He would have to live with the mistakes he was making. For some reason he was clearly listening to but not following my advice.

In any case, Rouseaux and Devereaux were impressed by Ohtsuka. They made plans to have dinner with him and me at 6:00 p.m. in the same restaurant. In the meantime, Ohtsuka would relax and wait on one side of Rouseaux's suite, while

Rouseaux would meet from 2:00 p.m. with the fired president, Motoyama. I asked for a crack at Watanabe to try and persuade him and the sales department to back down on their demand for Motoyama's return and to withdraw their promise of mass resignation should the demand not be met. No one was quite sure where Watanabe was.

We all went up in the elevator to Rouseaux's suite. As the elevator door opened Watanabe, the rebel sales manager, was sitting smack in front of us on a sofa in the mini lobby to the wing of suites. I must admit that I was not quite prepared for this awkward moment. Ohtsuka was also surprised and was hanging back behind the elevator control panel. Here was Watanabe still fervently attempting to get Rouseaux to take Motoyama back, and we were about to enter Rouseaux's suite with what all of us were thinking would probably be the next president. Rouseaux handled it extremely well with "Gentlemen, Mr. Watanabe is still with us. Mr. Watanabe, we'll move on into the suite and kindly wait about ten minutes and then have a chat with Mr. Nevins."

I was with Watanabe in the main hotel lobby for about two hours. Any people around us must have found our intense dialogue quite embarrassing. They certainly didn't stay around us for long. We had the deep end of the huge lobby all to ourselves. Japanese and foreigners alike seemed to realize that it was not right to get too close to us. At the time we couldn't have cared less what people thought.

Since there were no sofa chairs directly facing one another and my neck hurts if I have to talk for too long sitting side by side, I would alternate between kneeling at his feet and looking up at him or sitting cross legged on the rug in front of him. It made him feel uncomfortable to have me begging and imploring in this position. After at first trying to get me to sit up, he then came down on the rug and directly faced off with me. The hotel employees also instinctively kept their distance. Maybe they reasoned the little show with the foreigner so intensely and at times heatedly speaking Japanese on the floor might even attract foreign hotel guests to sign up for the "*shogun tour.*"

Actually I wasn't doing really well. It wasn't until about 4:30 p.m. when I suggested that we go and get a beer and some food that the atmosphere began to lighten up. Watanabe held back slightly saying that he'd join me for some juice or something. As we walked toward the coffee shop we were able to make some small talk such as the number of years I've been in Japan and asking each other about our family situations. After all the attention he was getting all day, first from Rouseaux and now from me, Watanabe was beginning to feel self-conscious and more willing to compromise. He was also quite sure that our having both lunch and dinner with the new president, Ohtsuka, was proof that all his efforts would be in vain.

I guess Watanabe was beginning to face the facts. I convinced him that he could now play the instrumental role of saving the face and the jobs of his subordinates.

As their leader, it was within his power to get them to withdraw their commitment to quit their jobs. He admitted that, in fact, Motoyama was by no means an ideal president. Watanabe's ears perked up a bit when I offered him the chance of being the first Japanese manager to meet Ohtsuka, the man who would likely be the next president. Watanabe would join us for before dinner cocktails from 6:00 p.m. upstairs.

I described Ohtsuka in depth such that Watanabe agreed that just such a senior and powerful Japanese executive was what the company and the Japanese staff most needed. He could also see that the head office must have surely learned a lesson from all of this, and that in the future the Japan branch would have greater autonomy. At lunch time Devereaux and Rouseaux had reacted positively to Ohtsuka's request that should he be hired, I would work on an ad hoc basis to solve any misunderstandings arising between the head office and the Japanese staff.

After hearing all this, Watanabe seemed more hopeful about the future of the company. Ohtsuka had, in fact, said that he thought 'Watanabe was a good manager, with a lot of guts—a man who really cared about the company.'

"Did he really say that about me?" Watanabe asked.

"He did indeed, How about another beer and let's order some food."

"I feel like some chicken dish."

"No Watanabe-san, after all your hard work today, you deserve a steak. I'm billing your company, anyway!"

"Then I'm taking you out to dinner Nevins-san!" he said laughing.

Watanabe pushed out his chest and ordered the waiter over. "Two steaks, please." His voice was much cheerier now that the crisis was over. He could relax for the first time in five days.

We spoke about nothing in particular for the remaining hour. Once again I extended an invitation to him to join us for cocktails from 6:00 p.m. "You can just meet Ohtsuka, say good-bye to Rouseaux, and leave early before they order dinner."

"I think it best that I pass that up. It wouldn't be fair for me to get an edge over the other five *bucho* in meeting the new president," he said with a big smile. "Anyway, the revolt is over, and the sales department will be business as usual tomorrow."

We parted and I made it to the upstairs restaurant by 6:05 p.m. Devereaux's attractive Japanese wife had joined her husband and Ohtsuka for dinner. Devereaux stood up and met me halfway across the dining room.

"Where is Mr. Rouseaux?" I queried.

Devereaux put his hand in his pants pocket and looked up at the ceiling. "Believe it or not he's been with Motoyama for over four hours. Once again it looks like Motoyama's strong English and forceful appeal to foreigners are helping him to get back his job."

I just shook my head in disbelief.

"How did you make out with Watanabe?"

"Everything is just fine. He's calling off the rebellion. Everyone will be working as usual tomorrow."

"You're kidding, how did you do that?"

"I think a steak billable to you was a big help." Devereaux returned my wink.

Rouseaux didn't join us at the table for another half hour. His face flushed beet red when he heard that I'd won Watanabe back. "Well that's a real feather in your cap, isn't it Mr. Nevins?", he said in a weak and wispy voice. Ohtsuka was the most surprised to hear of the victory. He looked at Rouseaux saying "Mr. Nevins should really be congratulated."

Rouseaux nodded slowly and carefully, looking over the wine list. After a long moment of silence, he added "I wish that we had had walkie-talkies to check each other's progress, but I have gone ahead and made a commitment to rehire Motoyama."

All I could say was "Oh really, I'm surprised. I think you've made a big mistake."

"We will see Mr. Nevins. We do the best we can. But why can you say that with such certainty?"

"It's true that Motoyama was not fired properly in the first place. Nonetheless, the fact remains that he caused a good deal of trouble in your organization. With the decision to fire him, and during the last five days, your organization was seriously injured, and the scars, will last for a long time. The company was scarred yet you have merely ended up where you started—with Motoyama as president. Nothing has been gained, not even a new president."

"But can't these things sometimes have the unexpected effect of building up morale and pulling the organization together?" Devereaux was trying to cover up and place some cushions around his boss.

"As you say, they are at best 'unexpected' effects." I retorted. "Motoyama himself, deep down inside was looking for a fresh start. I could have happily outplaced him, of course, at no cost to you. I'm sure he'll be careful of the way he treats other employees and managers. But after all the loss of face, he will not be able to fulfill his duties with the confidence and the psychological peace of mind he is accustomed to. From my experience I can assure you that he will voluntarily resign within one year."

"How can you be so sure Mr. Nevins?"

"Wait and see. I think it would be difficult for a Westerner to perform his job under these circumstances, let alone a Japanese. In any country and in any organization, once a final and irreversible decision is made, as was your initial position regarding the Motoyama firing, management does not gain the employees' trust and confidence by succumbing to such pressures. Top management can only look weak and ineffectual."

Rouseaux was on the defensive and was beginning to show some signs of irritation. "Aren't Japanese organizations supposed to be emotional and 'wet'?" he asked with a clearly perceptible smirk.

I managed to ignore this last comment. We made chit-chat for an hour and a half enjoying our dinner in the best humor we could muster. I had poured everything I had into their problem for the better part of five days and would also bill them for the initial investigation. Although we didn't make a cent in executive search fees, the exercise cost them dearly in my labor consulting fees.

This company would have been so much better off if Rouseaux had had the guts (or the good judgment) to stick by his initial decision to behead Motoyama.

Listening for the first time after a decision has been made and then changing the decision are certainly not characteristic of Japanese management style. The founder, president, and chairman of the great Matsushita electronic empire, Konosuke Matsushita, put it like this in his essay on "The Finality of Decisions."

"Whenever we take back a decision we have made, we lose ground, and it is hard enough to push onward toward our goals without additional difficulties brought about by our own mistakes. This is not to say that we should stand behind our decisions even when they are wrong; on the contrary, it is very important to be able to admit our errors and take measures to correct them. I simply mean that we should always exercise the greatest care in deciding, making each decision as if it can never be revoked. For often it cannot be."

6

If the Headhunter Could Cry on the Client's Shoulder— or What the Client Should Do for a Successful Recruiting Campaign so the Headhunter Can Make No Excuses

Although vendors do not usually coach their clients,
executive search is an art;
and the product thinks, has pride and emotions.
Our job is to make you and your firm successful,
so please accept the following in that spirit.

A few things that will help us to succeed for you

Other than the obvious client responsibilities, such as calling back the headhunter promptly, providing feedback on resumes, or why a candidate of resume is not met, having enough time or corporate recruiting resources to be able to meet candidates readily and flexibly, evenings (or even on weekends when necessary), we hope the following reminders may also be helpful (although they may not at all be relevant in our particular relationship).

1. On understanding that a scouted candidate is initially a rather passive (even disinterested) candidate.

Please remember that TMT has never run an advertisement to attract a candidate for a client, gets virtually no unsolicited resumes from Japanese. Thus, candidates are directly scouted, happily employed, and don't particularly want to or need to change their job. Therefore:

a) Please be friendly, congenial, and remember you will have to sell them by getting them enthusiastic about wanting to work for you and your firm. Even a few jokes can help immensely to get candidates to relax and look forward to working for you.

b) It is best to describe your company first before drilling with questions.

c) Please avoid asking, "Why do you want to work for our company?" "Why would you want to leave your current company?" or even "Why are you looking for a new challenge?" Candidates are just as likely to answer back "I'm only here because TMT scouted me," and the unfortunate misunderstandings begin, and a candidate can be lost.

2. Our consultants may hesitate to pressure you, but please do place pressure on us.

Although your search consultant should be aggressively working and propelling the search effort, experience shows that the client who pushes and pressures its recruiters while giving encouragement and a pat on the back, if deserved, gets the best results.

Recruiters will hesitate to make demands on your time for interim meetings, and they will hesitate to push you, get feedback on resumes or to set up meetings with candidates, especially if they've tried to call you and were not called back.

The assignment can fizzle out, and they will work with the responsive clients who give the search the top priority it requires. The following helps us succeed for you.

a) Call the recruiter often, at least once a week and tell him you're depending on him. He'll be sure to work on those assignments that he knows are open and where he knows he is being depended on, rather than on those assignments where there has been no such recently communicated pressure/encouragement.

b) Scheduling an interim follow-up recruiting meeting every month or two is also helpful to refocus energies and/or bring more TMT resources/consultants to the search effort.

3. Please be flexible and open to adjustments in position requirements.

The client must be realistic about how comparatively attractive his firm is along with the conditions surrounding the job including salary level, age, education, or qualifications, etc. If these elements aren't there, perhaps standards of candidate selection may have to be lowered or adjusted. Please keep the following in mind:

a) Sometimes a client may be mistaken about the kind of candidate he needs and where to find him. Although part of our job is to point this out, it will help if you open the door by asking, "Are you facing any particular difficulties with our search parameters?" "Could we use a different position specification or be more flexible?" "Do you disagree with the way I've positioned the search?" "Is there anything we could be doing on our side better to make your search easier and help you get better results?"

4. If you cannot offer a big enough increase, you won't get candidates, and your Executive Search Consultant will soon become demotivated and stop working.

a) Put yourself in the candidate's shoes. If you were happily (successfully) employed in a good company at ¥15,000,000, would you move for a 10% pay increase to ¥16.5? Probably not, and probably most others will not either. Increases of 15% to even 50%* are not uncommon and are necessary to build up your firm with good people.

(* 50% pay hikes and perhaps even more are required and typical when scouting young engineers etc. whose salary levels are at low levels in major Japanese firms. They are simply not willing to leave and take a risk if you are a small start-up operation.)

b) If your initial increase offer is too low, the candidate even questions our intelligence, and even if the offer is raised, he is concerned, apprehensive and may lose interest. This happened to us this morning when a client offered a candidate at ¥8,000,000 an increase of ¥400,000 for ¥8,400,000—an extreme but all too often occurrence.

c) There is nothing that will demotivate your headhunters more. Although they want to help you they realize it is fruitless. If salary levels are too low, and client interviewers of our candidates and decision makers don't realize that attractive increases need to be made, you cannot work with our kind of scouting based executive search firm.

d) You will have to resign yourself to gathering active candidates (generally unsuccessful and about to be out of work), looking at your newspaper advertisement, or you will have to work with a *jinzai-ginko* or personnel placement agency that similarly advertises for active candidates.

5. More tips on succeeding with your Executive Search firm in a competitive and tight labor market.

TMT has placed over 60 staff in one foreign capitalized firm here and over 25 in a number of firms. The recruiting effort doesn't always take off and mushroom to this extent, and there are often identifiable and understandable reasons why. These problems can sometimes be fixed. Clearly the following are critical to success:

a) Recruiting must be the clients top priority, because it all starts with people. Your interviewers must sell well; and your firm must have the resources, make the time, and have the budgets to take care of candidates and pay attractive salaries. Your business plans, corporate goals, and company vision or mission must also be attractive.

b) Try to meet candidates even if the resume does not have sufficient detail or hasn't sold the candidate to you. Here, at risk of being accused of requesting undue tolerance for our resume quality, you do need to know that the way that TMT works, directly scouting happily employed candidates, often we have all we can do to bring the candidate in for the TMT interview. Although we meet him hoping to get enough details to write a good resume, since candidates are passive, they get irritated and sometimes simply do not have the time or the willingness to allow us to explore their backgrounds fully.

Does that mean we have no business introducing that candidate to you, even if there was only one brief interview meeting with TMT? We don't think so, and we believe if you understand this problem we face, you will agree that since the candidate is more willing to give you detailed information (after you have fully presented your company and needs), we believe it is in your interest to in any case get that meeting set up.

As much as possible TMT is committed to getting solid performers on the front line, non-job hoppers with stable careers, preferably in major Japanese or foreign capitalized firms. Unfortunately, we can't always push the candidates too hard for career detail on their resumes.

c) You must willingly meet, quickly process and hire candidates readily. Although most headhunters would hesitate to say this, the truth is that we place priority on the clients where our chances of getting results (in the form of a placement) are greatest. We want to work for clients that treat us well, respect, and value us and our efforts, and decisively hire our candidates.

d) If you don't move quickly, you'll lose your candidate. The labor market is tight, candidates are conservative about job change, and competition is great for good candidates. You may lose him to a competing offer; or he'll get his nose out of joint, his pride on the line—no one likes to face rejection so he'll lose interest or pull away from you. Clients often come to us telling us about the big one that got away because he wasn't reeled in right.

e) In fact, in Japan we probably should say, "When in doubt, hire." If you wait for all the traffic lights to turn green before you leave the house for town, you'll never make it to town. You've got to get started and started quickly in Japan. You'll lose the better candidate while waiting for the best candidate and end up with a compromise candidate or no candidate.

f) In the meantime, your headhunting team loses its enthusiasm and works on the client companies that are decisively hiring. When an executive search consultant knows that the candidate is the best available, given the attractiveness of the client or the nature of the position, it is pretty hard to scout for more candidates and to stay motivated and keep producing.

Thank you for giving us this chance to present frankly some of the needs and challenges that face us as an executive search firm.

We want to continue to provide you with the most dynamic and effective executive search available in Japan. We hope to work even closer and better together. Thank you for letting us know how we can serve you better, and for taking a look at some of the factors that help us to succeed for you.

(From our TMT "How Are We Doing?" bimonthly client survey.)

VI

A Helpful Summary— So as Not to Forget the Key Concepts and Strategic Tools

1

A New Trend in the Japanese (Labor) Market— a Nationwide NHK TV Interview

Giving advice on personnel problems

Komatsu: How do you do, viewers? Labor and personnel practices are one of the frequent subjects that we very often talk about with people overseas because it is one of the important factors that has contributed to the success, or sometimes oversuccess, of the Japanese economy.

The rapid internationalization of the Japanese society, however, is bound to change that, too, because labor and personnel practices are, after all, very fluid, so today we would like to talk about the labor and personnel practices in Japan more from the viewpoint of the recent trend rather than the traditional, stereotyped thinking about it.

Our guest today is Mr. Thomas Nevins. Mr. Nevins is the well-known expert in this field. He is the president of TMT Inc. which he himself founded in 1978. He is a very aggressive businessman. I really respect him for that, and he is also a practicing scholar. He has authored many books in the field of labor laws and practices both in Japan and in the United States. The most recent one is this one titled *Labor Pains and the Gaijin Boss* (Japan Times, 1984). Mr. Nevins, it's nice to have you in this program.

Nevins: Nice being here, Mr. Komatsu.

Komatsu: Would you briefly tell us about how you got into this area in the beginning?

Nevins: It was basically by accident. When I was 20 years old, I was figuring out what to do with the summer vacation. Some of my friends said to me: "Why don't you go to India?" So I did that, and then a professor at Cornell—I was studying labor relations at Cornell University—she said: "Why don't you go to Japan and do a labor relations project for me, or with me, do research together?" I had already been studying labor relations in college, so I came to Japan that year and then I studied Japanese at the university. Then I came back when I was 22 sponsored by the Japan Institute of Labor, and I gradually started working in labor unions and in companies and then did quite a lot of translating and did some odd jobs, my share of odd jobs as well, and did some work for the ILO, for example, and translated for labor unions, and then began this company in 1978.

Komatsu: Now, what do you do in this TMT?

Nevins: Our clients are multinational firms here.

Komatsu: Foreign capital companies.

Nevins: Yes, foreign capital companies, and we help them with their setups, for example—set up their Rules of Employment, their compensation, and benefit packages. We also handle such difficult problem areas as terminations and staff reductions when the company isn't doing so well. We handle cost-saving programs, and also union relations as well as other staff relations in general trying to make sure that they can manage the Japanese well and effectively, and giving them the answers that they need and really giving them the sort of practical advice and plotting the strategy and actually getting them where they need to be. So it goes much beyond, you know, a theory and analysis practice, but a lot is based on practical nuts and bolts experience that the firm has developed over the years.

Characteristics of Japanese industrial relations

Komatsu: Well, now when those multinationals or the foreign capital companies try to establish themselves in Japan, they also have to know the labor practices and labor situation in Japan. What do you think are some of the special characteristics of the Japanese labor and management relations that they have to know?

Nevins: Well, I think they should always know exactly what Japanese companies have traditionally known and practiced. For example, they should know that there is a summer and a winter bonus, and they should be able to have a choice or an option as to whether or not they and their employees want to have a summer and winter bonus. They should know that a traditional Japanese company and many of the multinationals will pay family allowances and housing allowances, and they will have position allowances, you know, the *yakuzuki-teate* for *kacho*s and *bucho*s. They don't necessarily have to be involved with those practices, however. It may not be so necessary. After all, one reason for having such allowances is that they represent nonpensionable salary, so their presence helps to control the weight of pensionable income or the retirement liability that a company must pay on an employee.

Komatsu: So those foreign managers usually like those Japanese payment systems?

Nevins: Well, perhaps on reading my book they may be predisposed to believing that they should have them, and there are some areas in the book which are based on seminars that I have run, for example. It's a compilation of articles which have been published in America and Japan over the years. There are some strong positions in there for Japanizing a compensation package, but as we get more and more experience, we see that as long as a multinational firm is safe in terms of, say, the weight of nonpensionable income by having just a simple concept such as a percentage of nonpensionable income—instead of having all those nonpensionable allowances or introducing a *daini-kyuyo* of just a nonpensionable salary component—then they are safe. And they don't necessarily need some of those other allowances, but I think it's important if the employees decide themselves in the firm that they don't want the summer and winter bonus and, instead, want annual income divided by 12, and they feel that they don't want family and housing allowances, which, incidentally, are quite risky now. They are quite a dangerous thing to get into after the April 1 legislation this year which provides that you have to give equal treatment for the head of a household regardless of whether it's a male or a female, and so on, and provide those allowances.

Komatsu: Now, aren't there companies, I mean multinationals, which would rather continue to use their own practices at home rather than adapting to the Japanese practices?

Nevins: That is often the reaction that they have. When they talk with me they see that maybe some of the Japanese aspects of a compensation package are not necessary, although I do recommend that they pay summer and winter bonuses. For one reason, the social insurance contributions are smaller on bonus than they are on normal monthly pay, and also there is room for flexibility because you can have a performance range on a summer and winter bonus, and if the firm doesn't perform so well it helps to have that bonus. It provides flexibility, so I will recommend that they have that, but sometimes they are relieved to hear that some of these other more complicated allowances really are not as necessary as they might have perceived that they are.

Komatsu: So some of those typical Japanese labor or personnel practices, such as bonus, are advantageous to the companies from the manager's viewpoint, so that they can probably be transplanted in the foreign soils, too. Is that how they perceive it?

Nevins: In fact, we had a JETRO book which was published by JETRO in 1980, which was about American labor relations for Japanese companies. Japanese companies bought that book to help them with their labor relations on the American side. And in that book I recommended that Japanese companies should not forget their roots, should not forget that they came from Japan and that there were many things they were doing in Japan which were extremely successful from also a macroeconomic point of view, in terms of allowing the country to have a higher savings rate. This is because so much of the summer and winter bonus can go into savings, from the employee's point of view in that he gets accustomed to a certain standard of living with his monthly pay, and with his summer and winter bonus he can save that and he can buy consumer durables such as refrigerators or automobiles. So essentially I think what you always have to do is not just follow Japanese practice blindly, and Japanese going into America should not follow American practice blindly. Or American companies, when they look at Japanese practice now and they're studying many, many books and so on, they should try and even integrate some of those concepts into America.

For example, one of the problems that Japanese companies have when they go into the United States or into other countries, is that they complain that the turnover rate is very high among the employees, that the employees quit too soon, and they put investment into training which is a great strength of Japanese industry, and it is something that large firms can do here because of lifetime employment and because they can get their money back on their investment. But when they do that in the United States, the people quit.

Now, if you have a bonus and you tell a man, it's called "golden handcuffs" now. They have a little word in America, "golden handcuffs." It's a deferred income) concept, such as if you stay in your job for a certain period of time you'll have deferred income and it will be paid at the end, which is really what the Japanese bonus is like to a large extent, so it will be helpful.

Increasing mobility

Komatsu: Those practices that you mentioned, like bonuses and allowances, are, however, key to the more basic personnel practices as lifelong employment or the seniority-based salary system, and these things, I think, are gradually changing, too, as a result of the changes of the Japanese economic situation and so forth, and then that will also have the effect of changing those payment practices also. Don't you think that kind of change in the basic trend is taking place?

Nevins: Sure, I guess some of the changes taking place in Japan, above all else, the work force is aging, and that means that there are not enough *kacho* positions, for example, let alone *bucho* positions for Japanese managers to take. And it's very rare; it will become more and more rare for man to be able to get a line management position. So that means that people's work will not be so interesting. They will be put over on the side into specialist roles which may or may not be interesting, and people will begin to look to the outside. There are firms, in fact, that are and have been, to some extent, pushing older employees out. In fact, one of the characteristics, more unpleasant characteristics perhaps of Japanese management, is that there is really even a concept of first-hired, first-fired. So although there is something called seniority wages, in reality on a staff reduction, you know, *jin'in-sakugen*-type reduction where you get rid of employees, older employees are asked to leave first, whereas in the United States, both by unions or even in nonunion situations, to prevent unionization they will always make sure that they have the greatest loyalty and commitment to the older employees, who manage to maintain their jobs.

But the Japanese approach is excellent from management's point of view because, in fact, the oldest employees have the most expensive salaries. If you can get them out of the firm, you know, they are the least flexible in adapting to technology. If you get them out, there is a tremendous savings there.

Now, basically the closed labor market is really the secret to Japan's success. It hasn't been really stated that way.

Komatsu: What do you mean by "closed labor market"?

Nevins: Well, it's usually said the three pillars of Japanese labor relations: lifetime employment, seniority wages, enterprise unions. But the reason why a Japanese employee up until recently generally stayed in one of those large firms was because there was no mid-career hiring in an equally large firm, which would pay him the higher salaries because small companies don't pay as well in Japan, and would also guarantee him a job. The job could be guaranteed because of the contract employment in the second tier of the Japanese economy or because of subsidiaries and so on.

Komatsu: But that situation is changing, as you mentioned, because of the increasing number of aged workers and also because of the increasing number of foreign companies doing business in Japan providing opportunities to the Japanese people.

Nevins: Indeed, they are providing very exciting opportunities.

Komatsu: It is much easier these days to change jobs for the Japanese.

Nevins: That's right. But still, you know, a great characteristic of Japanese recruiting and manpower planning is the April 1 *shinsotsu*, you know, the entry of the new graduate. This is very important, and it's a great strength and something that Japan should not easily eliminate. In fact, everyone joins not only the company on April 1 but they also join the union regardless of whether they're white-collar employees with a tie and jacket.

In America employees like that do not join the labor union, and they're never paid overtime, whereas in Japan in a large firm all employees are paid overtime, for example, and are in the same labor union as the blue-collar workers. So this is really, to a large extent, a company union rather than a trade union in the Western sense, and that has also been a great strength to Japan because, to a large extent, the union is an appendage of the personnel department. We know that often the union leader becomes personnel manager and so on.

Komatsu: This practice of hiring young people on April 1 at one time—and those people will remain with the company for long, I guess—is also changing because many of those young people are getting impatient about the slow pace of promotion, and when they see that many job opportunities are available outside, I guess, they don't want to stay in the company as long as their elders used to.

Nevins: That's right. There is a lot of truth in that, plus they just look at the percentages. They look at the possibilities of getting on the board of directors. That was a traditional carrot that many people would work very hard for. And as you got older, it would become more and more clear that you would not be able to reach that kind of a position. Then in Japan, even in the past, all the workers became comparatively less motivated, and I think that that sort of thing will be happening more and more, and then in Japan it has always been changing very fast. I would not say that it is going to change any faster, but certainly certain markets, such as financial markets, are changing dramatically, quickly, in Japan, and even your traditional trust banks in Japan. You know, your Japanese trust banks have gone out with newspaper ads to bring in mid-career hires, for example. That happened a few months ago.

Komatsu: Yeah, that's a marked change, too.

Nevins: Right.

Multinationals in Japan

Komatsu: I would like to ask you what kind of people those foreign companies look for. Are they the same type of people that the Japanese companies value, or a different kind of people that those foreign capital companies look for?

Nevins: Well, I think that basically they are the same types of people. They may be wrong about what they're looking for, but what they should be looking for are people who can do good work. So we also have a very large executive search business now. In fact, that has become our main area of activity, and I guess we have about at this point 17 headhunters now in the firm. In one sense, headhunting in Japan is quite easy because if you identify a man who is a line manager in a major Japanese firm and if he has never changed jobs and if he is in fact a *kacho*, a *bucho*, a *jicho* with line responsibility, you don't even have to really test his references. You know that he is a very good, solid man, and it makes it quite easy.

Komatsu: So whoever is good in a Japanese company is also good in foreign capital companies, too.

Nevins: He generally is. Now, one thing that is often necessary at a high management level like the *bucho* level is English, so that is something we must find. But there are so many Japanese now in Japanese firms who speak English, and their quality of English is just as good, or better, than the quality of the English of Japanese in foreign firms. There is no difference now. Japan has become that internationalized.

Komatsu: How about this loyalty thing? The Japanese companies tend to value loyalty above other factors, above other ingredients in personnel talent. How about the foreign capital companies? They do the same?

Nevins: Loyalty is, indeed, valued, and I think it will be valued more and more as we reach some excesses in terms of people turning over jobs, especially in some of the financial markets. It's quite ridiculous now, but in a few years there will be so much change that I think people will become tired of it, and loyalty will be valued.

In fact, my father, for example, worked in one company for some 37 years, and that's quite typical. So you read a lot of articles in American magazines and newspapers about someone at a very high executive level moving from one firm into another, and it's quite shocking to the Japanese. But, in fact, the great majority of Americans are not moving and changing jobs as quickly. And even in Japan there is a lot of job change among the lower sector of the economy, the smaller firms, where they are not able to hire people and to make a commitment on April 1 to people and where they have to hire a man to do a job somewhere during the year. There the employment patterns and the labor relations in those firms are not that unlike the employment practices and compensation practices in the U.S. There is a large distinction, I think, in Japan between the top firms that have some of the traditional practices and some of the smaller ones.

Komatsu: Do you think the Japanese are becoming less loyal these days as a result of this sort of increased availability of jobs or increased mobility in the labor market?

Nevins: Yes. You know, loyalty, I think as we use the word, is a symbol which represents a lack of job change, but that's about all there is. When it becomes possible to change jobs, then we have to say that there is more job changing, which means that there is less loyalty. But I wonder if people were really ever that loyal as much as it was that there were no other good opportunities in an equally prestigious firm. Now they're willing to trade off a more rational life style, be able to spend more time with their children, with their families, having more control on their work, having to play less political games in the workshop, and have a richer personal life; and this is something that even wives, I think, will learn to enjoy. As more people do it, and then Japanese are not so confused or upset or embarrassed by showing a *meishi* which has the name of a company that people are not familiar with. Although even these multinationals in Japan, they may be small in Japan, but some of them are obviously very large—very large throughout the world. So there are a lot of opportunities, good opportunities, there.

Komatsu: So in that respect you say that the Japanese are the same as human beings, not very particular from the viewpoint of loyalty also. I think you know both sides of the ocean, I should say, and how would you compare Japanese as a labor force?

Nevins: Oh, they're good; they're definitely good. I mean you can watch a Japanese at a McDonald's or in a cabaret or any place, you know, the waiter there, the way he moves with the pride that he takes; this sort of thing is really excellent. I mean Japanese are definitely highly disciplined employees, and that's especially true in Japanese firms where they see directions and instructions and guidance coming within sort of a guise of legitimatized authority. Now, sometimes that breaks down a little bit when they work in foreign firms, but maybe that's all right, too, because they have some other tensions that they have to deal with.

Komatsu: Do you think those things will stick, that the Japanese will continue to be good quality workers?

Nevins: Yes, but I think it's comparative. Just last night I was in a restaurant with a Japanese who has been in and out of Japan over the last few years. He comes in once every two years or so, and he lives basically in the U.S. He said that he has noticed...and when he's here he stays for maybe one or two months and he goes to restaurants every night. He says that he has noticed gradually service has been going down in Japanese restaurants, and it's simply a product, I think, of prosperity. You know, some of the things that were deemed to be very important and critical in life become a little bit less important. The Japanese travel more, and they see how people work. They see how they're served in restaurants abroad, and they losen up a little bit and relax a little bit.

Komatsu: Do you mean to say that it is poverty that is behind this high quality of the Japanese as a labor force, or is there any other factor?

Nevins: That wouldn't be accurate, either, would it, because if you go to various underdeveloped countries the service is not at all good, is it? So it's much more than poverty. But I think it's authority, and, to a large extent, I think it comes up out of the school systems. No, the word cannot be poverty because you don't have that sort of discipline and that very crisp approach to your job and responsibility in underdeveloped countries. It can't be poverty, and it's not going to change that quickly. Also, a good businessman who's managing a good business and is watching out for these things can continue to keep his work force, I think, doing a good job.

Komatsu: So you think it is well-bred in the Japanese society and it will not change readily?

Nevins: Not that quickly. We're talking about change here, but everything is comparative. Compared to other countries outside Japan, Japan will still continue to be doing just fine, and, you know, the discipline will be there. I think they will be very careful not to throw the baby out with the wash water in terms of maintaining some of their good practices that they have carried out over the years.

Of course, so many of these traditional aspects of Japanese labor relations are really postwar phenomena, anyway. For example, the enterprise union. The union organization rate before the war, the highest point was only 7%, and then after the war within just one year in 1946 it went to its highest peak of 39.5%. The main reason was it was externally imposed by MacArthur because MacArthur's occupation policy was to have labor unions, and he said you will have labor unions. No one was about to oppose that, so the easiest place to organize was in the company, say, the company cafeteria on the company land. There was no opposition, and so what you had was—overnight you had—an enterprise union. It didn't go through that baptism of fire, you know, so it's rather, anyway, a union which understands management's needs very well.

Toward optimum blend

Komatsu: So for those multinationals, they have good, high quality Japanese people as their employees, and they have rather advantageous management practices which they can adapt from the Japanese tradition. So, relatively speaking, it is easy for them to have a good performance in Japan.

Nevins: It's not that easy because one of the problems that a multinational has is that the top management changes. I mean it is necessary for someone from the country to manage an enterprise. I think that's very important. But when you have top management changing every few years, there are changes in policies, for example, and the roots are not here to the same extent that a large Japanese firm will have them in terms of subsidiaries and the ability to hire people on contract or to farm people out into subsidiaries. You have to have very good back-up in sales support on your product, so it still is not that easy. But if they work hard, and if they do their job right, I think, they would be very successful.

Komatsu: I think, after all, what they aim at is the optimum blend of the Japanese practices, good Japanese labor force, and some good, interesting Western practices....

Nevins: Yes.

Komatsu:...and mix them together in an optimum way. That should be the success formula.

We only have one minute to go, so would you say what would be the best blend of two practices to be successful in Japan for MNCs?

Nevins: Yes, that's a difficult question. The best blend, I would say, is to always use your common sense. You must not believe that it's the same as it is in the United States or in Europe, but you also shouldn't believe that it is different. You should believe that if you know how to do it and you do it in the right way, you can achieve whatever you want to achieve. But you just have to do it differently sometimes. So it's important not to feel that everything is different, but also not to feel that everything is the same and to look at what you've done in other countries and see what was successful about it, and to look at what the Japanese are doing. Then I think it's probably also helpful to call a good labor consultant to get some more advice.

Komatsu: So use your common sense.

Nevins: Yes, I think common sense is important.

Komatsu: Thank you very much. It was very interesting.

(April 1986)

2

Strategic Tools for Managing Japanese Personnel— Local Practices, Policies, and the Law Using Them in Six Key Areas

Manpower Sourcing and Recruiting—Executive Search

Mid-career headhunting and college recruitment versus compromising with ads, employee loans, and "out-placement gifts."

If asked, virtually every expatriate businessman in Tokyo will moan that the biggest barrier as well as bottleneck, toward building his business is the inability to identify and attract a high enough caliber of employee and in the needed numbers. One firm can get off to a smashing success with a charismatic executive holding the reins who can attract other good people around him, going on to build a business through his management skills and vision, while another firm with an equally attractive product may never get off the ground. To some extent even luck is a factor here, and something as basic as the selection of the executive search firm will inevitably be an instrumental factor in launching a firm with its initial team of mid-career, seasoned managers. Indeed, the difference that one or two key men in an organization can make is awesome. How can a multinational firm in Japan go about building up its management team and other human resources? What are the options available and the strategic advantages and disadvantages?

It is often said that if you are building a company in Japan, you must recruit new school graduates from the university the way Japanese companies do. As far as the small, foreign firm is concerned, however, something has been left out here. Don't forget that even the small Japanese companies cannot attract the new graduates, nor will the university *gakuseika* or student out-placement office provide students (and certainly not good students) to small, unknown employers of low social prestige. There will always be someone left at the bottom of the academic roster or a number of students with personality quirks who did not interview well at major Japanese employers, etc. But you don't want to get stuck with these dregs. And if you believe the stereotypes about lifetime employment and fall into the all too easy (and understandably so) pattern of providing job security, good pay, and annual promotions regardless of performance, you are in a particularly tough spot when you've taken on one of these less talented graduates "for life." Just as no Japanese corporate start-up operation has been able to get off the ground with new school graduates, neither will your firm. The necessary training systems, leadership, senior workers, and corporate policies and culture needed to motivate and mold young new graduates won't exist. Energy and enthusiasm make young workers priceless, but a lack of corporate culture and leadership, particularly among Japanese youth, leads to debilitating disillusionment.

One other tip on new school graduates—don't do a selling job on the university out-placement people and professors until your firm has something to brag about. Recently a large multinational in the top 20 of the Fortune 500 visited our office. They were excited about starting a college recruitment program. Considering they had been in Japan for some 30 years tied up with some limited joint venture connections, they had little to impress young students and their parents. There were still no appreciable assets in Japan in terms of land and buildings owned or direct manufacturing. I suggested that rather than go out and unimpress the university people with their lack of accomplishment, leaving an unfortunate first impression, they should wait two or three years until their investment in asset and head count here becomes commensurate with their new plans and with their standing as one of the world's great multinationals.

Nonetheless, it is not true that "foreign firms" have a difficult time recruiting good Japanese. An equally small Japanese firm would have even a more difficult time recruiting good Japanese (particularly if English were a requirement). It is a question of business scale, security, and social prestige. Small Japanese firms also must compromise on the quality of their human resources, and certainly in order to get the same good employee, they will have to pay considerably more than will the large, prestigious Japanese firm.

Newspaper advertising

Whenever a client has any doubt as to whether or not newspaper or specialized technical publication advertising will be of assistance in recruiting key staff, we encourage him to go ahead and give it a try. Generally, people who are busy, productive and content with their jobs are not looking at help wanted columns. On the other hand, you can occasionally luck out and get an extremely good person. If one is willing to spend time screening and processing, secretaries, for example, can be recruited in this way. If a company has exclusively built up its human resources through advertising, you may not be aware of what you are missing, and your standards for judging Japanese managers, their productivity, and effectiveness may be too low.

If a manager is out of a job or senses that he shortly will have to be on the job market, the danger is that he may be desperate enough to compromise himself or to take on a job which he knows deep down inside he is not capable of handling. Furthermore, when people leave a job for negative reasons, i.e., discontent, lack of promotion possibilities, inability to fit in, or failure in current position, it is unlikely that the candidate will be any more successful in the next position. The good news about advertising is that candidates are not passive, and are thus likely to come in at a lower salary. Furthermore, for marginal positions, including lower level clerical, the unskilled factory workers, or older administrative employees who need only to maintain an operation or office environment, rather than build and create, you should be able to increase head count faster than is possible using headhunters or personal connections.

A word of caution, however! The Japanese are aggressive market researchers and carefully study the competition. Thus, the content of a simple recruiting ad could give away a major strategic plan. There is the story of when Wacoal began advertising for metallurgy specialists, which also gave the competition the signal to move to those metal ribs on women's brassieres.

Joint ventures, employee loans, and out-placement freebies

Since foreign firms see procurement and management of Japanese human resources as one of their biggest difficulties and challenges, there have been tendencies to place too much importance on distributors or joint venture arrangements. Be careful of the rather common form of joint venture, which for the Japanese is designed to get a piece of the action, but more importantly to control the speed with which the new product or technology from abroad enters the Japanese market. After many years in Japan, a number of clients has come to us, telling us that their joint venture arrangements effectively limited their presence here and kept them out of the action until Japanese had equal or better technology and were ready to compete. Since foreign firms often cut off relations with their distributors and go it alone when the product reaches a certain saturation point, distributors have learned to protect themselves by not putting adequate resources into the product such that it becomes successful enough for a direct entry.

Whether you're a bank or a manufacturing joint venture, don't depend completely on the human resources introduced from your partners or cooperating institutions. Hire a few of your own key people to keep an eye on the joint venture, and by all means make sure you're not stuck with the seconded employees, who initially may be helpful in getting you started. No firm will lend you its best employees, and chances are they will even be two grades below average.

Direct networking and headhunting

Being in the industry, you have excellent connections and know many of the players, but unfortunately company image and relations with competitors often don't allow direct approaches. Furthermore, to the given executive responsible for his organization, there is not enough direct incentive to scout key executives effectively. On top of this, contacts are limited and you risk opportunity lost by not meeting a more qualified person. The human relationships of introductions can also, get in the way and prevent and objective evaluation of the candidate. Thus, enter professional headhunters.

If you need to build up your human resources from the top levels on down, find a firm that will give you specific references, meaning the names and phone numbers of clients where that was accomplished. There should be the right balance between up-front commitment fee and payment on contingency, or success basis. No commitment fee means no obligation to come through for you or means a firm that is rather desperate for clients, and desperate men may do desperate and unethical things. On the other hand, a large portion of the money being paid up-front in advance and regardless of performance allows such a search firm to stay in business without filling assignments. And although this is an envious position for a search firm to be in, it is singularly and clearly not good for the success of your search in that the reward system is wrong; i.e., the necessity, excitement, and the carrot for doing a good job are coming too soon, taking all the fun out of the hunt.

Look for a search firm that puts money back into the business. To fill your assignments, it takes tremendous manpower resources, office space for expansion, and computerized data banks. It's a good idea to visit the search firm. There should be a healthy internal, synergistic competition among several consultants at the search firm, with all of the recruiters knowledgeable of your assignment. This way you avoid having one or two consultants sitting on your assignment and taking no action. Filling your assignments requires days and days of unglamorous work, research and telephone calling, recruiters to interview passive candidates who have never thought about changing jobs or writing a resume. It is rare that assignments are filled through the "industry connections" of the headhunters. Rather many man-hours of time are required to go in and get the best people in the companies which you have provided the headhunters as your list of targeted manpower sources. The truth is that special knowledge of an industry is not nearly as important as the energy, techniques, quality, and level of fresh scouting which is being carried out for you, and is a direct product of the number of recruiters in the headhunting firm, as balanced with the number of clients it is carrying.

It's a cruel world. If you are a smaller multinational, with no market position and little in the way of Japanese operations, you will have to pay a higher salary to attract the kind of people that can quickly build up your position. The level of the salary you are willing to pay is certainly important, for given the other abstractions, such as "commitment to the marketplace," competitiveness of a product or attractiveness of the business plan, the salary level is one thing which assists a man in rationalizing the move to himself, and even more importantly to his wife, who at best can only remotely feel some of the excitement that the candidate feels toward the new job offer.

And certainly one of the most important aspects of the recruiting effort will be the firm's ability to infect the candidate with the firm's own sense of vision and enthusiasm. The charisma and salesmanship of the senior executives doing the interviewing are critical in drawing in like a magnet good people to build up the organization. Just like any Japanese company, when you have a name in the marketplace, or perhaps own your own building and land, you have a strategic advantage when it comes to recruiting. As expensive as land is in Tokyo, it is still a good buy and will continue to increase in cost, as it has by as much as 50% annually in some recent years. There are also the hidden savings accompanying land purchase, such as the lower salaries which become attractive enough to bring in candidates because the purchase of that very land serves as evidence of commitment to the marketplace (as well as assures that the foreign firm will pay out the promised lump-sum retirement benefit even should the firm close up and leave Japan!).

Other strategic recruiting tips

Always make sure you have someone interviewing and screening who is on a different career path from the candidates. For example, an expatriate manager who will go back to the head office anyway has no reason not to welcome enthusiastically a man better than himself. This is not always the case of the top

Japanese man in the organization, who may be hesitant to bring in a heavyweight. Although you say that the inability to get the right Japanese is holding back your chances for success, keep in mind that in the midst of the search, clients often forget what should be their greatest priority. Remember, every time you don't call your headhunter back right away or you waste another day in meeting a candidate, or cancel an appointment, or are unreasonable about who you are and your ability to attract what level of candidate, you are losing valuable time in bringing in the very support people whom you need to make your job easier and to build up the organization. If you need people, your top priority must be to get those people on board as soon as possible rather than to handle even the most pressing matters cluttering your desk. Without those people, you simply cannot build your business, let alone delegate some of those pressing matters which now have you tied in knots.

Remember that when recruiting a president or general manager, the man suitable for heading your organization today may not be capable of doing it in another three or four years when you've reached a head count of tens or even hundreds of people. Thus, it's a good idea to avoid the title of president. But a man of the same caliber can be brought in by enrolling him in your vision and infecting him with your enthusiasm. Some creative compensation incentives also help, such as a signing bonus, adding a few years of service automatically toward the lump-sum retirement benefit or designing a deferred income or lump-sum scheme to get around the candidate's commonly expressed concern that he is losing out on his former employer's retirement benefit when making the mid-career change. For example, a 40-year-old could be promised a 20 million yen payment should he still be on the payroll at age 60. Twenty million in 20 years will be peanuts, but sounds good today. Furthermore, the nice thing about such schemes is that your headhunter does not have to bill on them, which keeps down your recruiting costs.

If you're not completely sure about a candidate and his compensation demands are much higher than you feel he may be worth, consider placing him on a one-year probationary period, backed up subtly with a one-year term contract. In certain situations this can be a strategically effective and efficient way to screen out less confident individuals who are not sure of their chances of succeeding after one year. If you are going to make a regular practice, however, of placing employees on one-year probationary periods or contract terms, you will face a trade-off. While you enjoy control over your human resources due to their limited job security, they will probably not agree to work with you unless their salary is higher, to compensate for the greater risk.

Be sure not to throw the baby out with the bath water. Don't send your organization spinning because of hiring from the outside a key executive. Be sure that the mid-career hire is absorbed smoothly into the organization. Before he is hired, it is helpful to have him meet with key associates so that they have "ownership" on the hire. Then you can expect and insist on mature cooperation between all parties.

Make sure references are checked, and it is common practice in Japan to investigate candidates using a *koshinjo*, or investigative agency. Obviously, this is impossible if an individual has only worked in one place. And the current employers should never be investigated, as this may compromise the candidate and his employer may find out he is looking for another job. The nice thing about headhunting in Japan is that if the candidate has worked his whole life in a major Japanese employer and has held down a key-line management position, by definition, he has made the grade; so there will be no need for such an investigation anyway. This also makes identification of solid performers surprisingly easy in Japan.

Probably one of the most strategic realizations which multinational firms in Japan should make is that, in fact, it is not impossible to shoot for the very best and brightest, even in the leading Japanese employers, and that it is not necessary for them to compromise their standards when it comes to recruiting. It is not impossible to hire executives who will make a difference in your organization and build up a considerable market presence here. If an executive search firm is doing its job, it should be able to put up candidates the client is excited about hiring within six to eight weeks (and often sooner). Employee loans, "out-placement gifts" or joint venturing are fine under limited circumstances, but these decisions should be based on merits other than as an outgrowth of a belief that it is otherwise impossible to hire directly highly-qualified human resources. There is no easy way out, and your business cannot be left in the hands of others.

Compensation and Benefits—
Design and Change at Multinationals in Japan

Pay smart and keep getting your money's worth.

What are some of the characteristics of strategically-sound compensation and pay practices in Japan?

It is only large Japanese employers (generally over 1,000 employees or more) who can realistically follow the Japanese standard model of providing salary tables based on age and years of service with the typical interplay with functional or job grades as exist in those large firms of bureaucratized career paths. The hiring and paying practices of smaller Japanese firms are not unlike those of the typical smaller multinational firm in Japan where a manager or employee may be hired at any point throughout the year when the need to fill a job with an experienced mid-career hire arises. It is virtually impossible for the small foreign or Japanese firm to recruit directly from the schools; thus, there are negotiations with individual employees, and there is the need to look and see what the individual is making in his former job. Therefore, it is an unrealistic goal for a smaller multinational firm in Japan (certainly one with under 500 employees) to create fixed salary tables based on age or years of service.

Simplicity is best (and often the only workable solution)

Also note that in Japan today age and service tables of even the largest Japanese employers tend to be confined within a narrow lower and upper limit so that the salaries of top performers are free to move well above the upper limit; while the lower limit is at a bare subsistence level such that the lower limit is not forcing the firm to pay a low level, marginal employee any more than it would need to pay, anyway. This aspect of the "tail not wagging the dog" is extremely important, for in today's competitive environment even for the largest Japanese firm it would be unfortunate and strategically disadvantageous to have a compensation system which dictated the employer pay salary beyond what demand and supply of labor requires. While it is true that there is underemployment of inefficient employees in the largest firms, and while these firms also lose some of their top performers to the competition due to the inability to increase salary level, in smaller Japanese firms and in a strategically-managed multinational here, there must be less tendency to be tied to an inflexible system which does not conform to the realities of job change and the open labor market as exists in smaller Japanese firms and, of course, multinationals.

If a multinational is unionized or feels some internal pressure to create a system, there's no reason why that system should cause you to pay any more than you need to to attract an unskilled and marginal employee, nor should the system prevent you from attracting a top performer at a high salary, regardless of comparatively young age or even some considerable imbalance with other employees in the firm. The other side of the equation, however, is to make it clear to the manager or employee who is being paid an unduly high salary that this salary can be frozen or even cut back should performance not meet expectations. Although this does not always have to be verbalized to the employee, the Rules of Employment and personnel system should be set up such that the employer has this kind of control over his human resources.

Understand the $ and ¢ of "Japanized" vs. Western practices

Another strategic question becomes whether or not the firm should adapt a so-called Japanese-style compensation package. Just what does this mean? The average combined summer and winter bonus in Japan is some 5.8 months. The strategic advantages for paying this are that there can be a rather broad performance range on this bonus. It can be flexibly adjusted according to business performance. Its presence reduces the weight of pensionable income vis-á-vis the lump sum retirement benefit. On another technical point, the social security contributions on the bonus amount are only about 1/3 that of regular monthly cash compensation. Thus, by paying bonus, there are significant savings on the employer's contribution to health, pension, unemployment, and workers' accident compensation insurances.

As for the traditional monthly allowances paid in Japan—namely the housing, family, meal, or perhaps position and work allowances—the main advantage to the employer for paying those is that their presence, once again, reduces the weight of the compensation, which is calculated into the lump-sum retirement benefit, thereby directly and proportionally reducing the lump-sum retirement benefit liability to the employer. Furthermore, when bonus and these allowances are paid the same base-up percentage increase will, of course, mean a smaller increase in the cost of total annual income, as it will effect only the base salary. With the exception of the commutation allowance, which is nontaxable as income to the employee up to the tax deductible limit (which covers the commute of most employees), there are no tax implications as to whether or not these allowances are paid.

Since many firms have only paid the spouse and children allowance, or family allowance, and often housing allowance only to married male employees, especially since the April 1, 1986, Equal Opportunity Law was passed, it will behoove companies to do some fancy footwork and to cash out those allowances into perhaps a single, nonpensionable second salary component of *daini-kyuyo*. If this is not done, female employees may request that the family allowance, or what is often the larger of two housing allowances, be paid to them as it has been paid to males in the past. In the case of many multinational firms here, that would create a considerable extra nonperformance-related cost, which can easily be avoided with a timely and simple adjustment in compensation practice.

Know your selling points

Thus, Japanese and many multinationals firms have strategically limited their retirement benefit burden by paying summer and winter bonus and having an array of nonpensionable allowances. Even in firms where summer and winter bonus is not paid and various allowances do not exist, it is still possible to keep all things equal in terms of the balance of compensation design and the quality (or burden) of the lump-sum retirement benefit. This can be done by designating a percentage of nonpensionable regular monthly cash compensation in your Rules of Employment. Actually, if no bonus or allowances are paid at your firm, this figure could be justifiably as high as 40 or 50%. If you are interested, however, in trying to make your firm more competitively attractive, the figure could be higher but certainly should be no higher than 60% (assuming that the lump-sum retirement table of months of pay for years of service is a typical benefit). If you are paying as much as 60% of 1/12 of annual income as the calculation base for the lump-sum retirement benefit, that is a factor of great advantage to employees. Also, you are losing out on the opportunity to strategically attract and appeal to employees if you are not aware of the built-in advantageous merits of your firm's compensation practices.

If you are paying no bonus and allowances, and a candidate complains that there is "no bonus paid at this company," chances are you are paying the same or greater annual income as a firm that pays bonus. And you should certainly make the most of the opportunity to state that "That makes your lump-sum retirement benefit so much richer," or "That means that your monthly pay is comparatively stabilized and your income is secure." Basically, though, I would certainly recommend that summer and winter bonus be paid for the other reasons outlined above. Although in lieu of allowances, it certainly is acceptable to define a percentage of nonpensionable regular monthly cash compensation.

The question often arises whether or not a firm should fund its lump-sum retirement benefit. This would mean in the form of a tax-qualified pension, or *tekikaku-nenkin*. Unless you are sure that your compensation design is properly balanced with a strategically sound lump-sum retirement benefit plan, you should not go out and fund your lump-sum retirement benefit. When funding has not as yet taken place, it has been possible for us to neutralize the adverse impact of redesigning compensation or the retirement benefit tables by arguing that this has been compensated by the fact that for the first time what was formerly a paper benefit is now a very real commitment funded by an outside party, with the moneys safely locked away for the employees.

Strategically smart compensation

Philosophically, I believe that it's strategically smarter to put money into cash compensation rather than to create a rich and burdensome lump-sum retirement benefit. This is because a candidate will make his decision to join a firm without seeing Rules of Employment and without specifically having any details on the quality of the retirement benefit. Also, make sure that your lump-sum is designed such that there is a significant penalty between voluntary (when they quit on you) and involuntary (when they reach retirement age or you dismiss them) benefits.

Handling the pay increase each year in Japan is actually quite easy. The results of *shunto*, or the Spring Wage Offensive, become quite clear by mid-May. And if you are a firm following the common practice of adjusting salaries from April 1, you need only look at the averages in the newspaper, which become clear by about May 15. Strategically, you should think in terms of paying that average, or maybe just a point or two more if you had a good year and perhaps to help attract employees to you. If you're a typical organization, however, with top performers, average performers, and some poor ones, there should be wide variance in the percentage increases at your firm. In Japan there is no legal reason why everyone should get a pay increase; ,in fact, freezes and even pay cuts have become more and more common. (It helps to have Rules of Employment language which backs this up.) Even if you are unionized, there is no reason to accept the union demand that there be standard increases based on age or uniform percentage increases.

Just as there are no laws which require that you pay a lump-sum retirement benefit, nor is there much in the law which talks about how you must pay your employees. There is no national minimum wage, though there are regional and industry minimums. Although in practice there is little in the way of job or hourly pay rates for salary workers in Japan, there is no law requiring that salaried workers be paid on a monthly basis. You are free to innovate in terms of commission and incentive systems; deferred incentive or compensation schemes, such as golden handcuffs are also perfectly legal. Contrary to popular belief, Japanese firms in certain sectors do much with commission schemes. Since there is a comparatively open labor market between multinational firms, an employee's destiny is not necessarily one in the same as that of the employer. Thus, unlike in the large Japanese firms where employees have traditionally scurried to come out as high up on the corporate ladder as possible, it may take some creative incentive schemes to elicit the same level of effort and effectiveness from employees in your firm.

Rules of Employment—Should Be Your Most Powerful Management Tool

*Set the shop up right—fair and strategically sound.
Fix it on paper.*

If you have a hard time sleeping at night, take home your Rules of Employment. They are boring and not much fun to read; but if they have been strategically formulated, they are the key document to assist you in establishing and maintaining a successful business. The employer is free to write them, and you should not ask your employees (or even your managers) to do the initial draft or make changes in that it's pretty difficult to be objective when the subject under consideration is directly affecting one's own benefits, job security, etc.

Article 89 of the Labor Standards Law reminds us that these rules are legally required when a firm reaches a head count of ten. The Rules must be submitted to the Labor Standards Office along with an *ikensho* or statement of opinion from "a majority representative" of the employees. In reality, in most cases the majority representative is or should be a helpful and effective assistant in the general affairs or personnel department. There can be disagreement on this statement of opinion, and, nonetheless, the inspectors at the Labor Standards Office are required to accept the Rules unless they contain illegal clauses or, more specifically, clauses which provide benefits inferior to those in the Labor Standards law.

Article 89 stipulates that Rules of Employment should cover virtually all rules of the work place, or practices, policies, and benefits affecting employees. While the Rules of Employment take legal precedence over the individual contract, if there is a union, any collective bargaining agreements will take legal precedence over the same position held in the Rules of Employment. This means that an employer must first attempt to negotiate over a change in a collective bargaining agreement. And after, in fact, doing this in good faith, we have guided our clients to move on to making the necessary changes by introducing them as adjustments in the Rules of Employment, maintaining that this was unavoidable in that impasse was reached after adequate collective bargaining negotiations.

The right rules give leverage on 60 to 70% of your costs

Although the Labor Standards Law requires that Rules of Employment be created after reaching a head count of ten, firms find themselves in a Catch-22 situation, in that in order to apply for placing their employees on the government insurances, the social insurance office will usually require the submission of Rules of Employment. Thus, in reality most firms find that it makes sense to create their Rules of Employment even before they hire their first employee, so that there are no special problems and no need to do special "grandfathering" later on. It is also a strategically smart idea to create the Rules first, in that by definition it precludes employee involvement, which is the wisest way to get these key benefits set up. After all, personnel costs generally amount to anywhere from 60 to 70% or more of operating costs. Rules of Employment are so important because compensation design, the quality of the lump-sum retirement benefit, and such key policies as those affecting paid holidays, sick leave, whether or not leave of absence for sickness, etc., is paid, as well as critical operation points, such as the existence of good, tight probationary and transfer clauses, as well as the ability to control behavior, discipline, and dismiss are all set out and defined in this most strategic (but inevitably most dull and uninteresting) document.

What are some simple checks you can make to evaluate your own company's Rules of Employment?

See if they are making special provisions instructing you to establish contracts for temporary employees while at the same time creating the right expectation in the minds of contract employees regarding their lack of entitlement to such expensive benefits as bonus, lump-sum retirement benefits, pay increases, family, housing, meal, and other allowances, etc. You should have a probationary clause of at least three months, and this should be renewable for another three months when in doubt.

It is perfectly legal to work employees from 9:00 a.m. to 6:00 p.m. with an hour off for lunch; although a more common schedule might be 7.75 actual working hours, rather than eight actual working hours. If you are only working from 9:00 a.m. to 5:00 p.m.; however, I would suggest that many outside Japanese and other parties will be frustrated with switchboards closing down, as will internal managers be in a bind as their support staff go home early. Note that when it comes to paying overtime, the Labor Standards Law itself would hold that unless an employee's actions are visible throughout the day, or unless his supervisor has specifically requested that extra work be done, and/or given written permission for overtime, there would be no reason to pay overtime to, for example, salesmen and other outside field staff, or even to in-office staff who may not be working efficiently during the day. There is no reason why the overtime rate should be over 25% unless there is an overlap with over eight hours of work and midnight labor after 10:00 p.m.

While there may be large Japanese employers and a number of multinational firms which do not cut back pay when employees exceed the number of paid annual holidays accrued, the vast majority of smaller Japanese employers will cut back a day's pay for sickness, or absence for any other reason, exceeding the number of annual paid holidays accrued. Probably not to do so is unfair to the responsible employees who maintain their health and always come into work rain or shine. This is a simple procedure, and you will be surprised how much attendance will improve. You can base the deduction calculation either on the number of days in each month or on a consistent factor of say 21 or 22 days per month. Thus 1/21 of monthly pay would be deducted.

Most Japanese firms, large and small, as well as multinationals, do not provide for a certain number of sick days. Paid annual leave must be used for the odd cold. Although there will be provisions for extended leave of absence for sickness or other reasons, note, however, that the employer is not legally required to pay an employee for off-the-job sickness or disability. And by all means, make sure that if you are making the employee's salary whole up to a certain number of months based on years of service (a maximum of six months after ten years of service should be reasonable), make sure that you claim the 60% of the standard remuneration salary tables which are due you from your employer contributions to the statutory social insurances, and don't tolerate the likely refusal you may encounter from the office—it's got to be unconstitutional highway robbery, and when pressed they will pay! They may initially argue that they won't meet their obligation because you are!

As for the legalities of working hours and paid holidays, it is legal to work employees up to 48 hours a week, or eight actual working hours six days a week, providing one day of paid leave is provided. This day, of course, does not have to be Sunday, and, in fact, even the national holidays are not Labor Standards Law holidays and need not be given. Likewise, if your Rules of Employment provide for a *kyujitsu-furikae* or holiday change clause, it is even possible to switch a holiday with a working day without paying the holiday overtime premium of 25%. The law also provides minimum paid holiday protection, stipulating that the first year no paid annual leave need be given, and after 80% attendance the first year, only six days need be given the second year, with an additional day for each year of service. We would certainly not recommend this, however, it is sufficient to meet these minimum standards. It is common practice to give as much as 8 to even 12 days of paid annual leave in a multinational firm on a monthly prorated basis even from the first year. Also nowadays employees don't much like working on Saturday, and you will lose a number of candidates when recruiting if you insist on Saturday work.

With the Equal Opportunity Employment Law in effect from April 1, 1986, the maternity leave clauses changed with the necessity to provide up to ten weeks of maternity leave if requested for multiple pregnancies and with a mandatory requirement on the employer to provide for six weeks of maternity leave after child birth (even if the young mother wanted to return to work earlier). Note, however, that the strategically smart firm will probably not guarantee full salary during these maternity leave periods but rather will do as most Japanese firms do, providing no pay, with the employee drawing on the 60% benefit from the social insurances.

Good rules are a source of control and power

A key strategic area of Rules of Employment should be good duties and obligations clauses which can be tied in as grounds to the gradual disciplinary clauses of the sanctions section of the work rules. Duties and obligations should talk about more than items such as coming to work on time or maintaining corporate matters confidential. There should be an emphasis on stipulating requirements for efficiency, high levels of performance, cooperation with fellow workers and supervisors, as well as responsibilities for improving one's own skills and training other, etc.

One of the most important strategic points in Rules of Employment is whether or not there are adequate detailed disciplinary measures with strategically formulated grounds to take disciplinary action against employees. Without going into too much detail, one key area absent in almost all Rules of Employment, but one that has given us tremendous leverage in working with our clients when it comes to weeding out poor performers, or in one sense terminating without terminating, is the creation of language allowing the employer to adjust the job junction or demote and permanently change the work assignment. This justifies a permanent reduction in pay, which can supersede the Labor Standards Law limitation of 1/10 of remuneration during the pay period for a specific disciplinary infraction. In other words, for a specific transgression, the statute itself only talks about a cut of 1/10 of monthly pay. But sometimes an employer must go beyond this in order to reorganize and rejuvenate the organization effectively and more particularly take action against certain poor performers. There is no law which says this can be done, and no law which says it can't. The right language in the Rules of Employment helps, and beyond that, it is a question of strategically finessing it and managing it in your firm.

Change your Rules of Employment and practices as required

On the compensation or salary regulation side of your Rules of Employment, make sure that the language does not indicate that there will be an automatic salary increase each year. Rather it should be termed a "salary adjustment." Particularly, if you're not paying bonus and various Japanese-style allowances, have a nonpensionable salary component percentage stipulated in the Rules. Likewise, bonus regulations with a performance range can be provided if you don't have them.

Make sure that you do not limit your reasons for dismissal to disciplinary reasons or the ten or so grounds which have become universally recognized as grounds for dismissal in Japan. It is a matter of common sense, and it is obvious that those grounds, such as serious lying on resume, theft, violence in the work place, etc., need not even be stipulated, and rather you should be concerned with language that talks about performance, ability, work efficiency, ability to learn, and adapt to new skills and jobs, and even more subjective calls, such as inability to cooperate and get along with co-workers or lack of effort or application to the task at hand.

It is the rare employee who steals and can be expelled from an organization for that reason. Rather the problems facing the largest Japanese firms where there is underemployment, and also a number of multinational firms, is management's inability or lack of propensity to seize initiative and to order the work habits of managers and employees such that there is enough effective hustle to compete, grow, and profit in this difficult marketplace.

Check and make sure your retirement age is not 65, and remember that in Japan 60 is just gradually becoming the predominant retirement age, where 55 had been the rule in the past. If for some reason your retirement age is 65, you should certainly consider freezing years of service, freezing pay, and/or even cutting pay after age 60 (or even age 58 or so) in order to cut costs, save on the retirement liability and make room for new blood in line management positions.

Although the Rules of Employment will largely take the place of the individual employment contract, with a new recruit make sure that the individual contract is also set up right. If you have a performance range on a summer and winter bonus, make sure you don't stipulate in the contract a total annual income figure. Rather mention that the monthly salary and allowances will be X, and with a targeted (but possibly fluctuating) bonus payment of X months, your annual income should be approximately X. Also be sure not to limit or define the duties of the employee in the contract, as it will then become difficult to, for example, get a secretary to do something other than "reception, writing correspondence, translating, reception duties, and filing" or whatever else you specifically designated. Also don't forget to mention about the probationary clause and your right to transfer in terms of either job function or place of work.

Hone your rules into your most strategic and effective management tool

Perhaps, most importantly, remember that if your current Rules of Employment are not doing for you what they could be and should be, the employer is free to adjust them and change them. It has always amazed me how little energy and attention is placed on these Rules of Employment. Yet as soon as an employer is hoping to be able to dismiss an employee or, for example, discipline an employee, should there be litigation, corporate counsel and the judge will always look to see if the specific language of the Rules of Employment allows the contemplated action against the employee. Why not get your Rules of Employment honed into an effective strategic tool which will support you and back you up in taking your organization in the direction it needs to go?

Problem Employee Solutions/ Terminations That Work

Non-performance can't be tolerated, and even in Japan "firings" can be good for morale.

But when we use the words termination and firing here, let's be clear. I have *never* recommended, I repeat, never advised and even fought desperately hard against a client's impulses to terminate an employee. There are wiser and safer ways to end up with the same solution more quickly, cheaply and without litigation.

What can happen if you directly fire someone in Japan?

If an employee (of course, including manager) is inclined to litigate against you, it is absolute disaster to terminate his employment. In Japan termination leads to a *karishobun*, or temporary restraining order (TRO) on the dismissal, generally resulting in virtually automatic reinstatement and with back pay until the time of that reinstatement. It is, generally, then, up to the employer to sue in court to take away the temporary restraining order against the employer's abuse of the right of dismissal.

Safer and more effective alternatives to termination

Inefficient, poor performers should rather be rehabilitated into a workable position commensurate with their abilities, or they can be assisted to move gracefully into gainful employment in another organization. Under few circumstances should it be necessary to throw a poor performer out into the street, and, in fact, it becomes much more difficult to find another job when one is no longer employed.

In cases of outrageous behavior with infractions that would be readily recognized as grounds for disciplinary dismissal, the employer can safely go for a disciplinary dismissal, although this will require the approval in advance of the Labor Standards Office. This approval is not readily granted, but when it is the employer can be reasonably confident that his position will stick. Although the terminated employee may still sue in court for abuse of the employer's right of dismissal.

And, in fact, in Japan the employer does have a right of dismissal. If we look at the statutes themselves, we have Article 627 of the Civil Code, which stipulates that two weeks' notice must be given. This is superseded by Article 20 of the Labor Standards law, which holds that 30 days' notice or 30 days' pay or any combination of the two must be provided. (Note that even during the probationary period, after the first 14 days it is necessary to give this 30 days' notice or 30 days' pay. Thus, if you can, try and screen out during the first 14 days.) The problem is that the maintenance of job security is considered a matter of public order. And, thus, if the termination is litigated against by the employee, it is rather rare that the judge will admit the employer's right of dismissal. In fact, in court case precedents and in the summary opinions of judges, there are many instances when *kaiko*, or termination, is referred to as *shikei*, or the death sentence.

The reality is that so-called "lifetime employment" is and should only be an expectation of employees in the largest Japanese or multinational employers. Lifetime employment is not provided for in Japanese law and statues. In fact particularly in small Japanese firms people are being dismissed all the time. But there is no litigation because most people play fair and square with each other, and it is unreasonable to expect lifetime employment security in a small firm or in a multinational firm here struggling to survive.

An ability to demote and manage out freely the poor performer without litigation can be your magic, too

One of the most important strategic factors which will determine the success or failure of your firm will be your ability to have control over your human resources to the extent that you can move aside a man who is blocking progress, since he is too small for the job or lacks energy or vision or the ability to display the charisma and leadership traits necessary to attract good subordinates in building up your human resources. Whether or not you can do something about that man or other mediocre performers will depend not so much on what Japanese labor law and practice says about lifetime employment and job security as much as will the dynamics of your own work group and the perceptions of other employees toward that manager or co-worker. Is he perceived to be a leader by others (although not by you)? Does he have their sympathies? Does he seem to be good enough and popular enough such that to take action against him would have a demoralizing effect in the organization? If he is alone and isolated, you have a comparatively straight path, clear of obstacles toward moving the man out of your organization.

And remember, when it gets to that point, one of the most strategic concepts you can keep in mind is to make that poor performer thing that you don't in fact want to terminate him or otherwise expel him from the organization. If you address the problem with the orthodox concept of termination or dismissal, he will sense that and you will be in a position such that you can only gain his consent at a large settlement cost in terms of extra severance or retirement benefit. This is a very bad message to give the rest of the organization. For it is saying essentially that you can be a poor performer at this company and contribute nothing, and on top of that, by merely digging in your heels and staying, you will be bought off with a large sum of cash.

It's better to get the troublemaker or inefficient poor performer to believe that you are completely satisfied to have him stay on in the organization, providing he clears the path for another manager and providing his pay has been reduced to a level which is in line with his lessened duties and responsibilities. This will take all the fun out of it for him and he will see that there will be no fight for him to win. Chances are he will resign just as quickly as if you had gone directly for termination. But if you directly terminated and he litigated against you, that termination would not stick, and he would be reinstated by a court of law, with you then being guided (but not ordered) by the judge to pay him a large out-of-court settlement to obtain his agreement to resign, when by wiser methods you could have achieved the same results in less time, at no extra cost, and without creating a bad precedent in your firm and significant loss of management face and credibility in the eyes of other employees.

This curious but extremely important concept is that you can gain complete strategic control over hiring and "firing" in your firm without ever having to terminate or dismiss staff.

Staff Reduction and Cost-saving Programs

The Japanese cut and slash like everyone else.
There's much to learn from them.

There is a predominant belief that Japanese firms do not lay off or reduce staff. This is a product of comparatively high rates of economic growth which made it unnecessary to reduce staff combined with what is comparatively speaking a greater propensity to maintain a commitment to the human resources within the firm. In the West labor is often seen as the most flexible factor of production. And lucky for Japan, comparative difficulty in reducing staff due to the reaction of the courts combined with a cultural disinclination to do so, have forced Japanese companies to diversify into new product, develop new technologies and essentially to work much harder rather than to fall into the pattern of all too easily reducing staff when business turns down. Such staff reductions as practiced in the West are an admission of failure. And every time an individual employer takes the easy way out by cutting back staff, the economy as a whole and its dynamic vitality are cut back by just that much.

Yet in structurally-depressed industries over the years indeed the Japanese have often restructured and reduced staff when unavoidable. This is more and more true today with the *endaka* or strong yen. For example, major steel and shipping companies are reducing thousands of staff with a goal to survive and build up new business areas and to even be profitable once again in as little as one or two years.

In general, it can be said that Western companies will tend to reduce staff before rationalizing other benefits and cutting back costs in other areas, whereas Japanese companies make staff reduction the last resort and before that will impose other sacrifices on their employees. One reason they were traditionally able to do this is that, at least among the large employers, there were comparatively closed labor markets such that managers would have no choice but to take a pay cut and would be unlikely to look for and to be able to find equally good employment outside.

In Japan it's first hired, first fired

Thus, the traditional pattern of a Japanese staff reduction/cost saving program would include such practices as initially eliminating overtime, stop hiring temporary workers, stop filling vacancies, discontinue existing temporary worker contracts, set up new manning standards (transfer to sales force, overhaul and repair equipment, reduce management salaries and bonuses, etc.), stop yearly recruiting, temporarily lay-off workers, cancel hired recruits, terminate *shokutaku* (part-time and contract workers), invite voluntary resignations, and finally terminate employment on what is called a designated discharge basis (usually conforming to recognized criteria of "hierarchial preferential protectionism"), this basically means getting out the old employees, secondary (primarily female) breadwinners first and as much as possible trying to keep all the young (and coincidentally) cheapest employees, who are also the ones who are adaptable to technological change and presumably the most energetic and productive. In fact, on staff reductions in Japan it is first hired, "first fired." And the court opinions back this up, justifying it by saying that the older employees are the most costly to the ailing firm; thus, such a selection is economically rational.

In reality, most Japanese firms and virtually any multinational facing the need to cut costs will think primarily in terms of staff reduction and will not fully carry out all of the practices outlined above. In fact, cutting pay of all managers is not always strategically wise, particularly in a foreign firm, in that with the open labor market you will lose some of your best people. When executing that staff reduction, it is absolutely imperative that the special or extra severance premium beyond the lump-sum retirement benefit not be made available to all employees and managers. In fact, rather than designating the poor performers and carrying out the *kata-tataki*, or shoulder tapping of poor performers, it is probably more strategically crucial for the employer to inform the best managers and most efficient employees immediately that the extra lump-sum retirement premium will simply not be made available to them even should they resign at the same time as the designated poor performers are receiving their lump-sum retirement benefit with the extra severance premium.

Simply don't allow your best performers to take the special terms

Some clients and their legal counsel have questioned as to whether or not this is possible due to its discriminatory overtones. I would argue that when a company is struggling for survival, it is absolutely critical that the best and most efficient managers remain in order to assure the continued job security of the poorest performers who would not resign from the firm and accept the extra severance benefit no matter how rich that extra benefit is. In fact, we have been successful in carrying out many staff reductions, have insisted on this strategically key policy of not subsidizing the departure of the best employees, and most importantly, we have been successful without a single case of protesting litigation.

When designing the extra severance premium, find a formula which will strategically get rid of the most undesirable employees at the lowest cost to you. In general, it makes sense to have the premium be a combination of a percentage increase on normal involuntary retirement along with several months of salary and perhaps a fixed cash compensation figure. The several months of salary and fixed compensation figure will be more attractive to younger employees who have few years of service, and thus stand little to gain from a percentage increase on a lump-sum retirement which is very small or virtually non-existent. On the other hand, if you want to keep most of your young employees, then the weight should primarily be on a percentage increase of normal retirement benefit.

In Japan age discrimination takes a back seat to economic rationality

Although there are age discrimination laws in the United States and other Western countries, here in Japan it has been standard practice and legally justifiable to pick an age over which employees can be asked to resign. Such common ages would be all employees targeted for early retirement after age 45 or perhaps age 50. In any case, when you follow the policy of not allowing the best and most efficient performers to receive the extra severance premium, you must be careful not to make this premium too rich. If it is too great, the best performers who are not allowed to accept it will resent you for preventing them from enjoying that extra severance benefit. After all, they are the employees who are in the best position to go off confidently and get another job.

When your company needs to rejuvenate and cut back costs, remember that this is the best strategic opportunity to carefully examine all your compensation benefits and personnel policy practices. Since staff reduction should be the path of the most resistance, you can use this opportunity to argue that in lieu of a more widespread staff reduction or wider cutbacks in head count you will instead make an effort to cut costs in other areas. The position taken can be that by doing so it is possible to reduce fewer staff.

When rationalizing, don't miss a strategic trick

Primarily look at such compensation practices as automatic age or service increases, the possibility of freezing or cutting back pay of poor performers, reducing overtime rates to the legal rate of 25% or cutting back overtime hours, possibly cutting the employer's contribution to social insurances to the statutory minimum (which should be your practice from the beginning anyway), introduce a greater penalty on voluntary retirement, cut out paid maternity or menstrual leave, reduce the number of days of sick leave or shorten the periods of paid leave of absence, or even increase the number of hours of work each day if you happen to be one of those unlucky multinational firms that started out with a short work day, such as 9:00 a.m. to 5:00 p.m. (whereas 9:00 a.m. to 6:00 p.m. would also be legal with an hour lunch break).

When carrying out a rationalization program, don't forget about your right to transfer employees and adjust job functions and pay levels. When business really gets bad, or even if it is not so bad, concepts of freedom of capital flow should indicate that an employer is basically free to close down its operation. In non-bankrupt situations, and when the funds are available, an employer is required to pay the retirement benefit provided for in the Rules of Employment. And in practice, usually something extra is paid out. Keep in mind that the law says nothing about these extra severerance payment requirements. Even when unions are successful in provisionally attaching a company's assets, the judge will only allow assets to be attached based upon the retirement benefit provided for in the Rules of Employment with no extra premium.

In real life, cutting and building often will go hand in hand

In the real life situation of many firms in Japan, including, of course, a large number of multinationals, there is a definite need to not only cut back staff but also to build up human resources at the same time. When it is necessary to do this, it must be done. And once again, there is no law which says that cutting and building cannot take place at the same time. Hiring new people would tend to make it more difficult to dismiss staff should there be litigation. On poor performer employee terminations, there would be no reason to risk forcing through a dismissal of staff even under circumstances of severe business difficulties and corporate or industrial sector economic shrinkage. Rather a firm will have reduced fears of litigation and will be strategically more successful if it dangles a sweetener of extra severance premium along with the prospect that failure to take the package by a certain date will lead to inevitable pay cuts of anywhere from 20 to 40% due to the poor business conditions facing the enterprise.

You will find that if pay levels come down far enough, people will leave and move into sectors where they can make higher or at least equally high pay as their new reduced pay level. At this point it then becomes important to offer hope to the good staff and managers who remain in an organization which has gone through such a dramatic staff cut and cost-saving rationalization program. In fact, notwith-standing possible claims of discrimination, in order to keep the good performers, I would even recommend that it would not be unjustifiable or impossible to offer pay increases to the best staff, while less efficient human resources were facing significant pay cuts.

Union and Staff Relations/Attitudes

Know what to do if the union knocks.
And don't let one slow you down.

The union organization rate in Japan is about 28%. But while the rate among large firms with over a thousand employees is probably in the order of 85% or more, for smaller firms, union organization rates rapidly decrease. Not surprisingly then, as is the case with small Japanese firms, most multinationals in Japan are not and will not be unionized. Nevertheless, unions can be extremely messy business here in Japan, so this issue does deserve some time and attention.

Don't tiptoe on eggshells around the union issue

Just as significant as the question of whether or not a multinational firm is unionized, however, is an examination of the behavior of that firm in an attempt to maintain the union-free environment. When it comes to setting up benefits, compensation policies, and your Rules of Employment, it is important not to walk on eggshells or to be overly concerned or feel compelled to set up unduly rich and generous benefits out of the threat of unionization, or a fear that to do otherwise might lead to unionization. In fact, from our experience, there is nothing which is more likely to quickly lead to a union organization drive than the perception of employees that management can be so easily pushed, influenced, or in one sense even blackmailed in this way. Our experience indicates that it is most rare for employees to entertain the thought of unionizing in work environments where benefits are comparatively minimal and where there is little fat, and a tight ship with a tough captain elicits high levels of performance, effort and often even dedication on the part of the staff.

Even if your firm were unionized, what should that really mean? Frankly it is bad management and poor supervision with the employees' perceived lack of leadership on the part of management that leads to union organization. Weak management will, in turn, give unions unnecessary power by giving in to demands. For example, if an employee or two suddenly walked into your office with a petition signed by the employees to participate in collective bargaining, you will be best off to have a cool and rational reaction to that. And by all means, the biggest mistake would be to offer the benefits or meet the demands which are being made. In fact, the time when management can least afford to give in to union demands is when under duress or in times of irrational and radical union behavior such as organization drives, demonstrations, sit-ins, and strikes.

Collective bargaining gives management freedom to negotiate away benefits

Remember a union organization drive with petition and demands for collective bargaining is at that stage often little more than a test of management mettle. You are free to point out to employees that they already enjoy a number of benefits and policies far exceeding the legal minimums. Although the law states that you are not to use the Labor Standards Law as an excuse or as leverage to reduce benefits, in fact, in a less direct way you are certainly free to point out to employees that collective bargaining or negotiation means that you can start with a zero-based table and that the employees will have to see if they have the power to negotiate back the benefits which you can take away.

You can reverse the syndrome of "ask, and you shall receive" by throwing the union off guard and by making counter demands. If the retirement age is currently 60 and there is a request to make it 62, you can, in turn, request that because business is bad it should be moved back to 58. This will inevitably eliminate that request from a future collective bargaining session. It is also important not to allow the union to become the center of attention and information. Don't deal or spend more time with the union than with nonunionized employees or managers. Likewise, never address issues exclusively with the union. Rather you can organize a task force made up of union, nonunion, and management members to take initiatives on a variety of issues and to keep your agenda of change flowing. Whether or not the union wants to join this group is up to them, but an invitation to attend can remain open. (Reasonably spaced meetings with the union only will also have to take place if they insist.)

Remember that you can throw the union off balance by changing many past ways or practices. For example, don't allow the union to dictate anything or to rest on past practice or precedent. By constantly raising new demands, unions can get management's conscience and perceptions diverted from much more essential and fundamental issues. In labor relations it is too easy to get caught up in past precedents, even though such practices may not be good for the company. If you seize the initiative and make demands of your own, the union will soon realize that it is a new ballpark with new flexible rules.

Change will have to be document drive— agreement will never be reached

On the other hand, in enforcing any agenda for change, such as getting away from age or payment based on years of service, don't expect to be able to reach agreement. And after a respectable period of collective bargaining, claim that you have reached impasse and then make the changes as adjustments in the Rules of Employment. In this way, you can keep any program for change on course and moving along by having it driven by the new policies and document, which you will go ahead and formulate.

Don't worry if promoted staff want to stay in the union. If the union is managed properly and is not given power (by giving in to its demands, etc.), it really doesn't matter who are members of the union, or whether or not managers are members of the union. It is also true that as more and more good promotable staff join the union, this in fact co-opts the union and it begins to take on the dimensions of the typical, reasonable Japanese enterprise union model.

Make sure that union membership offers absolutely no advantages in terms of greater job security, bigger pay increases, or other favorable conditions. If this is not the case, you will have a demoralizing and debilitating situation in which morale is low and union membership and leadership become attractive.

Employees must pay a price for work stoppages and disruptive activities

Remember that you can reduce monthly pay proportional to the degree or lack of efficiency or productivity during partial strikes or work slow-downs. This becomes a key point in your goal of rewarding the right behavior and making sure that the wrong behavior is not encouraged or reinforced. This means that you should be cutting pay not just under circumstances of full strike. In Japan the strike or collective action usually takes place within the company and during working hours. Thus, management must make its own decision as to what proportional amount wages should be cut back.

To avoid a charge of unfair labor practice, you should try to be fair and consistent and be sure a supervisor fills out some sort of a form and files a written record. Describe the type of interference with work that took place and give the date and time frames of such behavior, as well as the percentage to be deducted on each specific incident. These will all be totaled up on a monthly basis to determine by how much pay should be cut back.

Employees want to look toward management not the union for leadership and strength

And as for a key strategy, whether we're talking about a unionized situation or just normal staff relations, make sure that good, productive, cooperative people get more praise, psychological reward, informal recognition, pay and richer careers and advancement than uncooperative, mediocre staff, who merely collect paychecks. This, of course, must be true whether or not people are in the union and should also apply to all individuals in your management ranks.

There is no reason why unions should have a determining influence on salary systems; base up formulas; and who, when and how people get promoted.

When you are dealing with tough union leadership, you will get nowhere if you request something of your employees regarding a policy goal you have. It is probably better to inform in advance of the need to make a change; indicate roughly both through the grapevine and through formal distribution of memos to all employees what kind of a change is in the making; present the new policy with some room for flexible compromise; and give this whole process some time to sink in. After compromising within preconceived limits, go ahead and get the change ready. You would have already been through your prior consultation phase and have largely been through collective bargaining procedures. You will simply end up making the change by way of an adjustment in the Rules of Employment. Even when your firm has no labor union, the concept at work here is quite similar. You cannot expect the employees to draft the policy or create the change in a way which will be best for both them and the company. They look to you and your leadership to take these initiatives.

Manage and build your business firmly according to your own strategy and exactly as required, based upon your own desired reward structure. Let the result in growth, sales and profits pay (many times over) for any possible litigation or settlements that result from firmly handling the union and employees and making the various changes that are required to energize the business and build it up in this difficult Japanese marketplace.